Thomas Lister Ribblesdale

The Queen's Hounds and Stag-Hunting Recollections

Thomas Lister Ribblesdale

The Queen's Hounds and Stag-Hunting Recollections

ISBN/EAN: 9783337324506

Printed in Europe, USA, Canada, Australia, Japan

Cover: Foto ©ninafisch / pixelio.de

More available books at **www.hansebooks.com**

THE QUEEN'S HOUNDS

AND

STAG-HUNTING RECOLLECTIONS

BY

LORD RIBBLESDALE

MASTER OF THE BUCKHOUNDS FROM 1892 TO 1895

WITH AN INTRODUCTION

ON THE HEREDITARY MASTERSHIP

BY EDWARD BURROWS

COMPILED FROM THE BROCAS PAPERS IN HIS POSSESSION

WITH NUMEROUS ILLUSTRATIONS

LONGMANS, GREEN, AND CO.
39 PATERNOSTER ROW, LONDON
NEW YORK AND BOMBAY
1897

All rights reserved

DEDICATED

BY GRACIOUS PERMISSION

TO

HER MAJESTY THE QUEEN

BY

HER LOYAL AND FAITHFUL SERVANT

THE AUTHOR

NOTE

The Publishers desire to tender their respectful thanks to HER MAJESTY THE QUEEN for her gracious permission to select certain pictures from the Royal collections for the illustrations of this book. Also to H.R.H. PRINCE CHRISTIAN of Schleswig-Holstein, K.G., for his kindness in granting facilities in connection with the pictures at Cumberland Lodge. Similar acknowledgments are due to Colonel Sir A. COPE and Mr. EDMUND TATTERSALL; also to Colonel AUBREY MAUDE for his valuable assistance in the reproduction of the pictures.

CONTENTS

CHAPTER		PAGE
	INTRODUCTION	1
I.	GEORGIAN STAG-HUNTING	22
II.	THE NEW SCHOOL	48
III.	CHARLES DAVIS	59
IV.	DEBATEABLE LAND	82
V.	DEER	92
VI.	THE STAGHOUND	114
VII.	THE HARROW COUNTRY	142
VIII.	THE FOREST	158
IX.	BANKS AND DITCHES	172
X.	BLACK AND WHITE	189
XI.	KENNELS AND STABLES	200
XII.	ASCOT AFFAIRS	213
XIII.	PREDECESSORS	222
XIV.	VÉNERIE AND THE VALOIS	244
XV.	THE EMPIRE AND THE REPUBLIC	258
XVI.	FRENCH HORSEMANSHIP	278
XVII.	FRENCH HORSES	290
	APPENDIX: LIST OF MEETING PLACES OF ROYAL HUNT	303
	INDEX	305

LIST OF ILLUSTRATIONS

PLATES

CHARLES DAVIS ON THE HERMIT . . . . *Frontispiece*
From the picture by Byron Webb, painted about 1834.

WINDSOR PARK . . . . *To face p.* 38
From the picture by J. Wootton, 1737, in the Queen's collection at Windsor Castle.

LADY LADE 42
From the picture by Stubbs, in the Queen's collection at Cumberland Lodge.

EASTER MONDAY: A VIEW NEAR WINDSOR—GENTLEMEN
SPORTSMEN ENDEAVOURING TO LEAD THE FIELD . 48

CURRICLE 51
From the picture by Marshall, in the Queen's collection at Cumberland Lodge.

H.R.H. THE PRINCE OF WALES'S TWO CHESTNUTS . . 52
From the picture by Stubbs (1793) in the Queen's collection at Cumberland Lodge.

CHARLES DAVIS ON THE TRAVERSER 70
From the picture by Barraud.

CHARLES DAVIS . . , . . . 81
From a photograph by Hills & Saunders.

LORD COVENTRY 82
The present Master. From a photograph.

EASTER MONDAY: A VIEW NEAR EPPING—THE HEROES
OF THE DAY, MEN OF DETERMINED COURAGE,
RIDING HARD—UP TO THE HOUNDS . 136

LORD COLVILLE OF CULROSS 152
From 'Baily's Magazine,' March 1867.

BUT YOU SQUELCH AND SCRAMBLE ON 159
By C. E. Brock.

LIST OF ILLUSTRATIONS

A Humiliating Pursuit in the Grounds of the
Royal Military College at Sandhurst . . . *To face p.* 160
By G. D. Giles.

John Comins . . . . ,, 168
*Huntsman to the Queen's Hounds, appointed April 1,
1894. From a photograph by Hills & Saunders.*

More likely to sprain your Ankle than smash your
Hat . . . . ,, 176
By G. D. Giles.

Mr. Edmund Tattersall on Black Bess . . . ,, 182
*From the picture by Byron Webb in Mr. Tattersall's
possession.*

Lord Cork and Orrery . . . 184
From 'Baily's Magazine,' June 1870.

Lord Ribblesdale . . . . ,, 189
*M.B.H. 1892 to 1895. From a photograph by Hills &
Saunders.*

The Willows presented a scene of wild confusion ,, 195
By G. D. Giles.

Unkennelling the Royal Hounds . . . . ,, 200
From the picture by Chalon, 1817, in the Queen's collection at Cumberland Lodge.

The Prince went at the Top of the Hunt . 206
By G. D. Giles.

Lord Lichfield . . . 237
After Count d'Orsay, 1839.

Earl of Chesterfield, 1882 . . . . ,, 238
From 'Baily's Magazine,' November 1860.

Lord Granville . . 240
After G. Richmond.

Piqueur de la Vénerie Impériale . 262
After A. de Dreux.

ILLUSTRATIONS IN TEXT

The Cream Horse 25
From an oil-painting in the Queen's collection at Windsor Castle.

New Terrors were added by the Highwaymen 28
By G. D. Giles.

Turning out the Deer for the Royal Hunt on Windsor
Forest 40
From an old print.

LIST OF ILLUSTRATIONS

	PAGE
THE ACCOMPLISHED SPORTSWOMAN	43
From an old print.	
MOONSHINE, A CELEBRATED DEER	46
Frequently hunted by His Majesty George III. From an old print.	
CHART OF THE VARIOUS MEETS OF THE ROYAL HOUNDS, 1841	61
From the 'Sporting Review,' 1841.	
RIDING UNFAIRLY	64
By G. H. Jalland.	
TO RIDE JEALOUS IN A FOREST YOU MUST BE REALLY INTREPID	69
By G. D. Giles.	
THE HERMIT	76
From the 'Sporting Review,' 1840.	
HARRY KING ULTIMATELY STOPPED THEM	78
By G. H. Jalland.	
THE DEER SHOULD GO RIGHT AWAY OUT OF HIS CART LIKE THE 'LORD OF THE VALLEY'	96
By G. D. Giles.	
ROBERT BARTLETT	97
First Whip to the Queen's Hounds, May 1835 to January 1854. From an old print.	
WINCHELSEA, A FAVOURITE DEER	103
From an old print.	
GROVES, DEER-KEEPER	112
From a photograph by Hills & Saunders.	
LUXURY	118
From the 'Sporting Review,' 1841.	
ROMAN	119
By G. D. Giles.	
RHETORIC	119
By G. D. Giles.	
THE COUNTRY FAR AND WIDE IS UP IN ARMS AGAINST US	146
By G. D. Giles.	
HARRY KING	148
Huntsman to the Queen's Hounds, July 1866 to December 1871. From a photograph by Hills & Saunders.	
FRANK GOODALL ON CRUSADER	150
Huntsman to the Queen's Hounds, April 1872 to May 1888. From a photograph by Hills & Saunders.	

xvi   LIST OF ILLUSTRATIONS

	PAGE
THE HIDDEN PREHISTORIC RUTS	166
By G. D. Giles.	
CHARLES HOARE	179
Second Whipper-in to the Queen's Hounds, appointed July 1, 1894. From a photograph by Hills & Saunders.	
YOU KNOW WHAT IT IS TO BE REALLY CARRIED	184
By G. D. Giles.	
CHARLES STRICKLAND	185
First Whipper-in to the Queen's Hounds, appointed July 1, 1894. From a photograph by Hills & Saunders.	
THE FIRST WHIP'S HORSE SUBSIDED WITH ONLY HIS HEAD OUT OF WATER	187
By G. D. Giles.	
CHARLES SAMWAYS	191
Second Groom to the Queen's Hounds, appointed July 1, 1894. From a photograph by Hills & Saunders.	
IT WAS ALL I COULD DO TO GET 'WILLIAM' HOME	198
By G. D. Giles.	
THE OLD KENNEL AT SWINLEY	201
From an old print.	
PLAN OF THE KENNELS, ASCOT HEATH	204
PLAN OF THE KENNELS, ASCOT HEATH	205
JOSIAH MILES	210
Stud Groom to the Queen's Hounds, October 1843 to March 1894. From a photograph by A. F. Mackenzie.	
REUBEN MATTHEWS	212
Stud Groom to the Queen's Hounds, appointed April 1, 1894. From a photograph by Hills & Saunders.	
PLAN OF PROPOSED NEW MILE COURSE (1895), ASCOT, BERKS	215
SWINLEY LODGE, THE OLD RESIDENCE OF THE MASTER OF THE BUCKHOUNDS	236
From an old print.	
LE RENDEZVOUS	262
From 'Manuel de Vénerie Française.'	
LE RELAIS VOLANT	272
From 'Manuel de Vénerie Française.'	
M. DUTECH CLEARING THE GATE AT A LEVEL CROSSING UPON PAPILLON	285
By G. D. Giles.	

MAP

PLACES OF MEETING OF THE ROYAL HUNT (*at end of book*).

THE QUEEN'S HOUNDS

AND

STAG-HUNTING RECOLLECTIONS

INTRODUCTION

BY EDWARD BURROWS

Vixere fortes ante Agamemnona

FEW of those who share with the writer the memories of an Eton 'wet-bob,' to whom 'The Brocas,'[1] 'Brocas Clump,' 'Brocas Meadow,' and 'Brocas Lane' are 'familiar in their mouths as household words,' know the origin of the strange un-English name which thus lingers on the Eton bank of the Thames just above Windsor Bridge, but has died out on the opposite side where lay the manor, styled, at least until the beginning of the sixteenth century, 'Brocas in Clewer,' or 'Clewer-Brocas,' and where the position of the Brocas Chantry, founded by that notable knight Sir Bernard Brocas, may still be traced in Clewer Church.

Few of those who ride with her Majesty's Buckhounds are aware that the hereditary Mastership was held by the family

[1] Materials for this Introduction are taken from *The Family of Brocas of Beaurepaire and Roche Court*, by Montagu Burrows, Captain R.N., M.A., F.S.A., Chichele Professor of Modern History in the University of Oxford a work founded on the collection of original Brocas documents now in the writer's possession.

B

of Brocas for nearly three hundred years, from the middle of the fourteenth to the middle of the seventeenth century.

Fewer still among those who ride or row have ever heard of the connection between this long line of hereditary Masters and the ruined castle of Sault and a church and villages in South-Western France, still bearing the name of Brocas, far from the track of the modern traveller, and buried among the woodlands and sand dunes of ancient Gascony.

A brief account of certain of these Masters of old time may form a becoming introduction to modern incidents of stag-hunting, may bring to light picturesque details of sport closely mingled with war, may show that the Mastership can claim an ancient and romantic past, and add proof that in all ages good sportsmen have been staunch fighting-men and loyal subjects.

The lands held in ' Clyware, New Windesore, Old Windesore, Eton, Dauneye, Boveneye, Cokeham and Bray ' during the fourteenth and fifteenth centuries by this family of Gascon knights, transplanted into England by Edward II., were important and extensive. Some ten men of this name and blood occupied notable positions as favoured courtiers and trusted servants of the Crown in the brilliant and romantic period of the reigns of the second and third Edward and the second Richard, and in successive generations held such offices as those of Master of the Horse, Master of the Buckhounds, Chief Forester of Windsor, Warden of King's Castles, Gaols, and Parks, Captain of Calais, Controller of Calais, Constable of Aquitaine, Controller of Bordeaux, Royal Ambassador, Chamberlain to the Queen, Chamberlain of the Exchequer, and King's Clerk of the Works. It is, therefore, hard to understand the almost complete oblivion into which has fallen the real origin of the name that still survives under the shadow of Windsor Castle. So fantastic and so far from the truth have been the suggested

INTRODUCTION

derivations that they only prove how completely family traditions disappear amid the building of royal palaces and the founding of royal colleges. Sir John de Brocas acquired these lands before Edward III. began to enlarge Windsor Castle. His descendants had ceased to reside on them before the foundation of Eton College, and entirely relinquished them soon after that event. So long ago 'the knight was dust, and his good sword rust,' that on the spot where he dwelt not even

> a herald who that way doth pass
> Finds his cracked name at length in the church glass.

Yet the swords of these Gascon knights, among whom the most illustrious was the first Brocas Master of the Buckhounds, were kept bright for many years in the service of their adopted country, for we find them at Creçy, at the siege of Calais, at Poitiers and at Najara, while others of their kin met death in defence of the English shores.

It is singularly unfortunate that the painstaking author of a recent 'History of the Royal Buckhounds'[1] was ignorant of the Gascon origin of the hereditary Masters, or ignored the information that might have been obtained on this matter. It is, moreover, much to be regretted that in a history which shows so much research the foolish tradition is repeated that the ancestor of the hereditary Masters was Sir Bernard Brocas, who came into England with William the Conqueror, from whom, in reward for his military services, he received permission to select lands to the value of 400*l*.; that he chose these lands in Hampshire, and built thereon a mansion styled 'Beaurepaire,' and that the lives of three successors of the same name sufficed, by a startling assumption of longevity, to cover a period of 280 years from the date of the Conquest to the year when Sir John de Brocas served

[1] *History of the Royal Buckhounds*, by J. P. Hore.

with distinction under Edward III. at the siege of Calais.[1] Such a descent is too incredible to be recorded elsewhere than in that storehouse of many such apocryphal genealogies, the College of Arms, where it appears to have stood without question for a long period, and whence it emerged to find, unfortunately, place in the inscription, inserted only in the eighteenth century, above the ancient and elaborate tomb of this early Master of the Buckhounds, Sir Bernard Brocas, in St. Edmund's Chapel in Westminster Abbey. In fact, this Gascon origin is a matter of more interest than is generally supposed; for it was plainly in consequence of their knowledge of breeding and training horses on the turbulent marches of Gascony that so many members of the family of Brocas were well fitted to have charge, as Masters of the Horse, of the royal studs, and, as Masters of the Buckhounds, of the royal hunting establishment. Thus is furnished an early and significant instance of the obligations under which England has ever lain to France in all matters connected with the chase, and of the striking advantage which during the Middle Ages accrued to the former country from the ancestral possessions derived by her kings from Eleanor of Guienne, not only in the graver matters of state and commerce, but in the improvement of the breed of light horses.

The cradle of the race whence sprang the hereditary Masters is found on the borders of Gascony, where a considerable tract of land was once known as 'the Brocas March,' where villages still bear the name, and where still

[1] Strangely different from these false legends are the real facts. For the settlement in England of certain members of the Gascon family of de Brocas did not begin until the reign of Edward II., and it was not until the year 1353 that the uncle of Sir Bernard Brocas purchased Beaurepaire from John Pecche, whose ancestors had held it for several generations. The line of the family that remained in Gascony is still represented there by the Comte de Brocas.

stands the ruined keep of their ancestral stronghold of Sault, twice styled by Froissart 'a strong and good castle.' Here dwelt Sir Peter Arnald de Brocas, foully slain at Bayonne during truce by Earl Simon de Montfort, and here, during many years of incessant border forays, the de Brocas showed with other loyal Gascons their gallant devotion to their 'Roy Outremer,' by holding their fortress as a bulwark of the English rule in Gascony against the ceaseless attacks of their turbulent neighbours the Vicomtes de Béarn, to whose castle of Orthez the road still runs due south across the old border line. Wild tales of flight and hot pursuit, of desperate rally and midnight foray, could that old highway tell in the days when English and French knights, hard-riding Gascon borderers and swaggering Free Companions, mustered under the rival royal standards and the banners of de Montfort, de Béarn and d'Albret, while from the keep above floated the sable pennon of de Brocas. Strangely must old memories have been stirred when along the same road in later days, after the stubborn fight at Orthez, British squadrons pursued the flying French and Wellington received his only wound. Ruined at length by their loyalty to the English cause during the disasters of Edward II.'s latter years, the children of Arnald de Brocas, 'lately slain in the King's service in Scotland,' possibly at Bannockburn, were taken into the royal household and brought up at the English Court. As no less than three of these young Gascon officers of the King became Masters of the Horse, and by their length of service proved their aptness for the appointment, there are sufficient entries under the name of 'de Brocas' in the Record Office to supply almost a history of Edward III.'s equestrian organisation. Space only permits the mention of certain facts illustrative of the experience in this matter of the family which had charge for so long a period of the royal hunting establishment.

Edward is too often blamed for his large expenditure on horses, but it is forgotten that his mighty conflict with the hosts of France, his contests of chivalry, his 'hastiludes' and military Orders, which largely operated to ensure his victories, entailed an enormous and special provision for breeding studs, large sums for purchase money, and a great array of persons employed in the business. With the very beginning of this work the de Brocas [1] were concerned. Sir John superintended it for a great part of his life, and when the great war seemed to be over, it was to him and to William of Wykeham that the King entrusted the sale and breaking up of the war establishment. In the long lists which occur in the Exchequer Accounts of the Wardrobe of numerous classes of horses belonging to the King —coursers, palfreys, trotters, hobbies, genets, hengests, and somers—the 'dextrarii' or 'great horses' received most attention. Provision was made for 102 of their housings out of 441 ells of canvas and 360 ells of cloth, which was to come from Candlewyk Street in London. The boundary between the great cavalry establishments was formed by the Trent, the division to the north of this river having its separate 'custos' under the Master of the Horse. The studs were distributed among the King's manors, such as Windsor, Guildford, Odiham, Woodstock, and Waltham. The due proportion of expense necessary for corn, shoeing, litter, headstalls and bridles was borne by the sheriffs of the various counties. The keep of thirty horses by one of these sheriffs for sixty days in the year 1338 amounted to 40*l*. 12*s*. 6*d*., or about 5½*d*. per horse per day, while the keep of a hound cost ¾*d*. per day. Special provision was made for a tunic of blue and a cape of white Brussels cloth as the attire of 'John Brocaz,' styled in these records

---

[1] The deeds show that the 'de' before Brocas is gradually dropped as the family begin to acquire lands in England.

'Custos equorum regis' or 'Gardein de nos grands chevaux.' The prices paid for horses in 1330 are shown by the following sums which passed through the hands of Brocas. 'To Master Thomas de Garton, Keeper of the King's Wardrobe, in money paid to him by the hands of John Brocaz for the purchase of the three undermentioned chargers, to wit, one called Pomers, of a grey colour with black head, price 120*l.*; another called Lebryt, a dappled grey, price 70*l.*; and a third called Bayard, a bright bay with hind fetlocks white, price 50*l.*'[1]

The great cavalry department appears to have been kept at its full war complement for about twenty years, until the power of France, after the battle of Poitiers, seemed finally broken. Thus in 1357 the King commissions Sir John de Brocas, Edmund Rose, and William of Wykeham to sell off that portion of the stud kept in Windsor Park, and the next year the horses beyond the Trent which were of no further use were sold; while in 1360, after the Peace of Bretigny, all the royal studs south of Trent were disposed of and the proceeds handed to William of Wykeham, 'surveyor of the King's work in Windsor Castle.' Too soon were frustrated the fond hopes that it would never again be necessary to sweep over France with English squadrons, and great was the need of this magnificent cavalry before the end of the reign.

Many and various were the duties of this active Master of the Horse. After employment with his son Sir Oliver in buying horses for the King in Gascony before the great campaign of Creçy, he is found in command of a considerable company at the siege of Calais, and he was chosen as ambassador to congratulate Alfonso XI. of Castile on his capture of Algeciras from the Moors, and to negotiate concerning the marriage of Edward III.'s daughter to the

[1] The proper multiple for money of this date, for the sake of comparison with the present day, is approximately 20.

Spanish prince known as Pedro the Cruel. After one of these embassies he brought back two Spanish jennets as a gift from Alfonso to Edward. Amid all these public services he found time to add by degrees to his estates at Windsor and in Hampshire with the caution becoming one who was a Gascon and an alien.

The career of his son Sir Bernard, to whom came by marriage and subsequent direct royal grant the hereditary Mastership, is so full of stirring episodes and knightly deeds that it might well form the subject of an historical romance.

Certain picturesque points can only be glanced at here. As Chamberlain to the Queen, as King's Warden and Ambassador, as Constable of Aquitaine and Controller of Bordeaux, as Captain of Calais and Master of the Buckhounds, as a warrior at Creçy, Poitiers, and Najara, this illustrious Anglo-Gascon trod every stage of the brilliant times in which he lived. Twice was he summoned as a witness on high matters of chivalry. From his evidence given in the famous Scrope and Grosvenor Roll, it appears that he was first armed as esquire on the shore of La Hogue on the day when the Black Prince was knighted, and 'that he had fought in France, in Scotland, in Gascony, in Brittany, and in Spain, in the presence of kings, princes, dukes, counts, barons, and other great lords, knights, and esquires, during forty years.' On another occasion Brocas is found as a witness, with such renowned co-signatories as Oliver de Clisson, the Earl of Salisbury, Sir Bartholomew Burghersh, Robert Holland, and Thomas de Ros, to the claim that King John of France surrendered to the Gascon Bernard de Trouttes and not to the French knight fighting on the English side, Sir Denis de Morbeque. The Brocas pennon must therefore have been in the thick of that final furious *mêlée* which raged on the bloodstained field of Poitiers round the spot where the French king turned at bay, while his gallant stripling son stood at his side warning him of the blows rained on him by the ring of emulous Gascon and English knights. Well might the French chronicle quoted later on describe Sir Bernard as 'ung des hautz hommes et nobles d'Angleterre, tres bon chevalier qui moult grandement avoit servi le Prince.' In boudoir as well as in tented field his fame appears to have stood high. In the court of Venus as well as in that of Mars did the Black Prince befriend him. It has been generally received on the authority of the Metrical Chronicle of Harding that the Prince began his suit not for himself, but on behalf of some nameless comrade-in-arms, to that beauteous dame of royal blood the Lady Joan Plantagenet, best known as the 'Fair Maid of Kent.' We now learn from the 'Chronique des Quatre Premiers Valois' that Sir Bernard Brocas was the knight for whom the Prince thus pleaded, and whose fruitless suit became the direct cause of that romantic royal match.

The narrative is so quaint in language and so characteristic in incident that it deserves full quotation below.[1]

[1] "Apres le trespassement de son dit Seigneur moult de nobles chevaliers qui moult avoient servi le Roy d'Angleterre et le Prince son fils en leurs guerres vindrent requerre au Prince qu'il lui pleust à parler à la Comtesse de Hollande. En especial ung des hautz hommes et nobles d'Angleterre nommé Monseigneur de Brocas tres bon chevalier qui moult grandement avoit servi le Prince et pour lui tant en ses guerres que autrement avoit moult travaillié, requist le Prince qu'il lui pleust tant faire qu'il eust la dicte Dame et Comtesse pour lui a femme, et qu'il en parlast à la dicte dame. Le Prince pour le dit chevalier parla à la dicte Dame de Hollande par plusieurs fois. Car moult voulentiers aloit pour soy deduire veoir la dicte dame qui estoit sa cousine et souventeffoiz regardoit sa tres grande beauté et son tres gracieux contenement qui merveilleusement lui plaisoit. Et comme une foiz le Prince parloit a la dicte Comtesse pour le dit chevalier la Comtesse lui respondi que jamais espoux n'auroit. Et elle qui moult estoit soubtille et sage par plusieurs foiz le dit au Prince. "Ha! A!" se dit le Prince "belle cousine en cas que vous ne voulez marier a mez amis mal fut vostre grant beauté dont tant estes plaine. Et se vous et moy ne nous apartenissons de lignage il n'est dame soubz le ciel que j'eusse tant chiere comme vous." Et alors fut le Prince moult supprins de l'amour à la Comtesse. Et lors prinst la Comtesse à plourer comme femme soubtille et plaine d'aguet. Et donc le Prince la prinst a conforter et la prinst a baisier moult souvent en prenant ses larmes a grant douliour et lui dit "Belle cousine j'ay a vous parler

This episode must have occurred soon after Sir Bernard's divorce from his first wife, Agnes Vavasour, and he rapidly found consolation for the failure of his ambitious attempt to gain the Fair Maid's hand by marrying an heiress and a King's ward, Mary, daughter of Sir John de Roches and widow of Sir John de Borhunte. With her he acquired not only 'Hunter's Manor' and the hereditary Mastership, but other lands and manors in Hampshire, one of which, the Manor of Roche Court, still remains after nineteen generations in the possession of his descendants. To these lands he added the lordship of Beaurepaire, near Basingstoke, purchased from its previous lord, John Pecche, in the year 1353, which he received licence from the King to empark, and which was destined to be for so many centuries the chief seat of the Brocas Masters. At length, full of years and honours, after making elaborate arrangements for the foundation of the Brocas Chantry in Clewer Church, this

<sub>pour ung des preux chevaliers d'Angleterre et avec ce il est moult gentilz homs." Madame la Comtesse respondi en plourant au Prince " Ha Sire pour Dieu vueillez vous souffrir de me parler de cettes paroles. Car c'est mon entente que je n'aye jamaiz espoux. Car je me suys de tout donnée au plus preux de dessoubz le firmament. Et pour l'amour d'icellui jamaiz espoux fors Dieu n'auray tant que je vivray. Car c'est chose impossible que je l'aye, et pour la sienne amour me vueil garder de compagnie d'omme, ne jamaiz n'est m'intencion de moy marier." Le Prince fut moult en grant desir de scavoir cil qui estoit le plus preux du monde et moult requist la Comtesse qu'elle lui deist. Mais la dicte Comtesse plus l'en veoit eschauffé plus lui prioit qu'il n'en cerchast plus avant et lui disoit : "Pour Dieu tres cher Seigneur, en soy agenouillant, pour la tres douce Vierge mere vueillez vous en souffrir a tant."

'A brief rencontrer le Prince lui dist que s'elle ne lui disoit qui estoit le plus preux du monde qu'il seroit son mortel ennemy. Et lors lui dit la Comtesse "Tres chier et redoubté Seigneur c'est vous, et pour l'amour de vous jamaiz à mon coste chevalier ne gerra." Le Prince qui moult fut adonc enbras d'amour à la Comtesse lui dit " Dame et je voue a Dieu que jamaiz autre femme que vous vivres n'auroy." Et presentement la fiança, puis aprez assez briefment il l'espousa . . . . De laquelle chose Edouart le Roy d'Angleterre fut merveilleusement marry et dolent et voult qu'elle fust mise à mort. Car moult plus hautement se fust le Prince marié et n'avoit empereur roy ne prince soubz le ciel qui n'eust eu grant joye se le Prince de Galles se fust mist en son lignage.'</sub>

preux chevalier is accorded a magnificent funeral by his grateful master Richard II., and, in St. Edmund's Chapel in Westminster Abbey, a stately tomb, round which still runs in contracted form the inscription: 'Hic jacet Bernardus Brocas Miles T. T. quondam camerarius Anne Regine Anglie cujus anime propicietur Deus. Amen.' It is unfortunate that no solid foundation is apparent for the legend that Sir Bernard bore the crest, used by him in seals as early as 1361, and still extant, of a Moor's head wearing an Oriental crown, in consequence of vanquishing a Moorish king in battle.[1] Possibly he fought among those knights of renown who did battle with Moors ' for the good of their souls ' in the open space between the two camps at Algeciras, when besieged by Alfonso of Castile in 1344. At any rate, the tradition was so well known in Addison's time that the attention of Sir Roger de Coverley was drawn when in the Abbey to the tomb of ' the lord who had cut off the King of Morocco's head.'[2]

Thus, with the marriage of Sir Bernard Brocas and Mary, widow of Sir John de Borhunte and daughter of Sir John de Roches, begins the long period of the Brocas Mastership of the Buckhounds, and it becomes necessary to refer briefly to the early history of the office as recited in an ancient Brocas document.

List of the hereditary Masters of the Royal Buckhounds by tenure in capite of ' Hunter's Manor,' in Little Weldon, Northamptonshire.

1. Osborne Lovel, Chamberlain to Henry II.
2. William Lovel.
3. Hamon le Venour, by grant from Henry III. in 1216.
4. William Lovel.
5. John Lovel, *ob.* 1316.
6. Thomas de Borhunte, *ob.* 1340, *jure* Margaret Lovel.
7. William Danvers, *ob.* 1361, *jure* Margaret Lovel.

[1] Arms of Brocas: Sable, a lion, rampant-gardant, or. Crest of Brocas: A Moor's head in profile, crowned.
[2] *Spectator*, No. 329.

8. Sir Bernard Brocas (1363), *ob.* 1395, *jure* Mary de Borhunte.
9. Sir Bernard Brocas, second of the name, executed 1400.
10. William Brocas (1), *ob.* 1456.
11. William Brocas (2), *ob.* 1484.
12. John Brocas, *ob.* 1492.
13. William Brocas (3), *ob.* 1506.
14. John Brocas, 1508–1512.[1]
15. George Warham and Ralph Pexall, joint Masters 1512–1514, *jure* Ann and Edith Brocas.
16. Ralph Pexall (1514), *ob.* c. 1540, *jure* Edith Brocas.
17. Sir Richard Pexall, *ob.* 1571, son of Edith Brocas.
18. Sir John Savage (till 1584), second husband of Lady Pexall, widow of Sir Richard.
19. Sir Pexall Brocas, *ob.* 1630.
20. Thomas Brocas, who in 1633 sold Hunter's Manor and the office to Sir Lewis Watson, afterwards Lord Rockingham.

From the list of hereditary Masters given above it will be observed that one of the earliest notices of any regular establishment for the Buckhounds is the grant of certain lands in Little Weldon, a manor in Northamptonshire, near Rockingham, to Hamon le Venour, in 1216. It is certain, however, that the Lovels had held these lands at an earlier date, for certain territories and the lordship of the Manor of Little Weldon were granted by Henry II. to his Chamberlain, Osborne Lovel, from whom they descended to John Lovel, who died in 1316. Whatever were the original relations of 'Hunter's Manor in Little Weldon' to the royal manor of that name of which it formed a part, it assumed under the Edwards a position so entirely independent of the larger manor that it is styled in the Brocas deeds and official documents the 'Manor of Little Weldon,' with 'Hunter's Manor' sometimes prefixed as an alias. To this 'Hunter's Manor' was attached in Grand Serjeanty for many centuries the Mastership of the Royal Buckhounds. For the ingenious at-

[1] The tenure of this Master, omitted in the list given in *The Family of Brocas*, has been correctly noted in the *History of the Royal Buckhounds*.

tempt made by the author of a 'History of the Buckhounds,' to which allusion has been already made, to throw doubt on the antiquity of the hereditary transmission of the Mastership with 'Hunter's Manor'—an attempt apparently based on the fact that the Lovels and de Borhuntes, who held it before Sir Bernard Brocas, were styled custodians instead of masters —needs no further attention than the statement that in the Brocas documents 'magister' and 'custos' are frequently used as interchangeable terms of the same meaning, and that in an indenture of Elizabeth's reign the phrase 'Master or Keeper' of the Buckhounds occurs. Remote from King and Court the situation of Hunter's Manor may seem at the present day to those who forget the central position and historical importance of Rockingham Forest and Rockingham Castle in Norman and Plantagenet times. Here, within reach of the stronghold of Northampton, was the royal residence, fitted for retirement and the pleasures of the chase, until, with the increasing necessity of moving the Court nearer to London, Rockingham was superseded by the greater convenience and magnificence of Windsor. A vast extent of country was once covered by Rockingham Forest, which, when reduced to the limits retained almost to modern times, was twenty-four miles long from Oxendon Bridge to Stamford, and twelve miles wide from Rockingham to Thrapstone. Numerous woodlands, quaint forest names, peculiar customs, and a population that retains its forest character still mark the ancient limits. Local names, such as 'The Lord's Walk' and 'Harry's Wood,' still recall the memory of some forgotten royal and noble lover of the 'mimic war' of hound and horn. Though 'Hunter's Coppice,' last relic of the ancient 'Hunter's Manor,' was broken up some years ago, there still may be seen in 'Little Weldon' mounds and foundations of an extensive building surrounded by a quadrangular moat to which the peasants give the name of 'The Castle' or 'The Hall,' and which may mark the site of the hunting lodge and kennels of the hereditary Masters. Still do the Pytchley awake the same woodland echoes as were roused by many a princely Plantagenet, and still hounds meet on the border of Farming Woods near an ancient stone three feet high and now fast sinking into the earth, named the 'Bocase Stone,' marking the site of a yet more ancient tree, and bearing still the inscriptions, 'In this place grew Bocase tree,' and, lower down, 'Here stood Bocase tree.' No local tradition of the meaning of this inscription survives, and so quaint and unlikely have been the derivations suggested that leave may be taken to hold that here stood the 'Brocas Tree,' and that here, where the old forest tracks, still traceable, met near the ancient kennels, the hereditary Brocas Masters, surrounded by their huntsmen, their 'ventrers,' 'berners,' and hounds, and clad in the livery specially provided from the King's wardrobe, were wont, in successive generations, to await the royal hunting train emerging from Rockingham Castle.

While there is clear proof from public records and documents of the Brocas family of the chief importance of Rockingham in the early organisation of the Buckhounds, it is strange that no direct evidence of the application of this hunting establishment to the New Forest or other royal demesnes has yet been discovered.

The tenure of the manor and office by the early Lovels and de Borhuntes is so similar in most respects to that of later times, and so interesting from its antiquity, that reference may here be made to an entry dated August 15, 1316, wherein the escheator reported that Lovel had held one messuage and one carucate of land in Weldon Parva of the King *in capite* by service of keeping and feeding at his own charges fifteen 'canes currentes' of the King's for the forty days of Lent in each year, and to a later document wherein it is recited that Thomas Borhunte holds of the King *in capite* a chain of land in Little Weldon of the inheritance of Margaret his wife, daughter and heir of John Lovel, by service of being ' Venour le Roy des deymers ' (Master of the King's Buckhounds); that he has charge of twenty-four hounds and six greyhounds of the King's, receiving for the keep of each an obol or ½d. a day, and also of two under-huntsmen, whose wages are 1½d. a day, with a cloth coat or a mark of money by the year, and boots; that he also has charge of a ' veutrer,' or huntsman, at 2d. a day, who is also to have a coat or a mark of money and 4s. 8d. for boots by the year; that the Master is to keep *at his own cost* for the forty days of Lent, fifteen Buckhounds and one ' berner,' or keeper of the hounds, while the second ' berner,' the ' veutrer,' and the rest of the hounds are to be kept at the King's cost for the whole of the year; that the Master's salary is to be 7½d. a day when at Court and 12d. a day when absent on the King's business, with two robes a year or 40s.; that the ' seigne en malades ' is to have for daily livery 1d. worth of bread, a gallon of beer, a mess of ' groos,' and a mess of roast from the kitchen, and that the livery of the huntsman is to be at the King's will. The most important point in this ancient document is the absolute acknowledgment of the hereditary character of the office and of the power of its transmission through females—a power which in the next century was abolished by restricting the succession to males, but which was revived again under the Tudors in such a manner as to defeat the original object of the Mastership, and to end in its being bought and sold in the seventeenth century as private property, with the final result of the formation of the Privy Buckhounds, the Mastership of which was free from these feudal hindrances.

To the value of the Manor of Little Weldon, or Hunter's Manor, there was added, from the middle of the fourteenth to the end of the seventeenth century, a supplementary salary for the Master, amounting on the average to 50*l.* a year, charged on the revenues of Surrey and Sussex, and payable by warrant under the Privy Seal addressed to the sheriff of those counties. So serious are the delays of payment of this salary after the Lancastrian accession to the throne, so great is the risk of its not being paid at all, that public records and the Brocas papers are full of piteous appeals from successive Masters, such as that of the year 1449, in which ' To the Kyng and Sovain Lorde bisecheth mekely your humble servaunt William Brocas Squyer, Maistre of your Bukhounds. Forasmuche that he holdith of you and alle his Auncestres of tyme that no mynde is have holden to your noble progenitours, the Manior of Lityll Weldon in the Counte of North' by Graunte Sergeaunte that is to witte to be Maistre of your Bukhoundes, and to kepe xxiiij remyng houndes and vi grehoundes, and to find a yeoman Veautrer and two yomen Berners, which Office was of old tyme ordeyned for the pleasir and disporte of your noble progenitours and their successours. . . . Wherefore please hit unto your Highnesse as well tenderly to consider these premisses as the trewe contynuell service that your said Bisecher hath doon unto your noble progenitours as to your Highnesse . . . to graunte unto your said Bisecher the said wages and fees. .

' Responsio

Soit fait comme il est desire juxst le continue d'un Cedule a yeest Peticion annexe.'

So alike are these petitions and so unchanged are the general conditions of the manor and service during the centuries of its hereditary transmission, that we may well turn in search of more interesting matter to such personal details of certain Masters as concern their tenure of the office. Of the romantic career of the first and most illustrious

Brocas Master a brief outline has already been given. In the next generation the passionate devotion of the loyal Gascon blood to the failing cause of Richard the Redeless, son of the 'Prince of Aquitaine,' brought the rising fortunes of the family to the brink of ruin. For the second Sir Bernard Brocas, in consequence of his share in the desperate plot to seize Henry IV. at Oxford, lost not only many a fair manor, but his head also. Betrayed by the dastardly traitor Rutland, the conspirators made a dash on Windsor, missed Henry there by a few hours, and fled in hot haste to Cirencester, where they were forced to surrender. The earls implicated in the rising having been beheaded without trial, the knights were taken to Oxford, where the greater number were barbarously executed, but four, including (according to the statement of the most trustworthy chronicler) 'Sir Bernard Brocas Gascon' and Sir Thomas Shelley, were sent to London for trial. Thus accuracy can scarcely be allowed to Shakespeare's graphic narrative of the event wherein Fitzwater reports—

> My lord, I have from Oxford sent to London
> The heads of Brocas and Sir Bennet Seely,
> Two of the dangerous consorted traitors
> That sought at Oxford thy dire overthrow.
> *Richard II.* act iv. scene 6.

At Tyburn Brocas alone of the four was exempted from the degradation of being drawn and hanged, and there they suffered death with the composure becoming knights and gentlemen, refusing to the last to betray their associates. For, as stated in the 'Chronique de la Traïson,' to the question, 'Say amongst you who they were that belonged to your party,' 'la ne respondit nul,' none of them replied a word.

Although by the clemency of Henry IV. the forfeiture and attainder were with remarkable promptitude reversed, and the family restored in blood and estate, the descendants of the attainted knight, taught by bitter experience, seem to have shunned the dangers of the Court, to have studied woodcraft instead of statecraft, to have followed the buckhounds instead of the 'dogs of war,' and to have devoted tranquil years at Beaurepaire to the service of their county, by acting, during successive generations, as members of Parliament and Sheriffs for Hampshire. After keeping hounds impartially for the Red and the White Rose, the elder line of the Masters comes, early in the sixteenth century, to be represented by co-heiresses, Anne and Edith Brocas; and in their favour the power of transmitting the Mastership through females was again expressly granted, to the exclusion of their living uncles and other kinsmen of the name, and in spite of the limitation of the succession to heirs male made in the reign of Henry VI. No explanation of this remarkable transaction is forthcoming, but significance of favour in high places attaches itself to the facts that Ralph Pexall, husband of Edith Brocas, was in Wolsey's retinue, and that Richard Pexall was the Abbot of Leicester of whom the dying Cardinal on his last journey 'craved a little earth for charity.'

It is unfortunately impossible to find evidence that either Anne or Edith Brocas carried the horn or exercised in person any duties of their office. They were probably wise to act by deputy in the reign of that amorous sportsman Henry VIII., whose attentions in the hunting-field were apt to lead to the block. But, had they lived somewhat later, one cannot but think that a Mistress of the Buckhounds would have been in place when Elizabeth, Henry's

> Man-minded offset rose
> To chase the deer at five.

In the next generation Sir Richard Pexall's claim to the Mastership was granted by Queen Mary in letters patent, and the marriage of his daughter to her kinsman Bernard Brocas

of Horton brought it back to the old name. In their son, Sir
Pexall Brocas, there passes across the stage a ruffling spendthrift and a riotous braggart who seriously encumbered the
family estates, and brought the Mastership into such bad
repute that the beginning of the end drew nigh. The strange
nature and variety of his career, his habits and proclivities, may
be gathered from the facts that on January 18, 1603, a pardon
was granted by James to Sir Pexall Brocas, Knight, for all
riots and unlawful assemblies before March 20 last past ; that
six years later Sir Pexall conveyed by deed to trustees the
greater part of his estates, including Little Weldon and the
Mastership of the Buckhounds, for the purposes (1) of erecting a tomb to his honour in Westminster Abbey, near to that
of his grandfather, Sir Richard Pexall; (2) of founding a
college at Oxford, to be called 'Brocas College'; and that in
little more than three years from the date of this pious conveyance 'he did open penance at Paul's Cross, where he
stood in a white sheet and held a rod in his hand, having
been formally convicted before the High Commissioners for
secret and notorious adulteries with divers women.' A touch
of picturesque assurance is added to this swashbuckler's
career by the tradition 'that he was attended by thirty
men in scarlet that waited upon him to the Lord Mayor
when he went to demand a dinner after doing penance.' It
need scarcely be added that on the expiration of his penitent
mood the conveyance above mentioned was promptly
revoked. This notorious Master entered upon his office and
manor without licence from Elizabeth, a trespass which was
pardoned ; but it was not until nearly the end of her reign
that his claim to the ancient salary of 50*l.* per annum from
the Sheriffs of Surrey and Sussex was recognised by the
judges on appeal. To this petition Sir Pexall soon added
another, for among the claims made by hereditary officers
for places at the ceremony and procession at King James's

coronation, is found one made by him 'as seised of Little Weldon to be Master of the Buckhounds.' This claim was unsuccessful, as was that made at the coronation of Charles II. by Lord Rockingham, who had by that time acquired the Mastership by purchase.

The merely nominal character now assumed by the hereditary office, and the serious difficulty, largely increased under Henry VIII., of obtaining any salary, pointed to an imminent change in the constitution of an establishment that had become unsuitable for modern requirements. That this change had begun under Henry VIII. by the substitution of the Privy Buckhounds as distinct from the hounds kept by the hereditary Masters is clearly shown by an indenture, preserved among the Brocas documents, of great value and interest to the subsequent history of the subject. For it is from this Privy Pack, with its Masters, one of the earliest of whom was George Boleyn, holding office at the King's pleasure, and not from the hereditary and feudal organisation, that the present establishment and the modern tenure of the Mastership directly descends. In this important and decisive indenture, dated July 13, 1598, whereby Sir Pexall Brocas deputes Sir John Stanhope to discharge the duties of the Mastership, it is recited that Sir Bernard Brocas and his heirs became seised of the Mastership, and 'being so seised, the late King of famous memory, Henry VIII., by the sinister persuasions of divers of the then servants of the said King, seeking their own private gain, did erect, make and establish another office called the Master of his Privy Buckhounds, and the same office, together with divers new fees and wages for exercising the same new office, did give and grant to divers persons to the great damage, prejudice and disinheritance of the said Sir Richard Pexall and of his manor aforesaid, and to the great and extraordinary charge and expense of the said King.' It is further explained in this deed that Queen Mary did revoke, repeal, and make void the said new office, and did confirm Sir Richard Pexall and his heirs in the ancient hereditary office.

In spite of this strenuous opposition of the hereditary Masters, the Privy Buckhounds were re-established under Elizabeth and James, and for a time the old and the new systems bitterly contended for the mastery, until in the early part of the seventeenth century the hereditary office became practically obsolete. It was in this condition when Thomas Brocas, in the year 1633, sold it to Sir Lewis Watson for 3,000*l*., with the Manor of Little Weldon, held by his ancestors for three centuries. Thus ended at last the long line of hereditary Masters, but not the loyalty of their race. For it appears from contemporary authority that Beaurepaire, their ancient seat, was one of the last houses in Hampshire to hold out for Charles's hopeless cause. Surprised and surrounded at length by a Roundhead force from Abingdon, the Brocas troop, after throwing into their moat the last pieces of plate that had not been melted down for the King, cut their way through to Basing House, to reinforce their neighbour, the gallant old Marquis of Winchester, in his final struggle. There for a few more desperate months the descendants of the faithful Masters of the Buckhounds fought on under that Paulet motto which might well have been theirs also, *Aimez Loyauté*. For not many families can boast, as can that of Brocas, that thrice in their history, once in Gascony and twice in England, their fortunes have been ruined by devoted loyalty to their King.

CHAPTER I

GEORGIAN STAG-HUNTING

I summon up remembrance of things past

I AM afraid that a great deal in this book has little or nothing to do with the Queen's Hounds. Often and often they have, as it were, to be dragged in by the scruff of the neck. I am constantly running out of my course, and at the outset I must plead this as my excuse for the many liberties taken with the unities of time and place in the following pages.

History, according to the late Master of Balliol, is Biography, and tested by Dr. Jowett's standard, any strictly conscientious history of the Buckhounds must leave much to be desired. For many long tracts of years they want the breath of life. Like most institutions they are not palpable. Their existence is abundantly vouched for by warrants, salaries, and accounts, but this is a very sinister way of reaching history. Besides, the history of the Royal Buckhounds has been done already, and well done. In his work on this subject, Mr. Hore taps and samples every available source of official information. He has brought a trained and patient industry to bear upon much old English and dog Latin. Pipe Rolls and the penetralia of public offices have been forced to yield their increase and been turned into type and plain figures. But cheerfully as he threads his way through this valley of dry bones and the dust of ages, Mr. Hore laments over and over again the absence of authentic records of actual hunting incidents. Where as an investigator he has failed, I am not likely to succeed. Thus the lack of material might account for the short work made of several centuries, and be my apology for skipping the trunk-hose periods. I am further relieved from having to touch on the earlier associations of royalty and stag-hunting by the fact that my friend Mr. Burrows, who, as a descendant of the hereditary Brocas Masters of the Buckhounds, is the proper person to remind us of these vanished ages, has told us about them in the Introduction.

Mr. Lecky, in one of his most engaging chapters, comments upon the fact that countless Enclosure Acts and the spread of agriculture had led to much less wild stag-hunting. But, on the other hand, it may be noted that these very Enclosure Acts in Bucks and Berks hastened the dawn of civilisation in the shape of the deer cart. Although I cannot fix an Hejira with absolute certainty, the credit of this invention belongs as much of right to George III. and his hunting advisers as the credit of hunting at force—that is, of unharbouring and riding to a deer with hounds—belongs of right to Edward III. and his hard-riding Gascon Master, Sir Bernard Brocas. I shall, therefore, without further apology, begin with a short survey of Court and country hunting under the Georges.

There is really little to be said about stag-hunting under George I. The Buckhounds, Mr. Hore tells us, were not idle—they certainly cost money, and his pages will repay the attention of those who like comparing expenditure statistics of the past with the present. But George I., as everybody knows, never settled down in England. As Dr. Johnson explained to Boswell in the course of a panegyric upon Charles II., he 'knew nothing, and desired to know nothing; did nothing, and desired to do nothing.' The fine company on the Mall, the beauty of St. James's Park, impressed him not at all. The oaks of Windsor only made him regret the limes of Herrenhausen. He was over fifty

years old when he ascended the throne of his ancestors, as
he called it in his first speech to Parliament—too old to learn
a new language and new hunting ways. He never went out
if the weather was bad, hardly realised the Buckhounds, and
threw them and the Master of the Horse department into
commission and the greedy hands of the Duchess of Kendal.
An instance of the German complexion which pervaded everything at Windsor occurs in a picture at Windsor of George I.
out hunting in the Great Park with his suite, by Göhrde.
The names of the fourteen or fifteen personages are all given
on the tablet. With two exceptions they are all German.
Even one of these exceptions is Germanised, the huntsman
being handed down to posterity as 'Ned Finsch.' In fine
weather, however, the King went sporting occasionally. In
September, 1717, we hear of his diverting himself with hunting in Bushey Park. After which, alighting from horseback,
his Majesty walked above three miles with a fowling-piece
in his hand, and killed several brace of partridges flying.
During the summer of 1724 a stud of nice horses was got
together and sent to Windsor for the King's stag-hunting, but there is no account of his ever using them. He
went out pheasant-shooting in August of the same year,
earlier than even the writers of the first of October leading
articles begin their pheasant-shooting. From eight in the
morning till nearly five that day he only shot two and a
half brace, and one and a half brace of partridges. But,
besides the gratitude we owe to George I. for the passive
respect he paid a free government and a free people, we
must, with the picture of the Queen's Jubilee Procession
fresh upon our minds' eye, ever be grateful to him for
bringing over the cream-coloured horses and their scarlet
housings of velvet and morocco.[1]

[1] For very many years past the cream-colours have all been bred at Hampton
Court. The only new blood that has been obtained—at all recently—was in 1893,

According to Mr. Green, George I. had the manners of a gentleman-usher. Gentlemen-ushers are not clearly defined types of human nature, but I take them to be personages versed in the grave issues and nice points of Court ceremonial. At all events, when he fell out with his son the rupture was so decisive that the servants of the Prince of Wales's

THE CREAM HORSE
From an oil painting in the Queen's collection at Windsor Castle

children were not allowed to wear scarlet liveries, only yellow ones being permitted 'according to precedent.' However, the Prince of Wales and 'cette diablesse Madame la Princesse,' as her father-in-law habitually called her, made the best of it, and set up for themselves at Leicester House and

when a two-year-old stallion and filly were bought of Prince Schaumberg-Lippe. The Prince's stud was sold by auction in the beginning of this year, and I believe the Queen's and the Hanover stud are the only ones in Europe. Four brood mares are always kept at Hampton Court, and only stallions are used in the State coach.

Richmond Lodge, 'where,' says Walpole, 'the most promising of the young gentlemen of the party, and the prettiest and liveliest of the young ladies, formed the new Court.'

George II., soon after his accession, appointed Colonel Francis Negus Master of the Buckhounds. The colonel was to defray all expenses on a yearly salary of 2,341*l.*, and this stipend appears to have continued till 1782. The accounts as compared with the present day are chiefly remarkable for their variety. The responsibility of the Master of the Buckhounds covered, as Mr. Hore says, a wide field of action. Colonel Francis Negus had all sorts of things to do besides looking after the hounds and hunt-horses. He distributed King's Plates at race-meetings, fed the wild turkeys in Bushey Park, and managed the royal menagerie in Hyde Park, where the king's tiger accounted for six pounds of boiled beef and mutton daily. Extracts from other sources of information appal one by the number of hunting and other accidents. Thus we have the Duke of Grafton, at that time Lord Chamberlain, thrown into a mill-race near Datchet and very nearly drowned; and pages of honour, hunt servants, ladies of the bedchamber, physicians, and gentlemen and gentlewomen of all sorts and conditions are always coming to grief and having to be bled. One day a stableman was riding an over-fresh horse which took fright at a swan which flew out at it from the canal in Bushey Park. The horse ran away, impaled itself on some iron spikes, and had to be destroyed. Lady Suffolk said it was lucky the man was not hurt, on which the king snapped her up very short. 'Yes, I am very lucky, truly; pray where is the luck? I have lost a good horse, and I have got a booby of a groom still to keep.' Lord Hervey instances this as an example of George II.'s rudeness and want of feeling, but even kings are human.

On one occasion, Sir Robert Walpole's horse fell just in

front of Queen Caroline's chaise; it was on August 14, a hot and dusty day, not the time of year one would choose either for hunting or for falling on a hard road. Sir Robert was not hurt, and soon remounted. The Queen, however, ' ordered him to be bled by way of prevention.' Sir Robert was Ranger of Richmond Park, and hunted a good deal with the Buckhounds in a green suit, sometimes, Mr. Hore tells us, officiating as Field Master. No doubt he did it capitally. The best of hacks will fall, but possibly Sir Robert did not ride very well-bred ones, as Horace Walpole used to relate that his father rode two horses to a standstill between London and Richmond Lodge, on the afternoon of June 14, 1727, when he galloped down to tell the Prince of Wales that his father had died on his way to Hanover. Perhaps they were Norfolk hackneys.

New terrors were added to hunting at this time by the number of highwaymen who infested the neighbourhood of London. Thus, when Lord Tankerville, Master of the Buckhounds in 1733, sets out from London in June to make arrangements for the hunting season, he takes with him ' a guard of retainers and troops.' Little else is recorded of his Lordship's Mastership, but Sir R. Walpole had a good opinion of Lady Tankerville, and recommended her for the discharge of delicate duties. When in later years he advised the Queen to choose the king a mistress, rather than let him choose one for himself, as he was bound to have one, Sir Robert proposed Lady Tankerville as a decent and obliging sort of woman in preference to Lady Deloraine, who had two dangerous things, a weak head and a pretty face.

Mr. Ralph Jenison, M.P., appointed Master in 1737 and again in 1746, is the last commoner who has filled the office. As far as I know, Mr. Jenison was the only Master of the Buckhounds who was painted by Sir Joshua Reynolds. The picture is in the possession of Mr. Adair, who succeeded to it from Lord Waveney. It is a curious thing how few people Sir Joshua Reynolds painted in hunting or even in riding dress. I only remember one lady, a most distinguished and admirable picture of Lady Charles Spencer, in a scarlet habit, deerskin riding-gloves, with—it must be admitted—

NEW TERRORS WERE ADDED BY THE HIGHWAYMEN

a shocking grey horse. This picture is now at Ferrières. Of course there must be several others, at all events of men. At the same time Sir J. Reynolds did not look to dress for the breath of life as much as Velasquez and Gainsborough did. He is rather too prone to robe, or rather garb his women, and to pose them as saints or nymphs.[1]

But to get back to hunting: in 1735 the great crowds which came out with the king's hounds led to arrangements by which people could only hunt by ticket, which had to be

[1] Dr. Johnson criticises this: 'I should grieve to see Reynolds transfer to heroes and to goddesses . . . that art which is now employed in diffusing friendship, in renewing tenderness, in quickening the affections of the absent, and continuing the presence of the dead.'

signed by the Ranger of Windsor or his deputy. As the
Great Western, one of the motor muscles of the Queen's
Hounds, was not available in those days, Londoners could
hardly have got as far as Windsor; but be that as it may,
the London merchants and tradesmen have been fond of
hunting from old time. A charter of Henry I. entitled the
citizens of London to hunt deer 'as freely as their ancestors
had done' in the Chiltern Hundreds, Middlesex, or Surrey,
and the wolf in Middlesex and up to the northern gate of
the City. The Lord Mayor of London, who is still regarded
by many French newspapers and most French people as the
head of most of our institutions, including the House of
Lords, was the ex-officio master of the 'Common hunt,' and
riding to it was an ancient and cherished civic right. But
an 'inundation' of building, to quote a contemporary writer,
spoiled the Common hunt country in the reign of Elizabeth.
Deer were getting scarce, for the forest country was shrink-
ing away before the needs of population, and the fields
of Islington and St. Giles no longer witnessed the once
familiar spectacle of a hare or a stag pursued with due
solemnity by the sleek pack of some worshipful City company. With less hunting, gout, which was at this time
styled 'the enemy,' began to infest the well-to-do City men.
They soon became, like George Selwyn's friend, too 'able'
judges of a turtle. In his 'Pills to Purge Melancholy,'
D'Urfey makes fun—or what passes for fun in his estimation—of the Common hunts, and describes the City notables
riding through Cheapside and Fenchurch Street with their
spurs put on upside down and their backswords across their
rumps. Arrived at the fixture the master gets to business:

> My Lord, he takes a staff in hand to beat the bushes o'er,
> I must confess it was a work he ne'er had done before;
> A creature bounceth from the bush, which made them all to laugh,
> My Lord he cried, 'A hare! a hare!' but it proved an Essex calf.

And so on and so on.

This is not quite fair; as Mr. Hore tells us that the Common hunt, under the mastership of a Mr. Cuttenden, was showing good sport in 1723. By this time, however, many members of the Common hunt hunted with the Buckhounds, not perhaps at Windsor, but about Bushey and Richmond and Hampton Court, and Mr. Hore pleasantly describes a celebrated hunting alderman, Humphrey Parsons, twice Lord Mayor of London, and a predecessor of Colonel Thornton, Mr. Chaworth Musters, and 'Jacob Omnium' in the forests of Chantilly and Fontainebleau:

'Towards the end of the reign of George I., Humphrey Parsons became very conspicuous through an incident which took place when he was hunting with the staghounds of Louis XV. in the forest of Fontainebleau, in the month of September, 1725. On this occasion we are told that Alderman Parsons, "being mounted on a spirited English horse, contrary to the etiquette of the French Court, outstripped the rest of the field, and was first in at the death. The king enquiring who the gentleman was, one of the adulatory attendants indignantly answered that he was 'Un Chevalier de Malte.' The king, however, entering into conversation with Alderman Parsons, asked the price of his horse, upon which the Chevalier, with true politeness, answered that it was beyond any price otherwise than his Majesty's acceptance. The king could not resist the acquisition of so perfect a hunter, even upon such terms; consequently, it was duly delivered at the royal stables. As a *quid pro quo*, Louis XV. gave Alderman Parsons—who was a famous brewer—an exclusive monopoly of serving the French nation with his Extract of Malte, yclept in the vernacular 'London Stout.'"'[1]

Somerville, to whom the first Lord Fitzhardinge always

---

[1] *History of the Buckhounds*, by J. P. Hore, ch. xii. pp. 264–5.

declared he owed all his knowledge of hunting, was himself
a master of the hounds. He wrote his poem 'The Chase' in
George II.'s reign. It was still the age of elaborate similes,
and the poet seizes the opportunity of paying a tribute to the
king's military talents in a comparison of a level pack of
hounds to a body of troops :

> As some brave captain, curious and exact,
> By his fix'd standard forms in equal ranks
> His gay battalion ; as one man they move.
> Step after step ; their size the same, their arms,
> Far gleaming, dart the same united blaze ;
> Reviewing generals his merit own.
> How regular ! how just ! And all his cares
> Are well repaid, if mighty GEORGE approve.
> So model thou thy pack, if honour touch
> Thy generous soul, and the world's just applause.

But although he had his fixed hunting days, George II.
had very little complaisance for other people who wished
to go away from London for their hunting. Lord Hervey
tells us that when the king got back from Hanover
in November, 1735, nothing English suited him; no English horses were fit to be ridden or driven; no English
coachman could drive, no English jockey ride. The men,
he said, only talked of their dull politics, the women of
their ugly clothes. It is true that he had upset himself,
Lord Hervey adds, by travelling in 'a violent manner,
only for the pleasure of bragging how quick he moved,'
but on arriving in London he was annoyed at finding Sir
Robert Walpole gone off to Norfolk for his hunting 'congress,'
a thin Court, and a more or less empty town. This—Sir Robert
being away—he put up with rather crossly, as he said no
man worked harder than Sir Robert Walpole, and that his
mind wanted rest and his body exercise ; [1] but he had no

---

[1] Sir Robert Walpole only took thirty days' holiday in the year, ten in
August and twenty in November, when he entertained a large hunting party at
Houghton.

patience with the Duke of Grafton, who also wanted to be
off fox-hunting. The king told him it was a pretty occupation for a man of quality and of his age to hunt a poor fox.
The duke said he did it for his health. Upon this, the
king asked him why he couldn't ride post for his health,
adding pertinently that, with his 'great corps of twenty
stone weight,' no horse could carry him within hearing, much
less within sight, of his hounds.

This period marks the commencement of a radical change
which was gradually taking place in the relations between
town and rural society in England, and which could not but
have an important effect upon country sports. Hunting, and
especially fox-hunting, was now beginning to attract the
attention of the ancestors of the men who were later on to
inspire 'Nimrod's' pen and Ferneley's and Alken's pencil.
In the earlier years of the eighteenth century hunting was
the business of the smaller gentry and of the parsons, and
a rough, boisterous sort of affair. 'There he goes,' says
Diana Vernon of her cousin Thorncliffe Osbaldistone, ' the
prince of grooms, and cock-fighters, and blackguard horse-
coursers.' Here and there a great nobleman or considerable squire kept hounds, especially harriers.[1] At Badminton
and Brocklesby and Berkeley, at Belvoir and Goodwood, a
pack of hounds was part of the apparatus of the estate which
went on from father to son. But it is doubtful whether
the sort of people who hunt most now hunted much then,
and it certainly was never the serious occupation of the
Court in England as it was in France. During the last two

[1] 'I am very sorry,' writes Somerville to a friend, 'I must deny myself the
pleasure of your good company to-morrow. I was to-day with my Lord
Coventry's harriers, and I know Ball will not hold out two days together. I
meet them again on Thursday morning in Wilmcote Pasture, near Stratford;
and should think myself very happy in your good company. I must be there
at six in the morning. It may be that a little variety may please you, and
induce you for once to condescend to hunt hare.'— *Records of the Chase*, p. 156.

reigns a king over the water gave the zest, not only of self-interest but even of self-preservation, to the dreariest routine of Court life. Great people hung about the Court and kept themselves in evidence not perhaps so much on account of what they might be able to say or to do for themselves, but for fear of what others might say or do for them. Besides, an immense number of places, not merely of profit, but of influence under the Crown, were to be had, which entailed little ability or trouble. There were no Blue-books, no long speeches to read, no Press Association or Reuter telegrams—no public affairs or interests to keep in touch with. Politics were comparatively private transactions. Both in this country and in France the quick-witted, sharp-eared memoir-writers make us see that politics were then largely carried on by intercourse often of a gallant and agreeable kind, by conversation, and by the repetition of conversations. More business was got through in the corridors of St. James's or Kensington than in Whitehall. The Court backstairs teemed with better opportunities for parliamentary preferment than the House of Commons. The most powerful minister had often to square his accounts with a lord of the bedchamber or an attractive maid of honour, before he consulted his colleagues or gave the rein to his statesmanship. William III. had never let the conduct of foreign affairs out of his own hands. Up till the death of Anne, the Court to a great extent qualified the Cabinet. Anne presided with solemnity at her Cabinet. She kept up all the prestige of the appearance of a governing monarchy. But George I. and George II. were depressingly constitutional sovereigns, and were very much aware of Parliament and of the Whigs. George I. was preoccupied with the desire to leave well alone and to live out of England as much as he could; George II., although he was always crowing loudly to the contrary, was led by his wife, and his wife was guided by the

D

Whig Ministers. The place-hunter, inured alike to asking favours and to refusals, still flourished. He always will. But times were changing, and a gold stick was beginning to mean very little more than it looked.

London, and indeed town life generally, was very popular in the earlier years of the century. On the other hand, 'mere' was the adjective which seemed to belong of right to country life and country folk. In October, 1705, Mr. Pope writes to Mr. Wycherley from Bracknell of their character in Berkshire. Mr. Pope is very much out of humour with things in general, but 'methinks,' he says, 'these are most in the right who quietly and easily resign themselves over the gentle reign of dulness.' Then he comes to the hunting men of the district, ' a sort of modest, inoffensive people who neither have sense nor pretend to any, but enjoy a jovial sort of dulness. They are commonly known in the world by the name of honest, civil gentlemen. They live much as they ride—at random—a kind of hunting life, pursuing with earnestness and hazards something not worth the catching.' Lord Chesterfield's letters to his son abound in slighting references to these honest civil gentlemen. Tested by his standard of breeding and propriety, he has the least sympathy of all with fox-hunters. A good-natured fox-hunter, he says, may, of course, be 'intentionally civil,' but at the best he can only mean well. Capitals, which he likes extremely, are the only places to live in. There are only three capitals—London, Rome, and Paris—and London is the only possible one. The smaller men followed suit. Thus Dr. Warner, George Selwyn's chaplain, happening to arrive at Leicester in the race time, thinks it right to lament the poor show made by the country squires. 'God help them,' he says, 'with their triple bands and triple buckles to keep in their no-brain,' and he is disgusted at recognising a friend (Colonel Guise, of Highnam) with his hat decked with this ' post-boy ornament.' No doubt he pretended not to see him. In short, the doctor feels quite sick and sore about them, especially when he hears 'a well fancied oath from the mint of the metropolis' robbed of all its 'grace' by their vile pronunciation. 'Oh!' he cries, 'better is the corner of a housetop than an habitation amongst such tents of Kedar.'[1]

But about the middle of the eighteenth century a change in habits began to operate. It was partly due perhaps to Walpole's policy of proscription, and its political and social effect upon the Tories, but anyhow a larger country life came into fashion. The management of their estates, the breeding of stock, drainage, planting, and reclamation, as against the laying out of formal gardens and the posting of statuary, began to interest people. Lord Chesterfield's letters to his son, written with the object of making him a cunning and accomplished man of the town-world—for he was not to hunt like Wyndham, a Master of the Buckhounds, and only to eat, not to kill game—resulted in the best picture of him being the one in which he is talking over the points of a prize heifer with his agent in a straw-yard. George III. would have been delighted. 'For my part,' he said, when he read Lord Chesterfield's letters, 'I like more straightforward work.' The days of the country bumpkin who hunted all the morning, and, to Lord Chesterfield's disgust, appeared in the Pump-rooms at Bath in boots and spurs, a leather cap and a deerskin waistcoat, were numbered. He was no longer to be the interpreter of country life, and country life

[1] Dr. Warner, like many parsons, knew what a hunter should be. It was after the 'hard day's christening' that he writes, over-full of claret, to his patron about his travelling hackney: 'I was hunting yesterday on Bay Spavin, who astonished me with the discovery of qualities I never knew he possessed; agile as a spaniel and resolute as a lion. He wants thrashing along the road, but in the field, where I took him yesterday for the first time, he is all animation.'

was to take a new ply and tone from a very different type of man.

Turnips and seeds and sheep-shearings began to occupy the attention of great men. Towards the end of the century Burke's letters, as Mr. Birrell tells us, thrill with passion on these topics. Fox was never so happy as when in his fustian coat and white beaver hat he leaned over the palings at St. Ann's and talked to passers-by about the crops. Miss Maria Holroyd, whose letters so brightly reflect the ways of the political society in which she lived, writes of the farming rides she is looking forward to with her father, and Lord Sheffield himself, though detained in London by his official duties, writes fidgety letters about drilling turnips and taking advantage of the cooler weather and damp roads to send the waggon oxen to Lewes. Lord Althorp came later. But not the least of Lord Althorp's distinguished services to his generation were those he rendered to the management of grass lands and the breeding of sheep. High farming began to occupy the fruitful leisure of politicians in those days. In these days it is golf, or theology, or the unemployed.

I imagine that in memoirs written say since 1884 the term 'country party' would be meaningless. 'Coningsby' and 'Sybil' could not have been written without the country party, but Mrs. Humphry Ward finds no place for them in her admirable 'Sir George Tressady.' As far as political influence in the old sense of the term goes, the country gentlemen might just as well colonise the Gordon Hotels as live amongst their own people. Of late years neither party in the State has had to lull the suspicions or coax the prejudices of the 'Civis agricola' Montalembert admired so much. Except, perhaps, in Ireland, where, as Lord John Russell said, the land is still the life, the heart of politics has shifted from the country house to the streets.

In the latter half of the eighteenth century the fathers of the gentlemen in top-boots, who in Mr. Reynolds' picture are watching with gloomy dignity the last stage of the 1832 Reform Bill in the House of Lords, were just beginning to see where their real influence and interests lay. Even the great revolution families whom power and office kept constantly in London were always anxious to get away. Politics and hunting entered together upon a new phase of their existence. The former began to realise the country, the latter to catch the tone and fashion and style of the town. No doubt country life had always kept a strong hold of the English character, and the Court was neither splendid nor amusing. 'No lone house in Wales with a mountain and rookery is more contemplative than this Court,' writes Mr. Pope. But such a keen observer as Lord Hervey, quite as professed a lover of the town as Dr. Johnson or the Duke of Queensberry, speaks despondingly of 'the rural epidemic' madness which was becoming chronic.

I never came across any mention of the Master of the Buckhounds either in Lord Hervey's 'Memoirs' or in George Selwyn's letters. In the latter, however, there are frequent allusions to hunting, and the following witty description of a weight-carrying pony for sale might have been written yesterday. Writing to George Selwyn from Winchester, in April, 1767, Sir R. Smyth tells him that a Dr. Thistlethwaite is dead and his horses are to be sold:

'Amongst them is a little bay gelding, about thirteen or fourteen hands, with flaming full long tail, strong enough to carry you, the mayor, and all the money you ever spent in elections at Gloucester together. The Doctor, some forty-eight stone, always shot off his back, and the keeper killed all the deer from him. I mention this as a proof of his sedateness. He goes fast enough to carry you close to foxhounds in full chase; but if your affairs do not require so much attention a snail would distance him. His figure is such that if you were to meet a tailor on his back you would pull off your hat to him, though you did not owe him one shilling. I know twenty men of weight who want him, but the weight of metal will have him.'

I remember a horse-dealer saying to me at one of our periodical jingo high tides that a war would play the devil with hunting—he meant horse-dealing. In 1734 the Buckhounds played a very honourable part in our history. They helped to avert war. The affairs of Poland had led to a general international complication. The usual suspicion in this country was aroused as to the designs of France. 'I hate the French, and I hope as we shall beat the French,' said Lord Grantham, and everybody agreed with him. There were noisy appeals to national honour, and violent attacks were directed against the Minister. George II. was full of fight. His personal bravery was incontestable. He was longing to put on the hat and coat he had worn with distinction at Oudenarde at something more stirring than the public festivals at which they had hitherto appeared. Walpole stuck firm to his policy of neutrality and inaction. But Queen Caroline was inclining towards the war, and he wanted to bring her into his way of thinking. Lord Hervey hated standing armies with the holiest Whig hatred, and was entirely in Sir R. Walpole's 'interest' to boot. Luckily he had exceptional opportunities not only of learning the queen's sentiments, but of conveying to her his own and Sir R. Walpole's. Wednesdays and Saturdays were the king's hunting days. The king, who had the manners of a drill sergeant, always ordered the queen out, and she came out in a chaise. As this is not a lively amusement for four or five hours, she had undertaken to mount Lord Hervey the whole season, who, although he gave some promise as a jockey in his youth, tells us that he now loved hunting quite

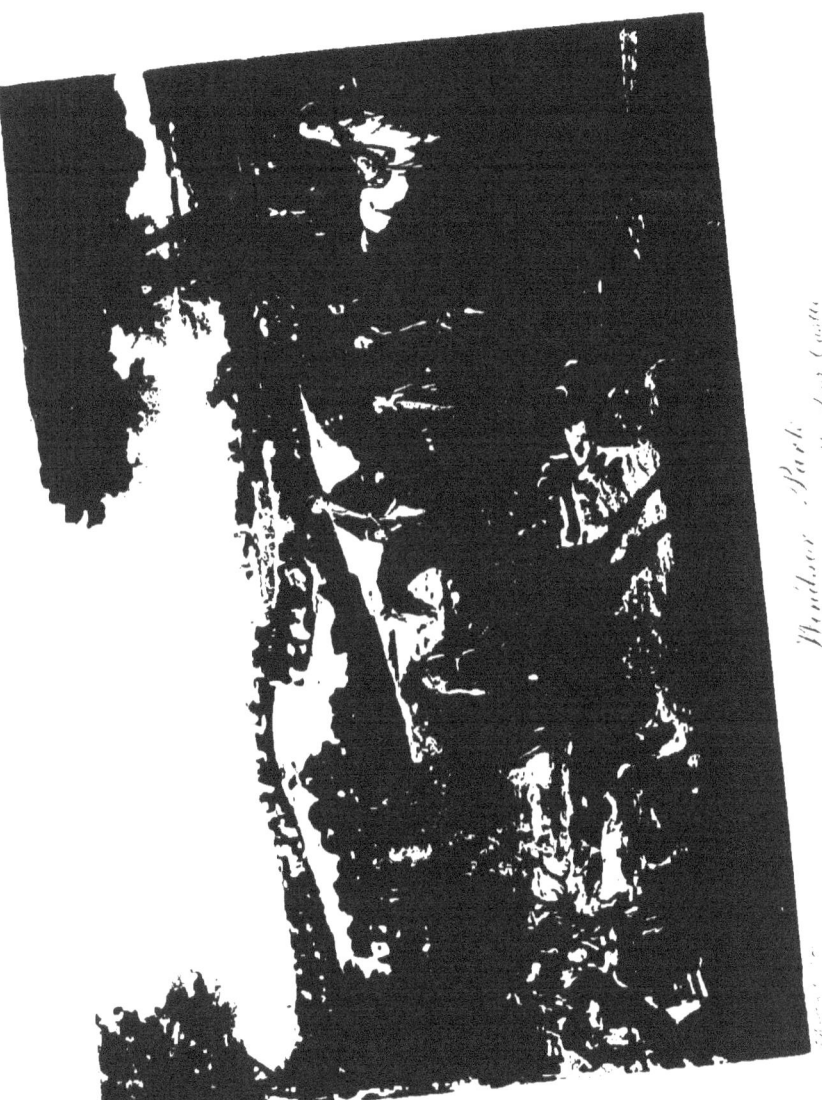

Windsor Park

as little as she did. By this arrangement he could ride
constantly by the side of the chaise and entertain her,
whilst others were entertaining themselves with hearing
dogs bark and seeing crowds gallop.' The most and the
best were made of one or two slow dragging stag-hunts,
whilst Sir Robert was keeping the field in order, or enjoying
himself at the tail of hounds. But Lord Hervey puts it in
a modest way. 'The queen herself,' he says, 'was enough
prejudiced too on this side [war], till Sir Robert Walpole
unwarped her from it, and made her see how much this
inclination jarred with her own interest.' This strange
Paul and Apollos planted and watered to good purpose.
'Madame,' Walpole was able to say to the queen one
morning in 1734, 'there are 50,000 men slain in Europe
this year and not one Englishman.' Surely that entitled
'le gros homme,' as the king called him, to laugh his heart's
laugh at coarse jokes and in coarse company. To call
spades spades, and take the world as he found it.

As far as I can make out, George I. and George II. confined their hunting operations to the parks, but George III.
was a stag-hunter of a very different mettle. His sport is
conscientiously recorded by the 'Brooksby' of the day in the
'Sporting Magazine.' The scribe's style feels the century; it
is elaborate and artificial. Still, in his own Court Newsman
sort of way he manages to tell us a good deal about the
stag-hunting. Here is his account of a run with a deer
called Compton: 'Lord Sandwich and his prime minister,
Johnson [the huntsman], on October 1, 1797, afforded such
a specimen of the superiority of stag-hunting as can scarcely
be found in the records of sporting history. Upon his
Majesty's arrival at Ascot Heath on the morning already mentioned, the deer Compton was liberated below the Obelisk,
and going off with the most determined courage and inexpressible speed, bid a seeming adieu to all competition. The

hounds were laid on with only five minutes' law, and the scent laying well they went away, breast high, in a style that "beggars all description"; eight of the fleetest horses only, out of at least a hundred, being enabled to lay anywhere by the side of them, till headed in absolute racing by Johnson, the huntsman, assisted by Nottage and Gosden, two of the yeoman prickers.

They brought him to view at Black Nest; here he repeatedly endeavoured to leap the high paling of Windsor

TURNING OUT THE DEER FOR THE ROYAL HUNT ON WINDSOR FOREST

Great Park, but without success, and the deer, hounds and horsemen were all intermixed in one general scene of confusion, when, by a most wonderful exertion, the deer reached the park by the hawhaw through the shrubbery, and plunging into the immense sheet of Virginia Water, passed entirely through it. Here his Majesty entered most energetically into the spirit of the chase, absolutely assisted in getting the hounds forward, laying them on where the deer left the water, and speaking to them in a sporting-like style.'

His Majesty's hounds hunted from September 25— Holyrood Day—till the first Saturday in May. On Holyrood Day they at that time always met at Charity Farm, Billingbear. Either harvests must have been earlier than they are now, or this was all grass or forest country. Tuesdays and Saturdays were the hunting days, and in Christmas and Easter weeks they hunted alternate days. Crowds of foot people used to come out these holiday weeks, and we hear of their delight and amazement 'at the leaps of unprecedented height and exhibitions of uncommon strength' of an unnamed deer in and out of the back-gardens and drying-grounds of Staines. Then, as now, a great many people drove after the Buckhounds, the 'surrounding spot,' as a contemporary scribe calls the turn-out, being embellished and 'beautifully variegated' with carriages containing ladies of the first distinction. I dare say the lemon-yellow post-chaises and the gay curricles and their smart cargoes looked very nice; and one day his Majesty was given an opportunity of exhibiting in a 'striking and public manner' his proper solicitude for the ladies. It was in October, 1793, and the ground was iron-hard. Prince Adolphus, a distinguished stranger, was out. The deer ran indifferently, and the hard ground lamed half the horses. A Mr. Griffin Wilson, however, drove his lady in a phaeton after the hounds in so daring a fashion that the king, who was a little out of humour, asked him whether he thought he had driven fairly or not. Mr. Wilson seems to have had nothing to say in reply to so pointed a question, whereon the king proceeded to say that whatever right a gentleman had to his own neck, he had none to hazard a lady's. This improving of the occasion met, we are told, with very general approval.

The ladies, however, were not always out in carriages.

Lady Mary Wortley Montagu apologises to Lady Mar for having neglected her correspondence by saying she has not a moment unemployed now she is at Twickenham. 'I pass many hours on horseback, and, I'll assure you, ride stag-hunting, which I know you'll stare to hear of. I have arrived at vast courage and skill in that way, and I am well pleased with it as with the acquisition of a new sense.' Lady Mary Wortley Montagu was at this time in her sixty-fourth year, and was enjoying the service and companionship of a really nice horse. 'I have got a horse,' she writes to Lady Mar, 'superior to any two-legged animal, he being without a fault.' I dare say her friends wished she had not taken to hunting. 'Her narratives,' Horace Walpole writes to somebody, 'become incomparably tedious.'

Now for the young ladies. Mr. Pope, as we have seen, tells Miss Martha Blunt how he meets the Prince of Wales, with all the maids of honour on horseback coming back tired and hot from hunting. These ladies can hardly have done themselves justice on the hired hacks provided for them. But the 'Sporting Magazine' speaks of Lady Lade and Lady Shuldham as always being well up. Lady Lade, who had started in life as a cook, after a good run in October, 1796, is declared to be the first horsewoman in the kingdom. In the picture at Cumberland Lodge she is in a lightish blue habit. The conspicuous horse is a bay brown against a very real Windsor background. It is a charming painting and the landscape is in Stubbs's best manner.¹ On

¹ This picture must have been a commission of the Prince of Wales—for we hear of her attracting the Prince's admiration out hunting at Windsor. Lady Lade was also greatly noticed at the execution of Sixteen-String Jack, a notorious and popular highwayman, who was hanged at Tyburn. He was remarkable for the originality of his dress, and for wearing a bunch of sixteen strings at the knees of his breeches. Neither she nor Sir John Lade can have been to the king's liking. Lady Lade was also painted by Sir Joshua Reynolds in a big hat. She looks very pretty and demure in this picture. Blue habits faced and turned up with red, and white beaver hats with black feathers, were the regulation for the queen, princesses and ladies of the Court in 1779.

another occasion when the Buckhounds met at the Blackbirds on Waltham Common, we hear of a young lady displaying 'a specimen of agility in following the hounds through the enclosures as would have surprised Lady Salisbury herself'— I suppose the same Lady Salisbury who wrote upon archery in the first number of the 'Sporting Magazine,' and who hunted her own harriers. She was burned to death at her writing table.

THE ACCOMPLISHED SPORTSWOMAN

George III. was 'critically exact to time.' At eleven o'clock he used to ride up on his hackney, accompanied by the master of the horse, his equerries and retainers, and any distinguished guests or strangers. His favourite hunters were Hobby and Perfection. The hounds were twenty-four to twenty-six inches, lemon pyes and black and white, with big ears, and could run for half an hour, giving tongue like Big Ben, but they never could have driven like the present foxhound pack. They were always being stopped to let his

Majesty get up, which is not surprising, as he rode nineteen stone ; but if the accounts of their runs are to be trusted, they seem to have dragged over great tracts of country. The story of George III. driving home to Windsor in a butcher's cart, after a quick run to Aldermaston, miles beyond Reading, is well known. On that occasion he surprised the butcher by his wise converse on beef and mutton. George III. wore a light blue coat with black velvet cuffs, and top-boots buckled up behind. An old workhouse dame told the 'Druid' how she had once seen the deer taken near Leatherhead ; years had created a confusion in her mind between the gay dress of the huntsman and servants and the simple insignia of the king. 'His Majesty wore a scarlet coat and jockey cap, with gold all about ; he had a star on his heart, and we all fell on our knees.' She was probably right about the cap. They came into fashion in 1786, when George III. discarded his three-cornered hat. The old Duke of Grafton, Lord Grenville and Lord Pembroke had always worn caps, and they now became general out of compliment to the king. The six yeoman prickers wore the scarlet and gold braid coats as they do now. The Master wore the same gold couples and belt he wears to-day, and I suppose scarlet ; but in a coloured engraving of the picture by Sir J. Reynolds of Mr. Jenison, the coat is green and faced with red, and more like the 'vénerie' coat of the Second Empire, which I believe was an exact revival of the Louis XV. hunt coat, except that the Bourbon coat was blue and the Empire green.

This is what happened after the deer had been safely taken : it is all much the same as now.

'The horns now repeat the musical prelude of the morning. This ceremony continuing a few minutes for the purpose of demonstrating to the hounds that they have obtained a victory, they are drawn off, and the deer conducted to the first farmhouse or receptacle of safety, from whence he is removed on the following day to the paddocks at Swinley Lodge, before described. The time and place of meeting for a future day being adjusted before the departure of his Majesty with his attendants, he generally proceeds to the nearest town where a post conveyance can be procured, and returns instantly to Windsor; and most frequently without taking the least refreshment, whatever may be the distance or the length of the chase. Instances have occurred when his Majesty had not reached the castle till eight or nine in the evening, at the dreariest season.'

George III. rode to a pilot. On one occasion they came to a place which the king did not quite fancy. He hung a little. 'John has gone over, your Majesty,' said one of the equerries, hoping no doubt that a hole might be made for him. 'Then you may go after him,' said the king, and jogged off to find a nicer place. But the king's personal attendants do not appear to have been great thrusters. Very possibly they were indifferently mounted; but Colonel Gwyn, one of the equerries, who married Goldsmith's and Hoppner's Jessamy Bride, was a brilliant exception, and we hear of his going so well in a good run (October 24, 1797), that he is complimented upon displaying when out hunting 'more of the genuine unadulterated sportsman than the effeminate courtier.' Moonshine, Starlight, Compton, and Hightflyer were great Georgian stags. The two former earned their names from so often running them out of daylight. Moonshine ran for seven—some say for nine seasons. The deer were established in the same five paddocks at Swinley as the deer of to-day, their housekeeping being conducted 'in a style of invigorating luxuriance.' George III. acquired the freehold of the present paddocks of Swinley in 1782.

I happened to re-read the 'Four Georges' just as we began forest hunting in 1892—my first season as Master—and Mr. Thackeray shall tell, in his own beautiful English, the sadness of the last few years of our stag-hunting king's life. 'He was not only sightless, he became utterly deaf. All light, all reason, all sound of human voices, all the pleasures of this world of God, were taken from him. Some slight lucid moments he had; in one of which, the queen desiring

MOONSHINE, A CELEBRATED DEER, FREQUENTLY HUNTED BY
HIS MAJESTY GEORGE III.

to see him, entered the room and found him singing a hymn, and accompanying himself at the harpsichord. When he had finished, he knelt down and prayed aloud for her, and then for his family, and then for the nation, concluding with a prayer for himself, that it might please God to avert his heavy calamity from him, but if not, to give him resignation to submit. He then burst into tears, and his reason again fled.'

The blue hunting coat had to be folded away. The early farming rides, the punctual hunting mornings, the kennels, the deer paddocks, the hunter-stabling passed away for ever out of his life. If he had a careful and affectionate valet, I dare say the queer old top-boots were put into grease against his getting better and wanting them. If not, I suppose that, like their master, they just perished away.

CHAPTER II

THE NEW SCHOOL

*The good of other times let others state,
I think it lucky I was born so late*

IN 1813 the historic Charlton hunt was broken up. The Regent acquired the Goodwood hounds by gift from the fourth Duke of Richmond, and Charles Davis went to the Ascot kennels as first whipper-in under Sharpe, his future father-in-law.

Mr. Mellish, Master of the Epping Forest Hounds, had been robbed and murdered one evening on his way home after hunting with the King's hounds and dining at the Bush in Staines; and from this time a couple of boys on horseback used to be sent out with the Buckhounds whenever George III. hunted. Each boy carried a brace of horse pistols, which at the end of the day they handed to the yeomen prickers who rode home alongside of the king. According to the 'Druid,' Charles Davis started as one of these boys. The 'Druid' in his own line, and within the very differing limits of his opportunities, was as felicitous a compiler of hearsay as Boswell. Take, for instance, his drive with Dick Christian in 'Silk and Scarlet.' He gives to everything he hears from others a visible flash of life and character which makes it, as it were, fasten upon the eye as you read. Sometimes, perhaps, he relates what he would have liked to hear in addition to what he heard. When his admirers gave him a dinner in 1859, Charles Davis himself told them

EASTER MONDAY. A VIEW NEAR WINDSOR
GENTLEMEN SPORTSMEN ENDEAVOURING TO LEAD THE FIELD

circumstantially about this 'unfortunate gentleman's' fate, and how from that time on, two yeomen prickers with pistols always accompanied George III.'s carriage back to Windsor. But as he gives no colour to this being a personal reminiscence, I must reject with regret a legend which it would have pleased me to preserve.

The arrival of the Goodwood Hounds at Ascot started a new period in stag-hunting. From this time stag-hunting of the present day may be said to date. The old order changed in many ways. Up till the end of the century the Royal yeomen prickers all carried French horns, which we may be sure they wound pretty frequently, and a great musicianing went on when the deer was first uncarted, 'an awfully impressive prelude,' says our chronicler. 'We comfort our hounds with loud and couragious cryes and noises both of voyce and hound,' writes a stag-hunter of 300 years ago. Even now stag-hunting is apt to be rather a noisy proceeding. Lord Chesterfield presented Frederick, Prince of Wales with a black boy named Cato,[1] who instructed the gentlemen of his household in blowing the French horn and the various calls and signals of musical venery. Africans were as honourably associated with the horn in those days as the French with cooking in ours. The celebrated 'Hellgate' Lord Barrymore kept four Africans in scarlet and silver on the staff of his Louis XV. hunting retinue; and I have a little picture at home of a fashionable early eighteenth-century *concerto*, with two Africans in the background making the utmost of their opportunities.

A sustained chorus of horns and vociferous hounds greeted the arrival of his Majesty at the meet, sped the

[1] Cato was the great *maestro* of his day. Sir Walter Gilbey has a picture by Wootton in which Cato in a turban and aigrette appears with his horn. *Vide* Hore, *Hist. of the Royal Buckhounds*, p. 322.

deer upon his way when first uncarted, and enlivened all concerned when he was taken. One way and another, says the sporting magazine of the day, a meet of the Royal hounds graced by 'the condescending affability and kindness of the Sovereign to the loyal subjects who love and surround him, may be candidly considered a repast too rich, a treat too luxurious, for a meeting at the side of a fox-hunting covert to be brought into a successful competition with.' But these ceremonies were now dispensed with, and the term 'yeoman pricker' gradually fell into disuse. Only the huntsman now carried a horn of the present bugle shape, and a fast foxhound pack cram-full of the stout Goodwood and Egremont blood—Jaspers and Dromos, Ledgers and Jumpers—took the place of the old Magpies and were entered to deer. 'It delights me,' George IV. writes to the 'gentleman huntsman,' as he always called Davis when, on Sharpe's retirement in 1822, he was appointed to that post, ' to know you have got the hounds. I hope you will get them so fast that they will run away from everybody.'

The purport of his son's good wishes on Davis's appointment would have made George III.'s flesh creep. But George IV.'s hunting notions and sympathies, even during his father's lifetime, were so entirely with the new school of stag-hunting that I have purposely made no mention of him in the chapter I have devoted to the Georgian period; this seems to be the right place to do so.

On New Year's Day, 1828, Davis notes in his diary that Dom Miguel of Portugal hunted an untried Windsor havier from Salt Hill. The Dom was attended by a distinguished company, including the Duke of Wellington, Lord Maryborough, who was Master of the Buckhounds at the time, and Lords Mount Charles and Albert Conyngham. The king himself had made very proper preparations to accompany this grandee out hunting, although he did not actually

grace the proceedings with his presence. When George IV.'s wardrobe was sold after his death, everybody was surprised at its variety and profusion. It was the history of dress for the last fifty years in this country, and an *édition de luxe* of the orders and Court costumes of every Court in Europe. Whips and canes alone amounted to several hundreds, and Mr. Greville, who was on most confidential terms with the king's valet Batchelor, especially notices a dozen brand-new pairs of corduroy riding breeches which he had ordered to hunt in with Dom Miguel. It was said that the time Louis XV. devoted to elaborating statistics and returns of his stables and kennels would have sufficed to post him up in the interior economy of his army; and George IV. appears to have spared himself as little when clothes were concerned. Baron Gronow tells us in his Memoirs of the hours of meditative agony which the Prince of Wales dedicated to the fashions of the day, and up to the last, as his pages lamented, he had a very wicked memory for clothes, and often upset them by asking to look at a coat which neither he nor they had seen for years. At the time of Dom Miguel's visit, however, he had become much too heavy to think of hunting; indeed, owing to his great weight and swelled legs, he had not hunted for a long time; so the order can only have been given from a sense of the eternal fitness of things, and by way of a tribute to the days when he lived at Kempshot and rode his dear Curricle,[1]

---

[1] 'Curricle,' according to the inscription on the back of the picture from which the illustration is taken, was a brown horse 'got by Trentham out of a sister to Gay, and was bred by the third Duke of Richmond as a racehorse; he was considered remarkably speedy, but neither slow in carrying weight nor running a distance. As a hunter, however, he possessed all the three rare qualities quite to perfection.' Stephen Goodall, the heaviest servant to hounds in the kingdom, rode Curricle for many years. He was bought at a very high figure for His Royal Highness the Prince of Wales, the Prince ever after declaring that Curricle was not only the finest but the best horse he ever saw, and that the best runs he ever witnessed were from the back of his 'dear Curricle.'

and when his name stood at the head of the list of the Hampshire Hunt.

George IV. then Prince of Wales—lived at Kempshot from 1788 to 1795,[1] and he had a pack of staghounds which were hunted by George Sharpe, who afterwards went to Ascot as huntsman, and whose daughter Charles Davis married. The stables at Kempshot were full of high-priced horses, but the stable management was bad and they never looked well. The Prince was already very gouty, and a stout, strong woman named Nancy Stevens acted as his nurse, and always helped him in and out of his bath. Whilst he lived at Kempshot he hunted regularly, and a little from the Grange and Crichel, where he lived when he left Kempshot. It was whilst he was living at Crichel that he rode home one day with a Rev. William Butler, whom he cross-examined upon the drinking capacities of various esteemed boon companions in the neighbourhood. He asked the reverend gentleman whether it was true that a certain gentleman was in the habit of drinking three bottles a night. Mr. Butler had no accurate information, but was inclined to give no credit to the story, adding that he would be ' as drunk as a prince.' When the Prince got home he told the story against himself, but he did not quite like it at the time. Many years afterwards Mr. Butler attended a levee, and the Regent was heard to mutter : ' The Rev. William Butler ; I sha'n't forget the Rev. William Butler.' Shortly afterwards he presented him with a fat Crown living. Once, when Mrs. FitzHerbert was staying at Kempshot, there was a great lawn meet and breakfast. Lady Jersey and Lady Conyngham followed the hounds on horseback ; but Charles James Fox —who once rode post part of the way to Newmarket on the wheeler behind the Prince of Wales on the leader, with the postillions inside— though booted and spurred, was so

[1] *Sporting Reminiscences of Hampshire*, by ' Æsop ' (F. Heysham, Esq.)

H.R.H. THE PRINCE OF WALES'S TWO CHESNUTS

FROM THE PICTURE BY STUBBS (1793) IN THE QUEEN'S COLLECTION AT CUMBERLAND LODGE

gouty that particular morning, that he could neither ride nor walk. In 1793 the Prince of Wales gave up his staghounds, and Mr. Poyntz of Midgham, who only gave 8l. for his unfortunate hunt-servants' horses, but always drove up to the meet with four horses and postillions, took over the direction of his hounds and turned them into foxhounds.

At this time, and indeed for many years later, George IV. never seemed tired of trying hacks and hunters; nor could he resist an invitation from Milton —the great horse-dealer of the day—or anybody else to give the company at Carlton House or the Pavilion a show. By all accounts he rode a hack well, his seat being so easy that it is said never to have soiled or ruffled his tight nankeen pantaloons; and his favourite hacks Tiger and Tobacco Stopper carried him to perfection. Tiger was light below the knee, and he was told he should give up riding him. He refused, saying, 'Tiger disdains to fall down.'

In 1786 Wraxall tells us that the Prince of Wales was in the full bloom of his looks and accomplishments, and that he led the way in every sort of fashionable pleasure and sport. There is a picture of him by Hoppner at Hertford House which fully bears out Wraxall as to the distinction of his good looks and the mantling bloom of his complexion; a lovely kitcat of poor Mrs. Robinson (Perdita) hangs in the same room. He is in a blue coat with a star, and wears his own wavy hair. The pose is instinct with the 'fascinating ease' Lady Jerningham admired so much. Even in those Florizel days he was under the ascendency of his uncle Ernest, Duke of Cumberland, whom he grew to dislike so much in later years. The Duke of Cumberland did all he could to widen the breach between father and son and to consolidate a Carlton House party. According to Lord Hervey, Walpole pursued the same tactics with George II. and Frederick Prince of Wales; but, whereas Walpole did his utmost to prevent them meeting in the peace-making circumstances of hunting, the Duke of Cumberland and the Prince of Wales were often out on the king's hunting days, not, however, to amuse themselves, but to annoy him. Neither of them ever spoke to him, and they made fun of his slow ways, slower horses, and homely clothes.

About this time the Duc de Chartres (afterwards Philippe Égalité) and several French gentlemen of high degree came over frequently and hunted and made love in this country. It was a period of Anglomania in France, and the Duc de Chartres took all his men out of the Louis XV. liveries and jack-boots, and put them into long skirted scarlets, top-boots and hunting caps.[1] There was a constant interchange of hunting civilities between the great hunting folk on either side of the Channel. The Marquis d'Argenson arranged with the Duke of Grafton for long hunting visits, and actually built kennels at Les Ormes —these arrangements, which earned the difficult approval of Arthur Young, being interrupted by the Revolution. Mr. Meynell got so tired of the visitors out hunting that upon one occasion he was heard to say that he wished we were comfortably at war again.

Horses of all kinds, even during his last illness, were always in George IV.'s thoughts, and he saw most of Ratford, his stud-groom, who came to him on the Duke of Queensberry's ('Old Q.') death. There was no lack of constancy wherever they were concerned. In the middle of a great State function he turned to Mr. Greville, who was taking an official part in the proceedings, with a 'Which do you fancy—the horse or the mare?' in an audible aside, and

---

[1] When the Duc de Chartres first came over in 1783, Lady Clermont arranged a great dinner for him. According to Horace Walpole, he came dirty and in a 'frock' with metal buttons enamelled over with hounds and horses. Sir Joshua Reynolds painted him the same year, being commissioned to do so by the Prince of Wales. The picture was burned in the fire at Carlton House.

THE NEW SCHOOL

excused himself laughingly afterwards to the Duke of Wellington by saying it was 'a little bit of Newmarket.' But with his racing career and its vicissitudes, with his debts and his indiscretions, with the sincerity of his selfishness and the half-heartedness of his attachments and his friendships, these pages have no concern. For all these things, and more also, he has been apostrophised and trounced by Mr. Thackeray with an energy which, to my mind, damages the literary and critical perfection of the last of the 'Four Georges.' Considering, too, that Mr. Thackeray felt him to be a dressed-up sawdust marionette, it seemed hardly worth his pains. Many of the foibles to which his critic brings a cudgel would have been better chastened with a riding whip. Let us remember that a very charming woman dignified him by her disinterested and abiding affection, and that the Duke of Wellington, who had the meanest opinion of his judgment and found him a difficult man to do business with, declared him to be very clever and amusing.

At all events, stag-hunters of the first fifty years of this century owe much to George IV. He brought Charles Davis to Ascot: he insisted upon a fast foxhound pack. In Charles Davis, as we shall presently see, he promoted the right man to form and educate a new school of stag-hunters.

The king can certainly have seen little of the hounds in the field after Davis's appointment; but I dare say he saw them now and again in kennel. He told a Newmarket trainer one day at Ascot that he was very happy with his hounds and his Virginia Water. He used to drive himself about the Park and Ascot and Swinley. There is a picture of him in Huish's Memoir, driving away from the Sandpit gate, where he had a menagerie of the better-disposed wild animals. He is in his pony phaeton, sitting well up in a tight [1] double-

---

[1] Mr. Cobden, whose family have been established in Windsor as tailors to the Crown since the reign of George III., tells me that his grandfather used to

breasted coat, white duck strapped overalls, and a white
beaver hat. A yeoman pricker acts as outrider on a natty
bob-tailed horse with a lash to his whip, and two grooms,
dressed much as the Royal procession grooms are dressed
now, are riding behind. None of the party carry their whips
quite right; and George IV. the worst of all, out like a fishing
rod: but this must be the artist's and not his friend Sir
John Lade's [1] fault, who had taught him to drive in their
palmy days. But to return to the hounds. George Bartlett,
Davis's feeder, tells me that George IV. liked a light-coloured
hound, and wished Davis to stick to the Goodwood lemon-
pye, which for some few years after they came to Ascot
distinguished the Royal pack, a notable lemon-pye named
Minos being a great favourite of his. 'But,' says Bartlett,
'Davis liked a good tan, and wouldn't have them'; and
Davis was the sort of man who got his way. I am sorry
myself the lemon-pye has been lost. I like an odd colour
in hound or horse; it gives character. Moreover, neither
Davis nor King was very successful as regards colour,

go up to the Castle every evening to see to the buttons and button-holes of the
clothes the king had worn; some of which were certain to have started from
the tightness George IV. insisted upon.

[1] The Lades (or Ladds) were a remarkable pair of people. Lady Lade I
have already spoken of. Sir John was Mr. Thrale's ward, and his extravagance
prompted Dr. Johnson to write a poem on his coming of age. When Dr.
Johnson lay dying he repeated this poem with great spirit to Mr. Windham,
saying he had never repeated it but once before, and had only given one copy
of it away to Mrs. Thrale. There are several four-line stanzas full of zest and
point. Two must suffice here:

> 'Loosened from the minor's tether,
> Free to mortgage or to sell,
> Wild as wind and light as feather,
> Bid the sons of thrift farewell.

> 'Call the Betsys, Kates, and Jennies,
> All the names that banish care;
> Lavish of your grandsire's guineas,
> Shew the spirit of an heir.'

When Goodall took over the pack in 1872, the 'good tan' was conspicuous by its absence. 'I found them,' Frank Goodall writes to me, 'bad colours, mostly black and white.'

Davis's diaries and manuscript books are very well kept, but the comments are lamentably few, and he confines himself generally to the bare facts of the day—where they met, how long they ran, the expenses, and so on. But on May 2, 1829, Davis enters in his diary—it is almost the only entry where he commits himself to an observation : ' Turned out an elk at Swinley ; he wobbled away—I could not call it running—for half an hour, and I took him at Bagshot. The hounds would not hunt him.' The elk was to have been fatted for his Majesty, but he was ultimately sent to the Zoological Gardens. I suppose he came from the menagerie. As far as I know, this is the last record of George IV.'s direct intervention in the affairs of the Buckhounds, and not a very proper one.

Very few words will suffice for William IV. As a boy he hunted when ashore, and I have no doubt rode with the dash of a seaman and the undeniable courage of his race. But I have only been able to trace one circumstantial occasion to his credit as a stag-hunter. In 1791, the French Revolution being at its height, Kempshot was crammed with French *émigrés* of distinction ; and 'Æsop' relates how a stag-hunt was got up by the Prince of Wales for their amusement ; post horses being hired from Hartford Bridge to help out the Royal stables and mount them. William IV. was at that time a middy at Portsmouth and came out on a pony ; but he got into a deep ditch early in the day's proceedings. This hunt nearly drove Sharpe mad owing to the crowd, the confusion, and the horns of the excited visitors, which they had stuck to in spite of the

French Revolution and the hurry of their departure from France.

After William IV.'s death, the Hampton Court stud, which, contrary to expectation, he had kept up well, was broken up in spite of a memorial from the Jockey Club and remonstrances in both Houses of Parliament. The yearlings made very poor prices, and looked wretched owing to a visitation of influenza—the crack Wings having gone blind from the illness, and only making 46 guineas. Three high-caste Arabian mares covered by a thoroughbred sire headed the list; they made 50, 150, and 105 guineas respectively. A black Arabian stallion made 580 guineas, being bought by the German Government; and a bay Arabian, 450 guineas, by the French. But Turks and Arabians were by this time going steadily out of repute. Eastern blood seemed to have done all it could for us : its direct influence, indeed, was held to be against a horse, and in 1782 the Jockey Club, in the conditions of the new Cumberland Stakes, gave the immediate produce of an Arabian an allowance of 3 lbs.

I have now brought up the historical part of this book to the accession of our present gracious Queen. As the Adam Smith of stag-hunting economics, Charles Davis must have a separate chapter to himself.

CHAPTER III

CHARLES DAVIS

Non omnis moriar, multaque pars mei
Vitabit Libitinam.

CHARLES DAVIS was born at Windsor in January 1788. His good looks gave him his start. It is true that his father hunted the King's harriers,[1] and that in any event he would probably have entered the Royal service in some capacity or other. But this is Dr. Croft's account of the beginnings of his conspicuous career, as related to him by a very old inhabitant of Bracknell (since deceased), who knew all the circumstances. I give it in his own words: 'Young Davis had been to school at Windsor or Eton, and on returning home one day, went into the cloisters at the Castle, where he was met by the King. Davis was a slim, good-looking lad, and the King took a fancy to him, spoke to him, asked him what he might be going to do, &c. Davis could not say what he was going to do. The King asked him if he would like to go hunting. Davis's father was at this time huntsman to the King's harriers, but the King did not know that he was talking to his huntsman's son. The boy said he should like to go hunting very much. The King asked him

---

[1] In Davis's diary several mentions of hare-hunting occur, but they are casual and uninteresting. On May 14, 1832, Davis notes that the Duke of Brunswick and his suite hunted with the harriers in Windsor Great Park. Considering the time of year, and seeing that they turned out three box hares and killed them, it is strange to find him noting it as a good day's sport.

what his father was. In this way it came about that he was made whip under his father.'

So it was settled, and hunting became Charles Davis's profession when he was about twelve years old. But I think he went on with his schooling. His feeder, George Bartlett, who still lives at Ascot, and whose memory is excellent, tells me that George III. gave him 1*l*. a week and sent him to a school at Windsor, which probably means that the king arranged that he should stay on at school for a little longer, before going into service at the harrier kennels. 'Stoody, stoody, stoody, always stoodying at thy books. Take, I say, my advice, sir, and stoody fox-hunting,' said Luke Freeman—Lord Egremont's kennel huntsman and a great character—to one of his master's sons, the course of whose education interfered periodically with his hunting soon after Christmas. Doubtless the young 'sir' would have been only too pleased to have done so. An open January is a sweet and bitter month to many a schoolboy. But Davis, in spite of such an early apprenticeship to business, must have found time for his books as well as for his hunting. A few letters of his which I have seen are certainly the letters of a man of education. They are written in a graceful, early Victorian hand, the sentences have originality and turn and precision, proper words fall into their proper places, and there are no mistakes in spelling.[1]

The following is quite as good an example of his style as anything I have seen. It is in reply to Sir John Halkett's complaint that his hounds broke away directly they

---

[1] His biographer in 'Baily' tells us that he had a great liking for reading and that Charles Kingsley and Whyte Melville were favourites. Mr. Bowen May tells me that he remembers Lord Dufferin giving Davis *Letters from High Latitudes*, and that Davis had told him he had enjoyed reading it very much.

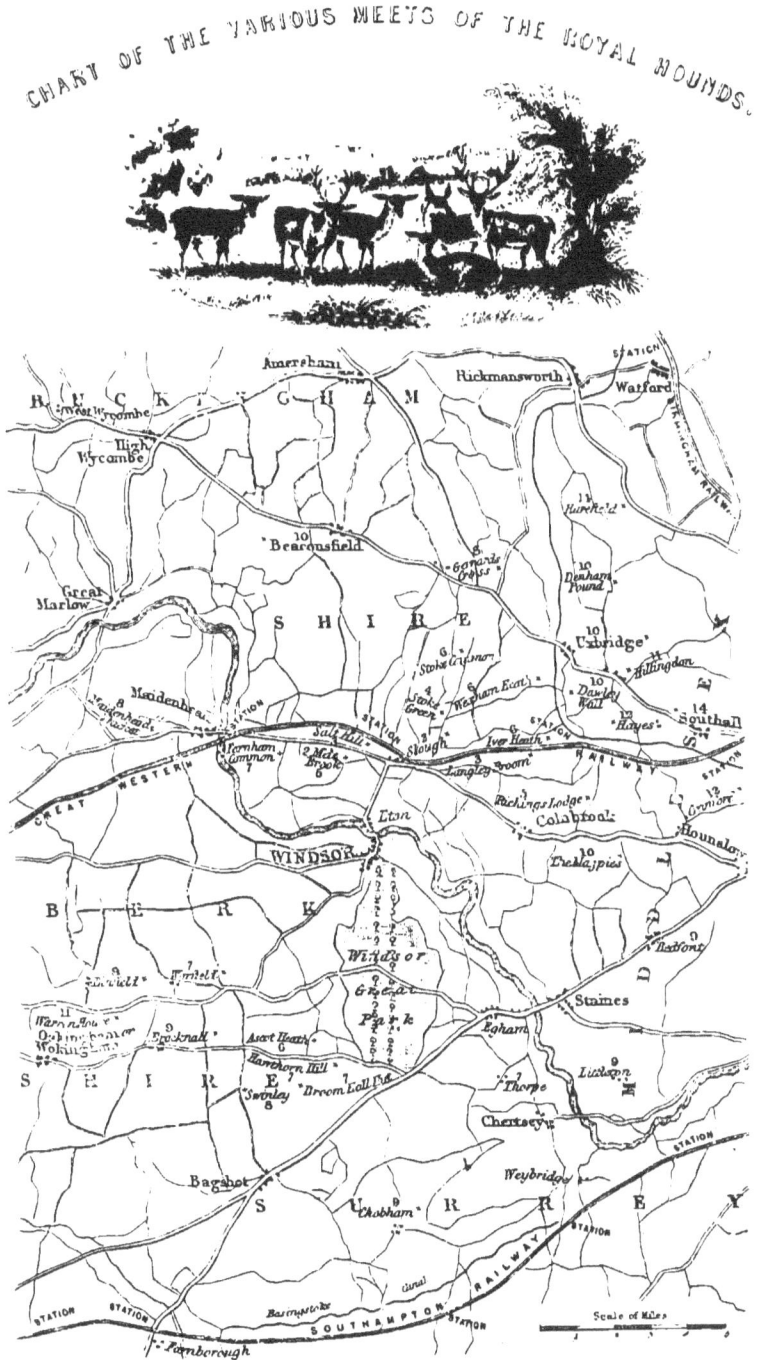

1841, FOR THE PROPRIETOR OF THE SPORTING REVIEW BY I. MITCHELL, 33 OLD BOND STREET

saw the deer van. Davis underlines heavily all the words printed in italics.

'Ascot Heath:
'December 12, 1839.

'Sir,—I am delighted to hear of your good sport, but am exceedingly grieved at your information respecting the Hounds breaking away: I always profess candour, and must therefore give my opinion thus. I really believe there is no cure for your grievance; it probably might have been *prevented*, the method of which cannot be put on paper, as it consists of a thorough knowledge of the temper, disposition, &c. &c. of each Hound—to so great a degree as to know what each intends to do, before putting their vice in practice—and at such times, speak not *harshly*, but kindly, and even *your countenance* must bear the impress of *friendship*.

'Correction I do not advocate, and it is equally wrong to say I *never* suffer the whip to be used—but certainly not when you are taking them to the meet; for by causing one Hound to cry out, the others would be off, "gadding o'er the plain." I am sorry to hold out no encouragement, but it is only an opinion after all. Hounds are sagacious beyond the belief of many, and man must use his own intellect, and learning too, to deceive them; therefore you must not try deception with them, but treat them with the greatest confidence, and make them know you are beholden to them, not *vice versa*. For instance, yonder is a cluster of people; they, the Hounds, know that the Deer is gone from that spot. You must *beg of them* to go there quietly, not say "You *shall* do so." If you saw me *trot* up to the spot, I must assure you it was an exception to my general way; for I creep as quietly and as slow as possible. Yesterday I did so, and stood some time within five yards of where the Deer left the cart. I never heard of any pack doing this but this one. Lord Derby's used to fly away in all directions; the Royal Hounds in the olden times did so too.'

There is always a natural and comfortable tendency, when a personality like Davis's is concerned, to take refuge in general terms. He was a perfect specimen of a royal servant: a thorough gentleman; a miracle in the saddle; an example everywhere else, and so on.

But as the present case is worthy of something more than mere generalities, I am indebted to many hunting men for personal recollections of Charles Davis—things they saw, things they knew; things they noticed and drew deductions from, and which had impressed themselves in colours, as it were, on the magic-lantern slides of memory.[1]

I shall first give extracts from Dr. Croft's and Mr. Cordery's letters in their own words. Both these gentlemen are excellent judges of hunting and of hounds; they are both Berkshire men; famous riders in their day, and were cradled, as it were, in the wildest and roughest part of the Queen's country, the forest and heathlands and the intricate Bracknell country. Writing to me from Bracknell, November 1895, Dr. Croft, in the letter already quoted, after telling me about George III. and Davis in the cloisters, goes on:—
'Davis's best time was before mine, but he was very good in my younger days. He left much in his latter days to his men, but he was always near enough to see what was going on. His hounds in the forest were as perfect in close hunting as harriers. They were left to depend on themselves, and so required but little assistance. "Let them alone" were his words to his whips at check. I never heard him say anything about a bad scent; he told me he would rather have a third-rate scent for his hounds, as the pace was then

---

[1] Especially to Colonel Anstruther Thomson, Sir A. Halkett, Captain King-King, Mr. Bowen May. Dr. Croft of Bracknell, and Mr. Cordery of Hall's Farm, Swallowfield.

quite fast enough for pleasure, as the pack would have to fling round occasionally and give you a chance to be nearer to them. The Bracknell country was very difficult to get over in former times—hedgerows very broad, and ditches wide and blind, much overgrown with grass and brambles. Davis had his field under good control, and he never minced the matter if he saw any man riding unfairly. His language was strong and not always parliamentary, but was most effective at the time, and, I have heard, lasted into the future.

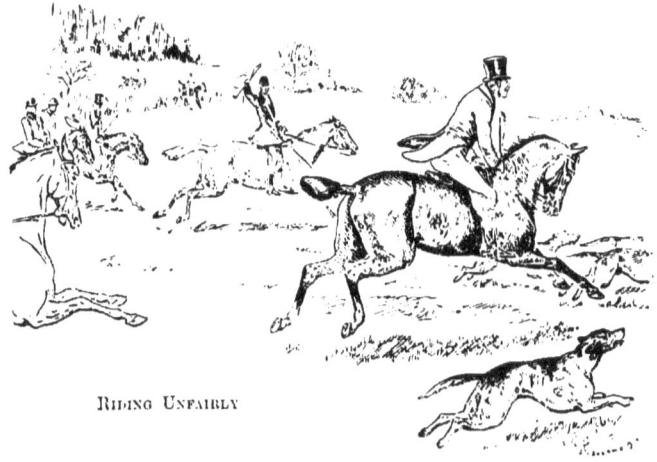

RIDING UNFAIRLY

If his temper was hasty it was soon over and forgotten. He was a perfect gentleman in appearance, manner, and conversation, well educated, and, I should say, of good ability.

'These hounds, as you know, from the first were foxhounds. I believe he bred from the best of his own and others, but he managed somehow to make them peculiarly his own, so much finer and more racy-looking than even the foxhounds of the present day. Getting them faster began, I dare say, when the King told him to make them fast enough to run away from the field. This most certainly he did, for they ran away from the field on several occasions in the Harrow country, and I have experience of their doing this in the Bracknell country.

'His hounds appeared to love him, and one of the prettiest parts of the day was, when a check occurred, to see them fly to his call, and all the pack cluster round his horse, and he take them to a holloa and plant them on the line of scent. I think this control was due in a great measure to his system of entering the young hounds in the forest in October. The deer were nearly always taken without injury, and many were hunted for years, and knew how to take care of themselves.'

Mr. Cordery first knew Charles Davis in 1835. He used to see him out with Sir John Cope's foxhounds—for Davis loved fox-hunting—and also with the buckhounds. 'I thought him,' he writes, ' as good as any one I ever saw on a saddle. Used to ride over a country very easy, and never seemed to distress his horse. He liked a clean, well-bred horse, and was master of him and his men and his field and his hounds. Respected by every one, his word was law, his hounds he loved, and woe be to the man who rode over one.

'Mr. Davis's hounds were not quite so high as yours. Bitches very neat, and smaller, I think. Perhaps your present pack goes a little faster than they did, that is because the country is so much more open now. Aldershot Common all open at that time, Wellington College and Broad Moor the only two houses. On each of these commons you could see hounds a mile off. Have been hunting all day and only have seen a man snipe-shooting. Very open and wild at that time ; much troubled with bogs where there were no rides. Mr. Davis did not ride fast at his fences ; good trot or canter he would ease his horse to.'

Catching your own again, as some one called hunting

the carted deer, lacks the inevitableness we prize in wilder sports of the field. All concerned know only too well, not perhaps quite what will happen, but what is meant to happen. Upon the other hand, the master and hunt-servants of a stag-hunting establishment—I speak from some experience —are always on the edge of novel and often ridiculous incidents.

Some people, however, seem able to invest the most untoward circumstances with their personal prestige. A few of this sort should be kept for stag-hunting. Charles Davis appears to have been one of these gifted personages. It is true that he hunted a very much better country, and that in other ways (which I shall refer to presently) he enjoyed substantial advantages which no Queen's Huntsman since his retirement has enjoyed or can hope to enjoy. Yet it cannot be supposed for a moment that he can have hunted the Buckhounds for the forty odd years he carried the horn without having to put up with his share of the tiresome things which attend upon stag-hunting. Some of these are difficult to suffer gladly;[1] and if record speaks true, we must remember that Davis had to satisfy a critical and superfinely mounted field who came out to ride, and to ride against each other. He must have been familiar, as we

[1] The following entries are, alas! familiar to most stag-hunters:

'February 5, 1824.—Paid two men 5s. 6d. for getting into the water at Uxbridge by Lord Maryborough's order.

'January 28, 1824.—Paid 2s. 6d. for a window broken by a stag.

'December 11, 1837. Met at Salt Hill; took in the Playing Fields, Eton.

'December 29, 1837.—" Seymour " destroyed himself in a conservatory at Taplow.'

This diary and a horse-book of Charles Davis were kindly lent me by Mrs. James King, widow of Mr. James King, a brother of Harry King's, who succeeded Charles Davis as her Majesty's Huntsman in 1866. Whether the amount of the fee or the 'getting into the water' was Lord Maryborough's 'order,' the amount is not excessive. I know the water at Uxbridge well. It used to affect me very much in the same way as the waters of Babylon did the Jews of the Captivity. About the worst place I know, to take a deer comfortably.

are now, with the good-natured but irresponsible foot people; with the deer which runs up and down the first fence, or prefers the haunts of men to the shaggiest heath or fairest champaign; with the gentlemen who ride the deer, override the hounds, or ride over other gentlemen. But I feel that Davis was able to invest all these things with a decorum as majestic as his neckcloths. Thus when we read of his lying in a Vale of Aylesbury ditch, after a run which for pace beggars description, with his arm round Richmond Trump's neck—a position full of restless discomfort to both parties—there is something chivalrous and romantic about it all which redounds to the credit both of Davis and the gallant Trump. Pictorially, it is all but a subject for Sir Edward Burne-Jones rather than for Caldecott or Leech. And the present Duke of Richmond tells me that he once saw him direct the operations of a whipper-in in a punt—a trying test—without the slightest sacrifice of dignity.

Mr. Bowen May, who began his stag-hunting under Lord Maryborough, and who still notes with an observant eye all that concerns his favourite pursuit, tells me that he once asked Davis about the pace of a pack of hounds. Davis, who had strong convictions as to the excellence of his own hounds, replied in a letter that the Queen's Hounds were the fastest pack in his opinion, and that nine miles in the hour was about their best pace. But this pace was far exceeded by Richmond Trump's day.[1] It was all over grass, and Davis only weighed about ten stone, and had it all to himself on the Clipper, an animal up to sixteen stone. When Mr. Davis lay in the ditch with one arm round Richmond Trump's neck, as already related, he pulled out his watch with his free

[1] I have found the entry in his diary, March 13, 1832: 'Richmond Trump at Lillie's, ran one hour, took at Twyford between Bicester and Buckingham— ran twenty miles in one hour.' In his horse-book I find that the Clipper was bought in the Christmas quarter of 1831 of Mr. Anderson for 120 guineas; he was sold again at Tattersall's in the summer quarter of 1834 for 24l. 18s. 6d.

hand, and timed the run. Nobody but Davis could have done so; but his skill and knack with deer were most remarkable. Colonel Anstruther Thomson told me he once saw Davis jump off his horse in a narrow lane ; a tired stag was coming up it slowly with all the hounds round it. He let it half pass him, caught its horn with his left hand and swung his whip round with his right, keeping the hounds at bay, and held the stag till some one came to help him. The Trump had been out twice before that season, and started on his career as the Richmond Knobber. After the Aylesbury performance, however, he was renamed Richmond Trump, after a popular fighting man of the day, who doubtless much appreciated the delicate compliment.

I spoke just now of substantial advantages which the best Davis period enjoyed as against the present day. Until well into the fifties the Queen's Hounds moved about and saw a great deal more of other countries than they do now— an excellent thing for everybody.[1] A run in the New Forest inspired their huntsman's Muse. She keeps very near the earth.

> At Vinney Old Ridge they found a prime stag,
> And ran hard for an hour, which caused him to flag.
> He was taken near Burley alive, safe and sound,
> But in less than ten minutes fell dead on the ground.

It is noteworthy that the New Forest deer hardly ever survived a run, although they were always taken alive, if possible, with the object of sending them to Windsor or Richmond for a change of blood. Upon one occasion Davis said, 'We shall kill every stag in the forest if we stay here long.'

---

[1] As well as going for a month or more every season to Aylesbury, they went for about a fortnight at a time to Sir Robert Throckmorton's at Buckland, near Faringdon, during Lord Granville's Mastership; and to Hampton Court, and on to Epsom with Lord Rosslyn ; the deer during these outings to Epsom being kept in loose boxes belonging to trainers. And for many years, as everybody knows, the Queen's Hounds used to go down to the New Forest late in the season.

They had not the condition which I shall insist upon in another chapter.

The New Forest hunting was no joke. In 1848 we hear of Lords Canning, Granville, and Rivers coming over to Heron Court from Highcliffe, disgusted with the danger of the ground, and declaring they will never hunt there again: a groom having been killed, three gentlemen badly hurt, whilst Lord Granville had had his face cut by the boughs

TO RIDE JEALOUS IN A FOREST YOU MUST BE REALLY INTREPID

of a tree against which his horse had carried him. Lord Malmesbury relates how, some years before this, Mr. Assheton Smith and Lord Cardigan rode jealous of each other with the Queen's Hounds in the New Forest. A large party was assembled at Mr. Compton's, and the night before these gentlemen glared at each other all dinner time, as if they were mortal enemies about to fight the next day. Lord Cardigan's horse after a 'regular race' outstayed Mr. Assheton Smith's,

To ride jealous in a forest, you must be really intrepid! 'Æsop' relates how on another occasion Mr. Smith was talking to Charles Davis, and not looking where he was going to, when his horse suddenly swerved, Mr. Smith falling on his back over the horse's shoulder. An officious well-wisher asked him if he was hurt—always a mistake when a man has tumbled off—on which Charles Davis turned round and said, 'He is much too hard to hurt,' an encomium which greatly pleased Mr. Smith.

I read somewhere or other that a great many pictures of Davis were painted at different times. His namesake and relative painted him several times on Hermit, the grey horse he is riding in the well-known engraving of a Meet of the Buckhounds on Ascot Heath during Lord Chesterfield's Mastership. Then there is another engraving of him on Columbine, a short-tailed mare which went to Badminton and bred some capital coach-horses. The Duke of Beaufort was telling me about her only the other day, and I have the entry now before me in Davis's horse-book. For the Michaelmas quarter 1831, under 'Horses sold,' he notes: 'Brown mare Columbine and foal to the Duke of Beaufort, 19l. 5s.'

I believe, though, that the most characteristic and best-known engraving of him is on Traverser, after Barraud. Without placing this picture in such company as Titian's 'Charles V.' or Velasquez's 'Don Balthazar Carlos' at Madrid, or Stubbs's 'Duke of Hamilton' in the green coat on the chestnut hackney, if the painting is as good as the engraving it must be a very charming and distinguished equestrian portrait. People who care for sporting engravings should buy it; it is getting very scarce. In my time the reduced photograph from the engraving was popular at Harrow. I had one in my room over the mantelpiece. How often have I looked to Mr. Davis for inspiration in the horrid

CHARLES DAVIS ON "THE TRAVERSER"
FROM THE PICTURE BY BARRAUD

stress of iambics, and wasted my time in thinking that Traverser was the sort of horse I should like to ride hunting on some day, and Mr. Davis's the sort of seat I should like to have! Traverser was bought for Davis by Lord Granville, and was one of his best horses. He made a noise; but a whistler of Traverser's scope and quality, ridden by an artist of Davis's weight and knowledge of the country, will always beat an average sound horse—at least, that is my experience. How well the artist has put him on the horse! His length of limb guarantees that smoothness of seat which Don Quixote impressed upon Sancho as being the peculiar attribute of a great gentleman. When some one asked Sir R. Sutton whether a stranger out with his hounds could ride, Sir Richard said he did not know, adding 'I should think so, for he hangs a good boot.' So did Charles Davis.

In the most literal sense of the word he was picturesque; and was becomingly aware of it. 'Davis,' a gentleman tells me who knew him well, 'was always fond of a grey if he could get one to suit him; I think he thought himself better looking on one.' George III.'s choice was inspiration. Nature had dedicated him to scarlet and gold, and had given him the right colouring and complexion for scarlet. In the February number of 'Baily's Magazine' for 1867 a pleasant *requiescat in pace* article appeared upon Charles Davis. The writer ('The Gentleman in Black'[1]) had known the subject of his memoir well for many years, had ridden for several seasons with the Queen's Hounds, and all he says has the value which nearness and the habit of personal intercourse alone can give. This is what he says of Davis's appearance: 'He was very tall and thin, probably 6 ft. 1 in. in height, and only weighing nine stone and a pound or two. He was a good-looking man, with a large handsome nose and good dark eyes and eyebrows. The ex-

[1] The Rev. C. Clark, of Sunningdale.

pression of his face was severe and serious, latterly with many lines about the mouth, unless when excited by conversation on his favourite topics. When not officially dressed he had a very gentlemanly, almost aristocratic, appearance, and always appeared to advantage amongst the frequenters of the stand at Ascot.'

Appearing to advantage in the stand at Ascot, or indeed anywhere else, is eminently satisfactory. But his biographer goes even further : ' In plain clothes, he looked like a peer of the realm.' This is a pleasant tribute to the good looks of the House of Lords, but it would probably be nearer the mark to say that all peers of the realm did not look like Davis. In externals, at all events, and indeed in character, he had the knack which Mr. Emerson somewhere or other lays stress upon, of never reminding us of others.

Davis kept his figure to the last, and was one of the few men whose legs were sufficiently straight and clean on the inside of the knee-joint to wear becomingly the skin-tight leathers which were generally the fashion in his best days, and which are still to some extent the fashion for the royal servants. In his day the hunt-servants wore very much shorter and closer-fitting coats than they do now—hardly any skirt ; the old yeoman-pricker tunic pattern of coat was retained for very many years ; and I remember thinking, when first I hunted with the Buckhounds in 1879 from Aldershot, that Goodall's tunic-like coat and tight leathers gave a rather postilliony look. Whilst I was Master I lengthened the coats very much, both in the waist and in the skirts—a long coat seems to seat a man better on his horse, and it is certainly comfortable and more becoming to the average figure.

The slimness and youthfulness of Charles Davis's figure up to the very last were in great measure due to the simplicity of his life and the regularity of his habits. Like a wise man he was very moderate in eating and drinking, and treated his digestion with constant deference. Colonel Anstruther Thomson tells me that one day, when the hounds met at the Crooked Billet on Egham Heath, Davis said to Lord Rosslyn when he arrived, 'I hope you will excuse me if I do not ride hard to-day.' Lord Rosslyn asked what was the matter. 'If you please, my lord, I allowed myself to be persuaded to take a bit of pheasant last night at supper. It was rather high and it has disagreed with me.' However, there was a scent. Davis was riding a horse he liked, forgot all about the pheasant and its effects, and went like a bird. He liked a little wine, and sometimes accepted presents of wine from his field, which he much appreciated. Dr. Croft tells me he never remembers him having anything to drink at a meet or on the road home; nor would he allow his men to do so.

Ladies going out hunting with the Queen's Hounds did not meet with much approval from Davis. He made an exception in favour of a Miss Gilbert, 'on account of her cheerful spirit and dashing riding'—qualities which are more often apt to inspire a huntsman with suspicion rather than confidence—but especially on account of her Spartan endurance of long rides home at hounds' pace, of which he himself was a great exponent.

He was very particular about feeding punctually, and would allow no noise in the kennel. The whips were sent in before feeding time to prevent a note. Those were the days of stern kennel discipline. The celebrated Tom Smith on one occasion tied twenty-five couples up in a row to the park palings and had them flogged till all hands were tired; and the same gentleman would couple a wild hound's forelegs under his neck and have him led for miles by a whipper-in. But Davis's striking control—some might say over-control—of his pack was due, as we have seen by his letter to Sir John Halkett, to the love which casts out fear and begets perfect understanding. Speaking of the wonderful discipline of the Royal pack, Sir Arthur Halkett writes me from Pitfirrane, N.B.: 'When I was quartered at Hounslow in 1857 with the 3rd Light Dragoons, I saw an instance of this, which I would not have believed possible, unless I had seen it. The hounds were running up a grass lane, and got a view at the stag, when Davis galloped along the hedge side of the field, jumped into the lane in front of the hounds, and drew his horse across the lane, holding his whip out at arm's length. Although they were in full cry at the time, not a single hound attempted to pass his horse—and when he considered the stag had got a decent start, he lowered his whip, and the pack dashed on again, on the line. It was the most beautiful and perfect example of hound discipline I ever saw.' He exercised his hounds all the year round, and went out himself with the young hounds four times a week, and with the old hounds twice a week. He took them chiefly into Windsor Park till July, by which time they were broken to fallow deer; and Davis used to go off to Newmarket to stay at the Palace with his brother-in-law, Edwards, the King's trainer and former jockey. So far, I have not been able to find out anything about his habits at Newmarket, but in his later years, if his biographer is right, he can neither have amused himself nor others very much at Ascot. 'He spoke,' we are told, 'of the old days when royalty was regular in its attendance, and when the aristocracy and beauty of England walked up and down the course between the races; rather of the glories of the past, Lords Jersey and Verulam, the old Duke of York, of Zingance, and the Colonel, and Mr. Petre's Cadland, than of the present. Racing had in his mind become vulgarised and common,' and so on, and so on.

A friend, who has hunted with the Queen's Hounds

regularly since 1862, writes me a less flattering account of them at that time. 'The first time I saw them we had over thirty couple out. We uncarted at King's Beech, and of course they tailed all over the place. He always stopped them at the end of the first ten minutes or so. Between Sandhurst and Swinley the ground had just been planted, so you could see hounds and ride to them, instead of brushing through jungles after them, as now. I thought his hounds very weedy and mute, and a bit flashy as well, but perhaps I didn't know much more then than I do now! The old man could gallop, and was pretty handy when wanted, though he didn't jump a lot. He rode Comus, a roarer, as often as he could. Davis always showed the deer to the hounds when taken. His horn was like a young trombone, and sounded like the roar of a rutting stag; but hounds came well and handily to it. At this time they were said to be flashy from being too often stopped and taken to holloas. I fancy very few were homebred; you can't get drafts like gloves, all one size or colour.'

Excepting the Hermit, Davis rode all his horses in a single-rein snaffle. 'His hands,' writes Dr. Croft to me. ' were quite in the right place, and his horses seemed to take hold of him just sufficiently to keep him in his favourite position. I consider he rode with rather long stirrups, and his position when galloping was standing. He was a fine horseman, with a most perfect seat. It was rare, when going fast, to see him sit down in his saddle; but his position standing in his stirrups was very fine, not to be equalled.' In the picture of Davis and Columbine, he is standing up in his stirrups. I am sorry to say he has his cap off, which I do not like; and in a little loose engraving I have of him, he is standing up to Hermit and going great guns. Once hounds are away and settled, I confess I like to see a long, thin-legged man sit right down in his saddle, even if he has not, like Mr. Varnish in 'Market Harborough,' the air of playing a favourite instrument. The standing-up seat, with your horse moving like clockwork and going right into his bridle, is to my mind the seat for a critical time, when it is a matter of lifting hounds and taking them on to a holloa. The late Frank Beers did this to perfection. But all agreed that

THE HERMIT

whatever Charles Davis did on a horse was right. You could not, by all accounts, get him out of drawing with his horse, your eye, or the circumstances.

Some people invest every horse they ride with character and morals. I do myself, and although I have suffered some literally stunning disillusions I shall continue to do so. Davis had favourites, but, according to his biographer in

'Baily,' spoke very little about horses or their peculiarities. He accepted them as horses, and turned them to their best account. But as he had no sentimental prepossessions, so he had no prejudices. The late Sir Tatton Sykes would never look at anything over 15.2. The present Lord Lonsdale has fixed an arbitrary weight—a horse must scale 10 cwt. as a minimum to carry him—but Davis told the 'Druid' that he had been carried equally well by horses of all heights from 14.3 to 16.2, although, as a long-legged man, he liked a tall horse. He spoke most of Hermit's performances, but often mentioned an instance of his having been beaten on Hermit by a little roan mare, nothing more than a pony, belonging to a trainer called Dessy.[1]

He considered Hermit the stoutest and best hunter he ever had. He was bred by Mr. Gates, of Brookwood Stumps, near Woking, from a white Arabian mare. Gates sent the mare to Grey Skim, who then stood at Petworth; so Davis was indebted to the Wyndhams for his favourite horse, and to some extent for his favourite hound blood. Hermit was six years old when he was bought of Gates in 1832 for 150 guineas. I have before me the entry in his horse-book. The horse had been leading gallops for thoroughbred horses. Harry King rode him the first season with the Buckhounds. Dr. Croft says he was a very wild horse at first, but King was a fine horseman with good hands, and soon got him right. The story is that on one occasion the field had been stopped by a canal somewhere in the Harrow country, and the hounds had got a great start over that fine vale. Davis, probably aware of some danger ahead, bade Harry King try to stop them. By this time

---

[1] The great Mr. Meynell's best horse, South, was only fifteen hands. He gave 300 guineas for him, and sold him to Sir H. Fetherstonhaugh for 500 guineas; and a Mr. Porter in Warwickshire achieved a great reputation with two mares, 14.3—own sisters.

they were flying like pigeons over the grass, more than a mile away. To his surprise he saw Hermit gaining on them; and Harry King ultimately stopped them. When King came back, Davis only remarked that the horse seemed to go a fair pace, which King admitted, and from that

HARRY KING ULTIMATELY STOPPED THEM

time on, King rode him no more. Davis rode him for nine seasons; he broke down through injuring his coffin bone by jumping down a deep place into a lane. His appearance is well known to most people who look at hunting engravings, from Sir F. Grant's picture of Ascot Heath. Hermit was a stallion; and in those days stallions were much more frequently ridden with hounds. Anderson the dealer, who kept a few staghounds at Brondesbury, had a milk-white stallion, said to be so handy that he could jump through a window. This animal was specially commended by 'Nimrod' for his cleverness in the suburban scenes of his exploits. It seems a pity that Hermit was never put to the stud, but he was one of many examples of a very good horse with very crooked forelegs, amounting almost to deformity. His heart weighed 21 lbs., eight pounds more than Eclipse's.

Hermit shows a great deal of Arab—a lovely head and a bump on his forehead. He carried, as the dealers say, 'two good ends,' and was a beautifully coloured horse, with no thickness or muddle in his white and markings. When a grey horse of that glorified rocking-horse type is as good as Hermit was, there is nothing, to my mind, so attractive or so becoming. Davis was quite aware of it. The 'Druid' noticed portraits of him on Hermit in nine positions when he went to see him at Ascot. Mr. Edmund Tattersall, who lent me the sketch by Byron Webb from which the Frontispiece is taken, declares it to be Davis's seat and look on Hermit to the life. At the same time, both the position of his left hand and of his saddle leave much to be desired. Mr. Tattersall, whilst he corroborates Dr. Croft as to the excellence of his hands, says that Davis always rode on a short rein. But Hermit's immediate Arab descent must be held mainly accountable for this. Arab shoulders seldom carry an English saddle becomingly. I don't say that they are necessarily bad, but they are often thick and inelastic; the wither wants line and drawing, and very few Arab horses lend their forehand to your seat and horsemanship.

Charles Davis's horsemanship was as stainless as King Arthur's morals. But I imagine his riding appealed to the head rather than the heart. As we have seen, the expression on his features was severe and serious, and I cannot help thinking that his riding to hounds may have been a little wanting in geniality—perfect in form and satisfying in result—but somehow wanting in that impalpable quality which makes riding over an intricate country with certain people so amusing. In a point-to-point steeplechase Jem Mason rode Lottery over a locked gate 5 ft. 6 in. high, off a newly-stoned road, in preference to a hairy bullfinch at the side. 'I'll be hanged,' he said to his friends when they were walking over the ground, 'if I am going to scratch my face, for I am going to the opera to-night'; and Lottery jumped it like an antelope. There was no shadow of turning about Davis, but he would never have said that. Doubtless, had it been a question of rescuing the Trump or the Miller, he would have ridden over the gate, but he would have done it with the somewhat dismal zeal of a permanent official, rather than the zest of a man of pleasure. I admit 5 ft. 6 in. high, and the take-off would make most people feel grave.

Perhaps, too, Davis took himself a little seriously. He read the newspapers religiously; went to church regularly; never had a horse out on Sundays; made an excellent speech; favoured the Whigs in politics. All these things contributed to make up a valuable and respectable citizen. Moreover, the even and deserved prosperity of his career, his converse—almost identity—with great personages, and the responsible authority of his position may easily have induced a certain semi-royal aloofness. I feel confident that he was never in anything like a scrape—this is of itself quite a misfortune—and I question whether he ever had much to do with the scrapes and shifts of others. Under the startling influence of gratitude, Tom Oliver once swore a great oath that he would fight up to his knees in blood for Jem Mason, who had won him 100*l.* with Trust-Me-Not, relieved him of

Charles Davis.

the pressing society of the bailiffs, and set him again on his rather unsteady legs. But it is doubtful whether anybody ever had occasion to enter into such savage covenants for Davis. We might have asked him to stand godfather to our first-born, or act as trustee to our marriage settlement—if in order—but we should not have dared to write to him as Tom Oliver did to Mason, to say we were in Short Street and entertaining the sheriff of the county.

For some years before his actual resignation, failing health and increasing years had led to arrangements with King, by which Davis only went out hunting and remained out for his own pleasure. But in 1866 he had a bad fall and hurt his leg, and at the end of that season he asked leave to retire, and Harry King was appointed in his place. He died at Ascot on October 26, 1867, of bronchitis, in his seventy-ninth year. Charles Davis left no family.

Il n'y a pas d'homme nécessaire, but within the possibilities of this unimpeachable aphorism it was manifest that his death had made a gap, and that his life had made a quite particular impression upon a considerable public. Davis's was a conspicuous career, many things conspicuously English had contributed to his renown. But the distinction of his looks and ways, the elegance of his seat, the scarlet and gold of his public duties, the bold serenity of his horsemanship are not of themselves enough to account for the vitality of his prestige and tradition. All these things we admire in horse- and hound-loving England; all these things will be associated with and ornament his memory and profession. But there is something else of Charles Davis which I like to think lives to inspire and to encourage. There is the staidness of his private life; there is the conduct of responsible duties; there is the example he has left us of endeavour to provide things honest in the sight of all men.

CHAPTER IV

DEBATEABLE LAND

As it was my privilege to think with my own reason; so it was my duty to see with my own eyes.—GIBBON'S *Autobiography.*

'THE great difficulty is the Master of the Horse.' So writes Horace Walpole in one of his most serious letters to Mr. Montague in 1760. Those were the braver days of Court appointments and Court influences. Yet a Walpole or a Charles Greville of 1892 might have written much the same of the Master of the Buckhounds. Although perhaps a little of the Bottom type, this ancient officer of state was quite a lion in the path of Mr. Gladstone's last administration.

The difficulty in 1760 lay in the choice of the office-holder and the rivalries of claimants. That was certainly not the case in 1892, for, if anything, Mr. Gladstone had more places than peers. The question was whether there were to be any Buckhounds. Their situation was precarious. Hunting has always been more or less associated with Tory principles and machinations, and the Buckhounds were represented in several party newspapers as being kept for the amusement of a dissolute and exclusive gentry. Social reformers both in and out of the new House of Commons were actively hostile. And it is not to be wondered at that the party wirepullers inclined to compromise.

In the event—in spite of the menaces and exhortations of an excited section of our press—it was decided to appoint

LORD COVENTRY, THE PRESENT MASTER

a Master of the Buckhounds upon the understanding that he was to prepare himself and those committed to his charge for their latter end. The process was to be gradual; as far as possible painless; but it was to be complete. The doomed office was offered me, and, mindful of Lord Lansdowne's advice to the most eminent of a long line of predecessors,[1] I accepted it with all its suicidal conditions. One Minister wrote congratulating me on my *moriturus* appointment, and I discussed in cheerful after-dinner converse the various aspects and possibilities of disestablishment with one or two of our most trusted leaders. There are kennel secrets just as there are Cabinet and stable secrets. But I must chance the charge of indiscretion this paragraph may bring up against me.

Threatened men, they say, live long. At all events a threatened placeman quickly develops new instincts of self-preservation. I made up my mind very quickly that the office and its responsibilities would be entirely to my liking. Ascot Races and the terrors of the Royal Enclosure were in a reassuring distance. Forest hunting, on the other hand, was already beckoning to me in the near and inviting foreground. After going through the stables at Cumberland Lodge with Lord Coventry, the most helpful and entertaining of predecessors, on a glorious day in August, and just making acquaintance with the hounds, the sun-bathed kennel green, the wisteria in heavy bloom against the yellow brick of the hack stable, I determined that life was sweet, and that I would die hard. Even a 'Star-man' should not rebuke me for these admissions, seeing that they illustrate the most malignant instincts of the Court-placeman.

I quite see that my having taken so naturally to my new

---

[1] Lord Granville consulted Lord Lansdowne as to whether he should accept the Buckhounds. Lord Lansdowne's reply was that he had never yet known it go against a man's political career to have something to give up.

duties is no evidence one way or the other in the case sought to be made against the Buckhounds. I only dwell upon this in order to make it clear that I saw a great deal of them, because I liked the whole thing. The first season I lived at Ascot till July, 1893. So, during the three seasons I had the honour of hunting the Queen's Hounds, it is hardly too much to say that I had almost daily opportunities of arriving at conclusions based upon personal experience and observation. Most people will agree that conclusions founded on practice must always have a slight pull when placed in the scales with conclusions based upon theory, hearsay, and conjecture—even granting the fullest credit for sincerity and *bona fides* to the opponents of stag-hunting.

May I add that, if anything, my prepossessions were not in favour of stag-hunting; and that even now I should not care to start a pack of staghounds myself, or to locate myself in a stag-hunting country? On the other hand, I have formed a definite opinion as to its possibilities and limitations, and I am quite clear as to what I think and do not think about the 'cruelty' question. If the Queen's pleasure and the vicissitudes of politics gave me the chance of doing so—say tomorrow—I would gladly hunt the Queen's Hounds for another three years. I should not say this if I thought it cruel, and, setting aside private and personal considerations, had I found myself in substantial agreement with Mr. Stratton and those for whom he thinks, I should, upon public grounds, have deemed it my duty to our gracious Queen to say so, when an opportunity was given me of stating my opinion upon the cruelty question at the time my three seasons' Mastership came to an abrupt end in the summer of 1895.

So now for a little controversy. Excepting sentimentally, I have never been attached to the theory that an institution should be upheld merely because it exists. That such and such a thing should go on being done because it has always been done, is a method of reasoning which may be held partly accountable for the catastrophe of agriculture and for the costly eccentricities of so-called estate management. Indeed, the lapse of years pleaded in its defence is often the most vulnerable point of an institution.

Tested by these proper standards, there is a weak point in the armour of the Buckhounds as an institution. Moreover, it is a weak point which cannot be adequately or intelligently guarded by any 'J'y suis, j'y reste' justification. At the best, any such justification is to my mind only a disengagement, and not a parry. Curiously enough, however, this real weak point to which I refer has never been attacked by the critics. As I am in a good-natured mood, I will just indicate the outlines of what I mean.

Wire in Middlesex, the villa in Berks, the pheasant in Bucks, all the apparatus of population and residential amenity have changed the face and the habits of the Queen's country. The Master is obliged to constantly bear in mind that in many parts of a wide district he no longer has the free warren essential to stag-hunting.

Disraeli was proud of London because its environs could not be reached with 'fatal facility.' I think the passage occurs in 'Tancred.' But this evidence of expansion is no source of satisfaction to the Master of the Buckhounds. When arranging his meets he will often regret the days when a lady friend of Mr. Rogers was made ill by a fright she got from an omnibus on her way from Richmond to London.[1]

Some day, the want of country must decide the Buck-

[1] 'At that time,' says Mr. Rogers, who had called to inquire after the invalid, 'omnibuses were great rarities, and while Miss ―― was coming to town, the footman, observing an omnibus approach, and thinking she might like to see it, suddenly called in at the carriage window, "Ma'am, the omnibus!" Miss ――, being unacquainted with the term, and not sure but an omnibus might be a wild beast escaped from the Zoological Gardens, was thrown into a dreadful state of agitation by the announcement.'—*Table Talk of Samuel Rogers.*

hounds question for friend and foe alike. Time is on the side of those who would like to see the Buckhounds given up, but the time is not yet. Middlesex I give up. But the pheasant people in Bucks only require occasional consideration: all about Ascot it would appear that the villa industry is suffering from over-production; on the Surrey and Hampshire side a wide extent of rough country can very easily be extended, with advantages which will be referred to elsewhere.

It has often been observed that those who attack institutions, and especially institutions resting upon the titles of time and custom, are usually better up in their case than the defenders. The sub-editor of any thoroughpaced progressive newspaper could 'arrange,' in the French sense of the word, the House of Lords in a fashion which would astonish and bewilder a respectable handful of average peers. The fact is that, unless perhaps the ratepayer can be directly interested in the matter, the conservatism of mankind has always to be reckoned with when any definite proposal is made to alter a usage or transform an institution. Thus, when any such enterprise is in question, the attacking forces have to take great pains. It is advisable to know the strong points before attacking the weak ones. In discussion it looks well to give these strong points full recognition.

But, in this matter of getting up their case, the agitation against the Buckhounds seems to me rather an exception to the general rule. I suppose it is a natural inclination to see what suits us, and to shut our eyes to what does not suit us. Very likely I shall often do so myself in the course of these pages, but the critics of the Buckhounds appear to have done this to a quite unusual degree, and their case has suffered in consequence. Either stupidly, or perhaps from the fact that their occupations and aptitudes do not permit of any practical knowledge whatsoever of stag-hunting,[1] these gentlemen have jumped into the error of generalising from exceptions, and they have tried to establish the exception as the rule.

Every now and again a deer meets with an accident, and has to be destroyed. Every now and again a deer may be killed by the hounds. I admit this in the freest and fullest way, and I will make the opposition a present of my own experience of these occurrences. In three years, on the whole fairly open seasons, I remember losing four deer; or let us say five, for I am not speaking by book, but to the best of my recollection. Certainly five covers it. Two of these are cases which I have seen instanced from time to time with great richness of circumstantial detail in the newspapers, and upon which the agitation still largely rests its case. These deer came by their death through being hunted, but I may here remark that not one of these four or five deer was killed or even touched by the hounds.

Let us, however, for a moment assume that they had been so killed or so hurt, is it fair to take these exceptional cases, and present them to the large public who have no possible means of arriving at any real opinions one way or the other as the regular incidents and accompaniments of stag-hunting?

I should protest against this tyranny of isolated texts, if I attached any argumentative value to the method, but I attach no such value. Indeed, the weakness of their case lies in the method adopted. Railway accidents are very terrible things. Why do we not, therefore, do away with fast trains? Why do not people give up railway travelling? Because accidents of this kind are exceptional; because they stand out in startling, and yet in a sense most reassuring, relief, as exceptions. Granted that there is no analogy

[1] The first petition (1892) was very largely signed by the hands in Huntley & Palmer's Biscuit Works at Reading.

between stag-hunting and railway travelling, there is in the reasoning process which should be applied to both.

And now for a moment let us turn from the opponents to the defenders of the Buckhounds, and see what they have to say about it all. The opposition to the Queen's Hounds, as I understand their case, concentrates upon a charge of colossal cruelty; the defence, speaking broadly, takes its stand upon a flat denial of cruelty, and a muscular 'all d——d rot' to any ethical considerations which may be advanced.

Rolands and Olivers of this build are as unlikely to compose their differences as opposite angles or the Irish party, and are best left to themselves. But speaking more particularly, I remember being told by several people who claimed to have given special attention to the subject, that the agitation against the Buckhounds was only the first parallel of a general attack upon all field sports, and upon hunting in particular. I confess that is not the impression I have formed. Here and there no doubt people may exist who, in the matter of field sports, are of the sour mind of Lord Macaulay's Puritans. Here and there an individual may be cited who, for some reason or for no reason, honestly dislikes hunting; I have read that the late Professor Freeman became so angry as to alarm his family whenever he heard the cry of foxhounds running. But at all events neither the Archbishop of Canterbury nor Mr. Stratton can be included amongst these eccentrics.

Let us devote a moment to the Archbishop in this connection. The Archbishop of Canterbury thinks a pack of hounds a very proper appanage of Royalty. And, with a superfluity of charity, he recently placed himself at the head of a number of well intentioned gentlemen who seriously recommend to Lord Salisbury the transformation of the Buckhounds into a National Drag-hunt. Now a National Drag-hunt

is no doubt an alternative, and that is about as much as need
be said about it. But this last petition—signed by the Archbishop—takes up fresh ground. It pegs out, as it were, a new
claim in the cause of the humanities. The horses ridden
by the hunt-servants and others after the Queen's Hounds
are now to be included in the area of organised cruelty.[1]
It is not explained how the National Drag Hunt is to get on
without horses; but we can hardly expect the Archbishop
to know all about drag-hunting as well as about stag-hunting.
When I took over the Queen's Hounds, the simpler form of
agitation was at its height. Under the leadership of Mr.
Stratton the horse argument had not been invented.

I made up my mind to make the acquaintance of Mr.
Stratton as soon as possible. Somehow I felt persuaded of
his sincerity; besides, the zeal and resolution of his attack
upon the scarlet and gold of our dynasty rather interested
me. I wished to hear for myself what he had to say
about it all. The opportunity soon came. Early in the
month of October we ran a hind out of the forest to
Wokingham. She ran into a little stream, and was safely
taken a few hundred yards from the many-gabled old redbrick almshouse of which Mr. Stratton is the warden. He
takes admirable care of the old people, and is much esteemed
by them. 'There,' said Harvey, the Queen's huntsman, to
me in a stage whisper, 'is the Rev. Stratton'; and there
he was, watching our proceedings. I at once introduced
myself, and we had quite a nice talk. On that occasion Mr.
Stratton assured me that he was no enemy to fox-hunting.
Quite the contrary; a Staffordshire man, he was brought up
to like it, one of his nearest and kindest relatives, as he told
me, being a great judge of a fighting cock or a foxhound.
After that we had some little correspondence of quite a

---

[1] 'Merciless riding of horses in the effort to save the deer for another day,'
is the way it is put: see *The Times*, Nov. 23, 1896.

friendly character, and, although we disagreed, we did not misunderstand. At least, speaking for myself, I certainly never misunderstood Mr. Stratton's attitude. Honest disagreement never hurt anybody. Mr. Stratton and I started and parted very good friends, as far as our personal relations at that time were concerned. I trust, though the exigencies of politics have severed us, we so continue.

But admitting the root and branch opposition to the Buckhounds to be honest in its sentiment and single-hearted in its aim ; admitting that it has no dark designs upon hunting, shooting, fishing, or any of our institutions, from beer to skittles ; is it quite honest in its argument ?

By all means let the case against the Buckhounds be stated with zeal and conviction. But let it be stated fairly, and—at the risk of repetition—I say it is not fair to represent the exception as the rule.

Hunting the carted deer has always had—and I suppose always will have—its critics and its apologists. I am not going to attempt any further controversial apologia. It would only be tiresome, and I dare say as unconvincing as apologias usually are. Plato—I am quoting the tainted authority of a sporting writer, and I have not been able to discover the passage[1]—laid it down that hunting was a divine institution. I do not suggest that Plato would have included modern stag-hunting, and I advance no such claim on its behalf. Tried by the purest standards of hunting, it cannot, to my mind, take rank with fox-hunting. But during the last four or five years the Buckhounds have become the villains of politics. Sins are laid to their charge which they know not of. Speaking as one most intimately connected with the establishment, I hope in the following pages to establish the exaggeration of the grave charge of systematic

[1] Probably he had in his mind the opening words of Xenophon's essay on Hunting.

cruelty brought not only against these loyal servants of the Crown, but also against the staff and against the field of the Queen's Hunt. The best way of doing this seems to me to tell my readers as much as I can of the everyday life of the establishment. We should all—men, deer, horses, and hounds—like the public to know all that there is to know about us.

CHAPTER V

DEER

Foot-people staring and horse-men preparing,
Now there's a murmur, a stir, and a shout,
Fresh from his carriage as bridegroom in marriage
The Lord of the Valley leaps gallantly out.

SUCCESSFUL stag-hunting depends upon two things—the condition and the humour of the deer you hunt. I put these in front even of country—upon which I have laid stress elsewhere—and very much in front of scent. Anxiety about the latter need never keep the stag-hunter awake. Some days of course there will be a better scent than others; every now and then circumstances, the only 'force majeure' which besets stag-hunting, may run you out of scent. But there is always scent enough for hounds to hunt a carted deer on days when they could not own a fox. I have often seen the Queen's Hounds make up what seemed an impossible leeway. As Davis said to Mr. Bowen May, 'The scent of a deer is much sweeter.' Country, as I have already said, I rank very high. It would be madness to start a pack of staghounds in many parts of nineteenth-century England which are hunted by foxhounds. But the condition and the temperament of your deer—for perhaps it is temperament rather than humour—come before country. Given these, and given anything approaching a decent country within a two-mile radius of your turn out—surely a very moderate postulate—you are all right. 'An amiable deer,' as the deer-keeper at Swinley described Sepoy to the 'Druid,' will have you out of the bad country in a twinkling. Upon the other hand, I must admit that the condition and temperament of the Swinley deer—certainly their condition—sometimes prevented us taking them. 'Where did you take him?' in a stag-hunting district is the equivalent of the 'Killed the fox, sir?' or the juvenile 'How many have you cotched?' which is put to the fox-hunter so often, so good-naturedly and so unselfishly, on his way home from hunting. Taking the deer is, of course, the proper conclusion of a day's stag-hunting. I admit that there is a certain flatness in having to tell these kindly and interested questioners that you have left the deer out. It sounds and is rather ineffectual.

Whatever may be said against the long pilgrimage-like dragging runs to which the athletic Swinley deer often treat their followers, there is a certain satisfaction in bringing such runs to their legitimate ending by taking the deer, and a corresponding dissatisfaction about having to give him up. It is nice, too, after a run like Bartlett treated us to on January 27, 1892, from Hawthorn Hill to Stanford Dingley, ten miles beyond Reading, to be able to bid good-night to your good deer comfortably housed in the best loose box about the place, up to his knees in long wheat straw. There you know he will stay, the honoured guest of pleased and sedulous hosts, until his carriage is announced some time next day.[1]

How well I can see and recall it all! 'Ex uno disce omnes.' As I run a rather unpractised eye for the third time over the pack I come to the startling conclusion—which however I keep to myself—that we have got a

[1] Bartlett did not get back to Swinley until past four o'clock on the Saturday, but he was not in the least stiff, and at once went in at his carrots, old beans, and clover-hay in famous fashion. This deer was named after a family which for a century had been associated with the Royal pack.

couple more than we started with. This turns out to be a mistake. We are really a couple short, as Needful was run over by a handsome landau and pair at the meet, and Wellington was badly lamed by a gentleman, supposed to be a captain from Aldershot, at the first fence. Bartlett is being attended to and refreshed in his comfortable quarters. The men's horses look a little tired; yet liberally ridden throughout, they have stayed. And here, faint but pursuing, come the second horsemen, who appear to have obeyed their instructions to 'keep following on' to the letter. As to my own, he turned up with William half an hour ago at a desolate cross-road. How he got there Heaven only knows, for we were by this time clean out of our own country and geography; but there he was, like manna in the wilderness, waiting for me, with the horse cool, and the stirrups ready altered to my length. William, considering the generous way in which he insisted upon being ridden from Hawthorn Hill to close against Loddon Bridge, still seems as fresh as a daisy. But it is getting late; the sunset has robed the sky in rose and lilac. And now the distances are fallen asleep, and the foregrounds are getting drowsy. We must be moving. Horses, however tired, hack home cheerfully with hounds; so do men. What though there are ten long miles between us and Reading, good stabling, gruel and linseed, and the welcome the Queen's Hounds can always count upon. Is there not also the nearer and nearer anticipation of the snug coffee-room of the Great Western Hotel, of the change you so prudently sent there, of the loin chop to which you know the head waiter—the best of my acquaintance—will give his particular and expert attention? There is even a reckless, thriftless sort of satisfaction in the calculation that you are short of horses, five-and-twenty miles from the kennels, and a good four more on to that from the hunt stables at Cumberland Lodge.

It is true there are sets-off against these pleasurable emotions. No one has seen or heard anything of the second whip since three o'clock. He was last seen dragging his horse through the Reading municipal sewage farm—a four-year-old with a future, one of the 'no one knows what this horse may grow into' sort—on trial from an austerely just dealer. The first whip's horse, who seemed quite himself but five minutes ago, has been taken 'queer.' He has just been half

THE DEER SHOULD GO RIGHT AWAY OUT OF HIS CART LIKE THE 'LORD OF THE VALLEY'

pushed and half supported into the empty two-stall stable of the Marquis of Granby, and, you are informed, has now 'started blowing.' The way to Reading seems perplexing; the locals, whom the spectacle of the hounds has gathered round you, not being agreed amongst themselves. There is no telegraph office, you are dining at seven to go to the play, and you do not know the name of the theatre. But what good fun it all was! Was there ever such a deer as Bartlett, or

such a pack of hounds as the Queen's, or such a country as
England, or such happy things as leathers and top-boots and
a plain flap saddle ?

I spoke just now of successful stag-hunting. I admit
the difficulty of exactly defining what this means ; it is a
pastime so full of paradox and anomaly and contradictions,
but at all events I know what I understand by it myself.
To begin with, the deer should go right away out of his
cart like the 'Lord of the Valley.' We had a deer called
Blackback, who would take off from the floor of the deer-cart
just as if it was a spring-board, and strike straight away into
his gallop. Mind you, it was not fear, it was courage made
him do so. Blackback was a most easily handled deer, quite
understood the nature of things, and never showed any signs
of terror or even anxiety. In the next place, I do not like to
see a deer often during a run. He should go straight away
in the Blackback style, and hardly be seen again until he has
had enough of it. I do not like to see or even hear any more
of a deer, once the inevitable cart business is over, than I
should of a fox, given the same conditions of country. In the
run I have just touched upon, I only saw Bartlett once at
Bearwood : hounds had turned back very short and sudden in
the fir woods near the house, and hearing them turn I got a
nick up the high road. I saw him jump in and out of it
three hundred yards in front of me as quick as thought—just
as you would like your horse to go in and out of a road
in a point to point race. That day we ran a point as the
crow flies of twenty miles—twenty-four a gentleman from
Slough, whose horse succumbed the same night, declared,
and it must have been thirty miles or more as the hounds
ran. This same deer pleased me in the same way when we
ran him from Aldershot to within a mile of Sutton, near Alresford, when H.R.H. the Duke of Connaught was out with us
and saw all the best of it and in the right place. In the long

distance covered by hounds that day after the turn-out I again only saw him once, a long way off from the turn-out, until we hunted up to him on some juniper-studded downland near Lord Ashburton's place. I can see him now, standing

ROBERT BARTLETT, FIRST WHIP TO THE QUEEN'S HOUNDS,
MAY 1835 TO JANUARY 1854
[*The head of the family from whom the celebrated deer takes its name*]

haunch-on to us against the steely blue afternoon sky, looking back to see if we were coming. It was an inconvenient place to take a deer, and there was nowhere to house him. We were all the best and most understanding of friends. My

second horseman and I just moved him along two or three
yards in front of our horses to the nearest homestead, half
a mile or so away in the valley below. He went much
more kindly than many a Craven shorthorn or any Lonk or
Herdwick wether would have done.[1]

At the risk of redundancy, I will insist again upon mettle
and fettle as the things most profitable to stag-hunting.
The ridiculous and unseemly things which sometimes occur
out stag-hunting may usually be traced to the want of the
one or the other, or of both. It is foolish to hunt a
weak deer, and wrong to hunt an unwilling one. A stag-
hunt does not depend upon the mere capture of the deer—

---

[1] Mr. T. Nevill, of Chilland, says in his MS. journal written in 1870: 'I so
far succeeded in taming a red deer presented to me by the Duke of Beaufort in
1855, that I turned him out on Winchester race-course and other open places,
and after giving us an excellent chase, when he had gone to bay and the hounds
were whipped off, he came at my call and followed me home, trotting alongside
my horse. Once he took soil in a pool after a very good chase: the moment I
called him he came out with a great bound, and galloped alongside of my
stirrup iron, to the astonishment of my sporting friends. My hind Princess
was just as tame. She fed in a field with our cows, started away when she
heard the deep note of two couple and a half of hounds, when I laid them on,
ran thirty miles and was lost, the hounds and horses being quite beaten. Three
weeks afterwards I heard of her whereabouts, took the same number of hounds
and hunted her—racing pace—for an hour, when she ran among some cows.
The huntsman called to a labourer to open a farmyard gate. In she went with
the cows. I dismounted, and the moment I called she came and pressed so
closely to me that I was afraid she would tread on my feet. A fallow deer
presented to me by the Earl of Portsmouth was made equally tame. This deer,
although so frequently chased by the hounds, would come up at feeding time,
and eat meal out of their trough.' But Mr. Nevill's command over animals
was extraordinary. Notwithstanding his apparent helplessness, for he was a
cripple from youth, he could hold horses that ran away with other people, and
thought nothing of putting a half-broken thoroughbred colt in harness, and
driving him alone for the first time. Many savage dogs, which their owners
dared not go near, were given to him on condition that he unchained them, and
took them away; and a jackal given him by a friend from India would follow
him about like a dog, range the fields a long way in front, and come back on
being called and roll round his feet. 'I repeatedly hunted him,' says Mr.
Nevill in his MS., 'with my bloodhounds. If closely pressed, he would frequently
get his back to some bank or knoll and fiercely keep them at bay, showing his
white teeth till I came to the rescue.'

I give this part of the business credit for many practical and sentimental advantages—but, after all, the run is 'the true pathos and sublime' of the game. Yet, given that your deer is as fit as a fighting man, and as great a votary of his profession as a game-cock, he requires sympathetic handling.

A deer must not be hunted as you hunt a fox. Catching him as soon as possible is just what you do not want to do. The huntsman of a pack of staghounds must disregard opportunities which are often hurled at his head. No healthy-minded fox-catcher ever gives a fox a chance. He would as soon think of casting forward. But to press home your advantages with a deer means that you run great risks of bewildering and so spoiling him, or even killing him. In any case, you will disappoint an eager field by depriving them of what they conceive to be their full rights: that is, plenty of galloping, jumping, and tumbling about. Moreover, it is well to bear in mind that a deer is quite as easily killed by over-driving at the beginning of a run, before he has had time to take his bearings, as at the end. 'Nimrod,' indeed, disapproved of bursting a fox. A celebrated exponent of this operation was Mr. Thomas Smith, of whom an admirer said, ' If I were a fox I'd sooner have a pack of hounds behind me than Tom Smith with a stick in his hand.' In reference to him, ' Nimrod,' in his hunting reminiscences, says : ' What is called bursting a fox, and hunting him to death, are very different operations, and on this subject I can state an incident to the point which I witnessed with Lord Kintore's hounds in Scotland. We had run a fox about twenty minutes into a small cover, whence we viewed him breaking away again. " Pray help Joe to stop the hounds," said Lord Kintore to me, blowing his horn at the time. " Let him get well away, and we shall have a run." He did get well away with the body of the pack on his line, and the result was a beautiful fifty minutes. I call this fox-hunting.'[1] Lord Kintore would have made a capital Master of the Buckhounds.

The best deer run to points, and I think concern themselves little about wind, although their preference is said to be to run on a side wind; but it is as well to uncart a deer with his head up wind, and give him time to make up his mind. It is customary with the Queen's Hounds for the first whip to ride the deer for a few hundred yards, to keep him away from the country which you do not want him to take over, and to edge him into the country you do. Davis liked to point him towards any conspicuous hill, such as Harrow, if he could, with a good stretch of country before him, and believed in giving him a sort of cynosure. In the sequel, I think it makes very little difference.

With certain deer, however, I got to know where to send my change or my hack almost with certainty. I remember turning out a havier named Lord Clanwilliam just under Maiden Earley. He ran us out of daylight to Easthampstead. We had him harboured in one of Lord Downshire's woods and found him there a fortnight later. It was a very pretty find, quite like the real thing, and he gave us a good run. He ran the last six or seven miles almost stick for stick of his old line the reverse way. We must all have jumped several fences in exactly the same places—I know I did—and we took him in an outhouse in the very next field to the one we had turned him out in. It is related of the Miller, a noted deer in Davis's time, that if he got two or three hundred yards out of his old line he would take the greatest pains to right himself, and would then set to in earnest. The Miller ran for eleven

---

[1] 'Nimrod' cites, in proof of the advantage of letting a fox get well away in his own way, and at his own time, the fact that a woodland fox which has stolen away, and only been viewed when well away, will stand longer before hounds than a fox found in a gorse cover.

seasons, and made them stop out so often that Davis used to put an extra guinea in his pocket whenever he was hunted.

Davis, much as he enjoyed and reverenced fox-hunting, was, as it were, cradled in stag-hunting. Thus, as we have seen, a fine perception of the ways and habits of deer had grown with his growth. Dr. Croft tells me that his deer were nearly always taken without injury. Season after season found the old names in the Swinley paddocks. 'The science of stag-hunting,' a friend of long experience writes to me, ' lies in the management of the deer: the rest is a matter of a bold, fast horse and an adhesive buckskin.' At all events, everything depends upon the old deer, the deer who know their points and have learned how to take care of themselves. Thus a man may be a good huntsman with foxhounds, and fail from his very qualities as a huntsman of staghounds. An apologist of the last century—for hunting the carted deer has always had its Strattons and its Bowen Mays—puts it in this way : ' Here our chase differs from every other of the field, and proves itself worthy of the title Royal, for as it is the sport of majesty, it is also strictly the seat of mercy ; for in all other sports of the field, as each individual considers himself the hero of the day for being first in at the death, here the arduous determined struggle is who can most exceed in his exertions to save life.'

Thus, one of the most difficult things for persons in authority out stag-hunting is to know when to stop hounds and when to press a deer. Some deer, as I have said, go away with a bang, make up their minds and yours in the first field, and prosecute their point with the determination of a Deccan boar ; but I have known deer which have given us capital runs make very poor starts. The weather or some accident or caprice may have something to do with it, but there are good sulky deer just as there are good sulky racehorses. Guy Fawkes,[1] a great celebrity of my time, was usually a little bit tricky at first—what a hansom-cab driver means when he tells you that his horse is 'nappy.' From the cabby it is all but a commendation, and the nappy ones are nearly always stout ones. The racehorse Lanercost, it was said, would make a race with a donkey, and I call to mind several good deer who had a little of the Lanercost indolence about them. I have had before me an old hunting diary of Freeman's, who was whip to the Queen's Hounds in the forties and fifties: invariably good runs for several years stand to the credit of a deer named Sulky. Sometimes the names of the Swinley deer had and have no connection with anything in particular; but in this case, I imagine, a deer would hardly have been given such an ugly and undeerlike name, unless it was in some way or other appropriate.

I have heard it said that hunting the carted deer, if not a science, requires a system. I cannot quite agree. You never know what deer are going to do. They will run up and down the fences, stand in the corner of a field looking at you, trot back down a road into the pack instead of galloping away from it, and altogether behave in a most un-Landseer-like way. They oblige you often to trust to luck or to the inspiration of the psychological moment as it arises. Either of these plays the deuce with a system. Sometimes, if the deer is disporting himself in the road, it is best to let the pack go right up to him and let him canter along in the middle of them under the safe escort of the whips until he jumps out. Then stop hounds till he has got his start. This looks bad, especially if the huntsman is at all excitable and fond of blowing his horn. The master in such an emergency should, if he can persuade his

---

[1] Mr. Gladstone took an interest in Guy Fawkes. Only the other day he asked me after his welfare and recent performances. Alas! *multis ille bonis flebilis occidit.*

horse to understand, pass sideways down the road at the head of the field, restraining the wagonettes and the hard riders by voice and gesture as well as he can.

If, instead of being in the road, the deer is trotting up and down the fences, it is usual to send on a whip with a couple and a half, who generally have to be dragged to the scene of action with backward and protesting glances. This does not look well either. It is a curious thing—I am now supposing

WINCHELSEA, A FAVOURITE DEER

the deer to be looking serenely at the impatient hunt from the angled corner of the same field—that hounds never seem to realise the deer on these occasions. They cannot bear leaving their companions, and dread missing some fun. Once they get there, however, the reluctant couple and a half enjoy themselves amazingly. A bitch called Cheerful was ridiculously fond of this guerilla duty. She never forgot a delightful quarter of an hour she once had all alone with a deer we had brought from Bramshill. After a great deal of dodging about she succeeded in driving him single-handed into a small wayside pond near Elvetham, when we took him. Ever afterwards she always tried to sneak on whenever hounds were stopped. I never discovered the qualities of heart and head—except I suppose that they could be easily stopped —which recommended particular hounds for this duty; but particular hounds were always selected by the huntsman. Cheerful and another great favourite of mine, a bitch called Notion, also an adept, were exceptions to what I have just said about hounds not seeing and realising a deer. It was always difficult to keep either of them with the pack. In any difficulty, whether indeed they saw the deer or not, they were always rushing forward, longing to show off and be of use.

But in all these seasons of perplexity, unless you know from experience that his behaviour is mere self-consciousness, I am sure that the best thing to do is to make up your mind, and not be too long about it, that there is nothing to be got out of the deer. Leave him to his devices, waste no more time, send for the deer-cart and turn out a second deer. Although, as I have already said, I did not like being beaten by a deer at the end of a good run, any legitimate excuse for establishing an outlying deer is to be welcomed. One thing must always be borne in mind. It looks best, and, indeed, is best in all emergencies, to show no symptoms of hesitation, to appear to take whatever happens as matters of course and calculation, and to reject all advice.

I said just now that hounds did not seem to realise a deer at times. It is curious too that in the case I have just outlined, that of a fresh deer cantering along in the middle of the pack—I mean a deer that has not given anything like a run—hounds do not try to get a hold of him. I have no distinct recollection of ever having seen a hound in such a case jump up at a deer, or even snap with any determination at his hocks. Even if he is standing still, a strong fresh deer with the slightest advantage of ground will hold his own, and the hounds will not go in at him. No doubt the men are usually there or thereabouts, and the thongs in near earshot; no doubt, too, most of the hounds have had reason to acknowledge at some time or other the flashing accuracy of a red deer's forefoot; but making due allowance for these considerations, this can only be accounted for by the force of education and example. The courage of individuals cannot be doubted. A hound called Falkland, a three-season hunter which I sent in a draft to Baron Houdemarre in Normandy, went straight in at a wild boar the first day in a way which the Baron described to me as heroic; so did one or two of the others, but Falkland would not have done this with a deer. Like most people do, he conformed to public opinion. Not because he was in the least afraid of the deer, but because he, the individual, had been merged in the pack. But a deer must have the advantage, or at all events not the disadvantage, of ground. In a ditch, for instance, he at once loses all his prestige, and is in a fair way of losing his life. The best of deer have a great liking for deep wet ditches, and seem to forget all sublunary things in their enjoyment of them. A wired country is bad enough; a wire fence sometimes throws a deer in a most disagreeable way to see; it prevents the men riding to hounds and being there to help him if he is in any straits; but I declare water-meadows are worse, and hounds should always be stopped at once.

I spoke just now of the value of old past-master deer, but it is only fair to say that an untried deer will often give you a fine run. Indeed, as a rule, I think, a deer tells you all about himself the first time you hunt him in an open country. He may not give you a good run the first time, but by the pricking of your thumbs or some other esoteric communication you know that it is in him to do so. Thus every deer should be given a second or perhaps a third chance of winning the affection of the establishment and the esteem of the public.

I see, by some notes taken in 1892, that the Swinley herd consisted in the middle of the hunting season of twenty-five deer altogether. We had eleven stags, seven hinds, four polled haviers and three haviers in the paddocks.[1] This may be taken as the average constituency. Most of the deer at Swinley are Windsor-bred deer, with the exception of one or two from Richmond Park. At that time I remember the only really intractable deer we had was a Richmond stag, and, from a hunting point of view, a very

---

[1] I am indebted to Mr. F. Simmonds, of the Woods and Forests Department, for the following rather technical particulars of Swinley Paddocks, which are in his charge :—

There are five separate deer paddocks at Swinley, comprising altogether an area of 12. 0. 35. acreage. The paddocks are supplied with water from a stream flowing out of a neighbouring pond, small bays being made for the reception and storage of water. A certain acreage of the paddocks is manured, harrowed and rolled every year, and the deer are shifted about from one paddock to another, as occasion may require. If deer are left to graze the same pasturage year by year, as at Swinley Paddocks, the herbage would go back unless well manured and attended to by manual labour, although deer manure is of first-rate quality. Deer are not good farmers, because they will only feed upon the very best grazing to be had, leaving the rough parts untouched. The paddocks are fenced by an oak fence standing eight feet out of the ground, five feet of this being a close pale fence from the ground, and the upper three feet open palisade. An iron ground sheet at the bottom of the fence is let into the ground about nine inches, and an iron sheet about three inches wide is laid along the fence where the close pale fence and the open palisade meet. The average price of the fencing, including banking, is 8*l*. 12*s*. 6*d*. per rod. The paddocks are treated as permanent pasture and never meadowed. Fencing for deer paddocks must be strong and kept in constant repair. In September, 1889, a very high wind broke down several rods of the fence, and when Goodall began forest hunting, all the deer, with one exception, were lying wild in the forest, but he took them all by degrees. The area of each paddock is—

acres	rods	poles
3	1	28
2	3	31
2	0	8
2	2	25
1	0	23

moderate animal. When it was a question of carting him, he used to rear up on his hind legs and strike in a most unfriendly way and with painful celerity.

The 'Druid,' in one of his books, attempts to draw distinctions between different breeds of deer from the hunting point of view. The Woburn deer, for instance, he speaks of with admiration; the Chillingham deer, imported by Lord Kinnaird when he was Master of the Buckhounds, with faint praise. I think it very doubtful myself whether the strain has much, if anything, to do with deer running well or ill. Yet, if I do not attach importance to how they are bred, I do attach it to *where* they are bred, and I should always prefer deer drafted to the paddocks from large parks like Windsor and Richmond. The larger and the rougher the better.

Except for an occasional drive in the deer-cart—in reserve —many of the Swinley deer are mere walking ladies and gentlemen,[1] or at best understudies for the leading character parts. 'Fruges consumere nati,' they are bovine in their habits and interpretation of everyday life, preferring the quiet plenty of the paddock to the distinctions of the chase. However, they justify their existence very tolerably as venison. A fat saddle helps amazingly to repair the gaps in Farmer So-and-So's fences, or even the depredations of Lord Suffolk's 'turnip tramplers.'

In my time only the good deer were hunted—deer that I knew could go and would go. This has always been the rule in the Royal establishments. I hear they were better than ever last season. It is difficult to say whether a deer will run well or ill. Much depends upon temperament and accident, a good deal upon the state of the ground, and a little upon the weather. Like other professionals, deer

[1] Our crack deer come out four or five times a season. Bartlett one season was out six times, I think, and never had a scratch of any sort; but this is an unusual number of times. Three would be about the average for the good deer.

have their days. It would also be difficult to say whether stags or hinds do best. Stags are, of course, the stronger, and the great long-distance runs have almost invariably been after stags or haviers. But towards the end of the season, say about March, when the country dries up and the fallows look pale and the pastures sallow, I like a hind best. They are gayer, and run the roads less than stags or haviers. I remember a wonderfully good fifty-five minutes with a hind named Hawthorn. The meet was unfashionable—Ascot Heath, which at that time of year means the Forest. We turned her out on the verge, close to South Hill Gate. She went straight out into the open towards Wokingham, and we never saw her till we took her after an eight-mile point. There may have been one or two natural checks, but I never stopped hounds once, and we were galloping all the time. Mr. T. Donovan, of Cork, was much delighted. He was at that time living and dealing at Reading, and a famous neighbour; for if, as often happened, we were short of horses, he would always lend us one. The South Berks woodlands and Mr. Garth's heather were little to his liking. He frequently took his gods to witness that the Queen's Hounds kept him alive, and he used to assure us of a cordial welcome if the Royal establishment could be permanently transferred to Ireland. I remember that day particularly, as we both rather mismanaged our hunting seats over some strong black rails which a small boy on a white pony with a crupper had jumped like an antelope. Timber is an unusual fence in the Queen's country. It seemed unjust; and a nervous surprise is not the frame of mind in which to ride at this sort of obstacle.

It is often impossible to account for a deer's actions. In 1892 Lord Clanwilliam, a havier named after the distinguished Admiral who assisted in capturing him in Englemere pond the first day he was ever hunted, ran us out of daylight after delighting an immense concourse at Cobham, where we had met by invitation of the Master of Old Surrey and the farmers of that sporting part of the world. We were nearly forty miles from kennels, and hounds and horses had to sleep out. After the stag had been outlying two or three weeks, I sent the hounds to try to catch him, as we could not afford to be without so good a stag. They found him on the hills above Boxmoor, and ran him fast for an hour and a half in a most distressing country for horses, having to whip off in consequence. Lord Clanwilliam, however, behaved magnanimously, and having seen the hounds out of sight retired into the porch of a limekiln. Some children saw him standing there and rushed off to tell their father, who was anchored in a neighbouring public-house. But, according to the account given me, it was nearly four hours before anything was done by the company in the public-house to secure him. The porchway was, however, eventually blocked up, Lord Clanwilliam having been good enough to remain there the whole of the time. I saw this deer two or three days later at Swinley, looking very well, but not in such good condition as before he lay out.

Loss of condition is always involved in lying out. If they gain in wildness they lose in wind and muscle. An outlying deer is a bad neighbour. They are wasteful feeders, and the lean tillage about Bagshot and Bracknell would quickly suffer if many deer were left out. I remember an outlying deer behaving very badly to the asters and carnations in a villa garden, and I am bound to say the massacre of domestic picotees and malmaisons by a so-called wild animal would quite have justified a Berkshire adaptation of Ansdell's 'Crofter's Revenge' from the best bedroom window.

In the paddocks the stronger stags hustle the weaker, and a good deal of bullying goes on. There is always a master deer.

Bartlett was master deer during my time, having bested a deer called Blackback. Attached as we all were to Guy Fawkes, who had quite as much guile as his namesake and more personality about him than the others, I think Bartlett was the best and the most reliable deer during my Mastership.

The other crack deer in my time were Lord Clanwilliam, Blackback, and Runaway. The latter got his name from a remarkable exploit. Half an hour after his first arrival at Swinley he was startled by the crack of a whip, and jumped out over eight feet of oaken paling. He was out for some weeks before he was taken after a capital run. I remember seeing Guy Fawkes jump a frowning, tarred, Masterman Ready-ish palisade within which the proprietor of the villa so often sees fit to entrench himself, which must have been over seven feet high. I also saw a deer jump a solid brick wall out of the high road near Chalfont St. Giles, off the footpath. It was a continuous brick wall, coped at the top, and looked quite unjumpable.

> The beasts which roam over the plain
> My form with indifference see ;
> They are so unacquainted with men
> Their tameness is shocking to me.

But the tameness and indifference which often shock the stag-hunter can hardly be accounted for by Alexander Selkirk's theory. The Windsor deer are as accustomed to civilisation, the Queen's lieges, and the latest fashions, as the sheep in Hyde Park. It is just the same when they get to Swinley ; there is lots going on past the paddocks. Ascot week is quite a gala, and the deer pay an inquisitive and pleased attention to the smart ladies and gentlemen and carriages driving past their pleasant precincts on their way to the races. I mentioned elsewhere the 'exhibitions of uncommon strength' of an unnamed Georgian deer in and out of the back-gardens and drying-grounds of Staines. Perhaps this particular deer was a specially selected holiday cheap-jack, as it was Easter week, when crowds of holiday-makers used to come out. There are always one or two of the back-garden sort at Swinley. But why are deer so fond of premises and people?[1] I have never made out whether the deer is a bold animal or a timid one. I am told that even the wild deer on Exmoor will run into farm-buildings like the carted deer. Not so very long ago one was killed in a dining-room and another in a conservatory. It is true that the latter was a Quantock Hill deer, which, as they live on a very small tract of country, are really more like park deer. I understand, too, that the Exmoor stags will trot down a road towards the field just as the carted deer do, the only difference being that the field, instead of standing still and letting the deer come through them, as we do in Bucks and Berks, gallop as hard as they can away from the deer.

I have already quoted from an old sporting magazine of the last century the statement that the deer of that day lived at Swinley in great luxury. This standard of comfort is still scrupulously maintained. The sweetest second cut of clover-hay (the first cut is too tough for deer's teeth), the glossiest old beans, the juiciest carrots are very specially chosen for them. I think the Swinley deer lead quite happy and contented lives. A Black Mount deer would pine for the shrill breezes of the tops, the sun-clad face, the cool stone and shadowland of the long corries. But these are the park-bred deer of Mrs. Hemans's stately homes of England. I won't say anything about heredity and evolution, but they would find the conditions of a Scotch forest very uncomfortable and inconvenient.

Any hurt or mischance to a deer is a matter of poignant regret to the whole Buckhounds establishment, and to the

[1] Pliny observes that a deer pressed by hounds often takes refuge in the haunts of men; so does Du Fouilloux.

stag-hunting public. Lord Cork and Goodall once got wet to the skin in a five-foot-deep pond in the interests of Harkaway. When Bartlett was in difficulties one December day in the ooze of the Loddon, the men went in nearly up to their necks in icy cold water and mud to rescue him. And I could give several conspicuous instances of the same kind which happened during my Mastership.

GROVES, DEER-KEEPER.

Diet and solicitude, however, will not do everything for condition. Whether a Master holds himself, his huntsman, or his deer-keeper responsible for the condition—that is, for the fitness—of the deer, the actual responsibility and credit largely rest with the deer-keeper. Looking after deer may not be as rare a faculty as, say, water divining, but a man who really understands deer under the artificial and high-feeding conditions of deer kept for hunting in paddocks is a very valuable factor in a stag-hunting establishment. Nor is it altogether a question of care and regular diet and ways. There must be the sympathy of secret understanding between the care-taker and the cared-for. The deer-keeper must be, as it were, their familiar. I remember its being said of the head-stableman in a livery yard, who seemed able to make a bad doer thrive and to alter an ill-tempered horse's nature from the moment he had anything to do with them, that he told the horses little stories. A good deer-keeper must have something of this about him, and at Swinley we are fortunate.

I will conclude with a word as to exercising. The few times a deer is hunted in a season will not keep him in sufficiently good wind for the deep country he is expected to show sport over. To my mind, deer should be exercised in the paddock. During my time we had a bob-tailed lurcher called Charlie. I think he was half greyhound, half collie. Harvey bought him for a sovereign of a travelling tinker. This was a wonderful dog to exercise deer, and such a mover! The deer and he were famous playfellows, and I do not think you could have got him to touch one. Poor Charlie, I heard the other day, had to be shot, being suspected of dumb madness. I was very sorry, and I shall always remember the good-humour of his innocent pursuit.

CHAPTER VI

THE STAGHOUND

Nobleman. Huntsman, I charge thee, tender well my hounds :
Brach Merriman, the poor cur is emboss'd ;
And couple Clowder with the deep-mouth'd brach.
Saw'st thou not, boy, how Silver made it good
At the hedge-corner, in the coldest fault ?
I would not lose the dog for twenty pound.
Huntsman. Why, Belman is as good as he, my lord ;
He cried upon it at the merest loss
And twice to-day pick'd out the dullest scent :
Trust me, I take him for the better dog.
Nobleman. Thou art a fool : if Echo were as fleet,
I would esteem him worth a dozen such.

LORD FOPPINGTON in 'The Relapse' declares that in his opinion a man of parts and breeding can do without books, and amuse himself very well with the 'natural sprouts' of his own imagination. But there are times when we should think of others as well as ourselves, and Lord Foppington had not undertaken to write a book about the Buckhounds. He was much too sensible. So at the outset let me acknowledge that a considerable portion of this chapter is the result of books and reading. The literature of the subject is large and rather formidable.[1] Scribes are not always authorities, and many of the best authorities are not scribes.

[1] Xenophon's *Cynegeticon* runs into twelve books, and in many respects is curiously modern. A passage occurs in the sixth book beginning: ἐπειδὰν δὲ περὶ τὸν λαγῶ ὦσι, δῆλον ποιήσουτι τῷ κυνηγέτῃ σὺν ταῖς οὐραῖς τὰ σώματα ὅλα συνεπικραδαίνουσαι, πολεμικῶς ἐπιφερόμεναι, φιλονείκως παραθέουσαι, συντρέχουσαι φιλοπόνως, συνιστάμεναι ταχύ, διιστάμεναι, etc. etc., describing a run on the Attic Highlands which might have been written, say, by the late Mr. Dear of Winchester of a run with his pretty harriers over Worthy Down.

However, I have levied upon other writers' researches and recollections the odds and ends which seemed most likely to season an excursion on the predecessors of the modern staghound. From first to last, except some shreddy personal experiences, there is nothing new nor original about anything I have to say about these antiques. A foot-note is not an enthusiastic expression of gratitude. But I see no more handsome way of acknowledging the heavy debt of gratitude I owe to the many excellent writers whose works I have consulted. From some of these, encouraged by Mr. Fox's observation, that Hume's practice of quoting from other writers gave an agreeable variety to his style, I have here and there given passages in their full text.

Since Lord Wolverton's hounds were sold to go abroad, and Mr. Thomas Nevill's pack was broken up by his death, as far as I know there is no pack which can lay claim to being distinctively staghounds.[1] Dr. Collyns writes in the past

---

[1] According to Turberville, we owe the staghound to one Brutus, who, having got into serious trouble in Italy for killing his father, settled in Britain near Totnes, and brought with him some hounds which were so staunch that, 'a hart once found, they would never leave him till his death.' Brutus must have been a country gentleman in advance of his time, for, notwithstanding the graphic scraps in Horace, *Od.* i. 1, 25, *Epist.* i. 2, 65, the popular form of 'venatio' with the Romans was the hunting spectacle, in which hundreds and sometimes thousands of wild animals were slaughtered in the amphitheatre to gratify the populace. It seems to have come at last, in the days of the Empire, to pure delight in shedding blood, *e.g.* King Bocchus sent 100 lions to Rome in Sylla's prætorship, 'with the proper number of javelin men to destroy them' in the circus. Sometimes a number of large trees torn up by the roots were planted in the circus, and the less savage animals being admitted into this extemporised forest were given up to the people, who were allowed to rush into the arena and carry off what they could. At the consecration of the Amphitheatre of Titus, 5,000 wild beasts and 4,000 tame animals were killed. At a venatio given by Probus there were 1,000 ostriches, 1,000 stags, 1,000 boars, 1,000 deer slaughtered, and on the following day 100 lions and 100 lionesses, 100 leopards and 300 bears, and we hear of a hippopotamus and five crocodiles in tanks in the amphitheatre, eighteen elephants, camelopards and giraffes (Scaurus, B.C. 58), a python sixty cubits long, and thirty-six crocodiles contributing at different times to the popularity of Empire (Augustus, 29 B.C.).

tense of the old Devon and Somerset staghounds in his interesting book on the chase of the wild red deer. 'A nobler pack of hounds no man ever saw. They had been in the county for years, and had been bred with the utmost care for the express purpose of stag-hunting. What the exact origin of this breed was I am unable to state with accuracy. The bloodhound and old southern hound, however, were beyond doubt amongst the ancestors of the pack, which when sold consisted of about thirty couples. In height, the hounds were about twenty-six to twenty-eight inches; colour generally hare pyed, yellow, yellow and white, or badger pyed, with long ears, deep muzzles, large throats and deep chests. In tongue they were perfect, and when hunting in water, or on half-scent, or baying a deer, they might be heard at an immense distance. Even when running at speed they gave plenty of tongue, and their great size enabled them to cross the long heather and rough sedgy pasturage of the forest without effort or difficulty. The hills and woods of Devon and Somerset will never again ring to the melody of such a pack.'

Mr. Fitt, in his capital 'Covert-side Sketches,' accepts a comparatively modern hound called Windsor, described in the 'Sporting Magazine' for April, 1840, as the true staghound. He even goes further, and accepts him as the type of the staghound of George III.'s pack in its best days. This Windsor was a distinguished member of the Massy Buckhounds, a crack Tipperary pack of that day, and was presumably entered somewhere about 1820. This is what his biographer has to say about him: 'Windsor, who deserves the name of 'Ultimus Romanorum,' was the noblest buckhound I ever saw, although I have been in their celebrated company almost from my infancy. His colour was white with a small spot of yellow upon each ear, heavy dew-lap, immense forepart and somewhat cat-ham, which belonged to their pristine

form.' With the requirements of modern hunting the whole
conception of the staghound has changed. No two animals
in the matter of points can be more different than the staghound featured and characterised in these graphic extracts,
and the ideal a Master of the Buckhounds sets before him to-
day. As to the points of these ' vieille roche ' aristocrats, it will
be seen—again I quote—that they were not arrived at without care and meditation. The cross is as complicated as a
Chinese puzzle, and is worthy of a pigeon-fancier. 'They
were a cross of the Irish wolfhound, the Irish bloodhound,
and the Spanish dark red bloodhound ; and they were afterwards crossed upon the large English bull-dog, and partook
of that animal's appearance in their silky (*sic*) coats and
large and deep-set underjaws.'

Colonel Thornton bought the best of the Royal hounds
and removed to France in 1814. I imagine they were not
anything to boast of. George's III.'s illness must have taken
a great deal of the heart and spirit out of the hunting. Sharpe
was an old man. In-and-in breeding, and the habit of constantly stopping hounds for a quarter of an hour or twenty
minutes to let the king, who would go no faster than he
liked, get up, and yet having very long days and dragging
over miles of country, had demoralised the pack, both in
the kennel and in their work. By this time, according to
a correspondent of the ' Sporting Magazine ' (March 1814),
men, horses, and hounds had ' dwindled by rapid degrees
from splendour to decency, from decency to poverty, from
poverty to inability. Those,' he adds, ' which don't eat are
going mad, and those which are not going mad can only
eat.'

The Colonel, I suppose, had formed his estimate of French
taste in hounds during his hunting tour in France, and he
no doubt knew where to place them. The King's hounds
were not his sort if the pictures and the record which

appeared in Daniels' 'Rural Sports' of one of his own breeding named Merkin speak true. There is nothing to choose between the Colonel's Merkin; Luxury, a crack hound in the Royal kennel in Davis's best period, and which

LUXURY

he considered faultless;[1] and Roman and Rhetoric, a dog and a bitch now in the Ascot kennel.[2]

[1] Charles Davis in a letter to the 'Sporting Review' in 1841 wrote: 'Luxury is now six years old, and was bred by me: she is twenty-three inches high, and I consider her in every respect perfect; her sire was the royal hound Lightning; her dam, the Duke of Rutland's Syren. Lightning was descended from the blood of the late Duke of Richmond, which I consider the stoutest of any in England. Syren's Belvoir blood is sufficient guarantee for its excellence

[2] Roman is by Warwickshire Rhymer out of Lord Leconfield's Rosemary; Rhetoric, by Roman out of Ruby.

THE STAGHOUND

The foxhound was not a fresh creation at the time fox-hunting first came into fashion. Side by side with the

ROMAN

RHETORIC

southern hound, which we may take to be the original Georgian staghound, the northern hound had by this time (say 1814) flourished for upwards of a century.[1] Originally a distinct Yorkshire breed—as a Yorkshireman, I insist upon keeping alive this most honourable tradition—this northern hound is the modern foxhound. The northern hound was an established breed in Yorkshire in Gervase Markham's time. As against the southern hound, Markham praises him for his 'swiftnesse,' and describes a most racing-like animal with *round* feet and many other precious foxhound characteristics. On the other hand, then as now, silence was the price which had to be paid for pace. 'To speak of their mouths, they have only a little sharp sweetnesse like a jigge, but no depth or grand-like more solemn music.' Their nose Mr. Markham thinks as good as, indeed, because more sensitive and responsive, better than that of the southern hound. 'You shall understand that these swift hounds are, out of their haste and nimbleness and metal, more subject to make default than other hounds, yet full as curious and full of scent as any other, as you shall perceive by the quick knowledge and apprehension of their own errors, casting about and recovering the scent, and so going away with the scent before any huntsman can come up to help them.' M. de Ligniville, a great French veneur and writer of the seventeenth century, speaks constantly of the excellence of the Yorkshire hounds; they are, he declares, the best in the world. He himself possessed a white northern bitch called Mouille, which could not be beaten. The hounds, not only in Wootton's, Stubbs's, and Sartorius's more important pictures, but in most hunting scenes to be found in old country houses, are in appearance to all intents and purposes foxhounds, excepting in colour, for Belvoir tan was still a luxury; they have all the points of the modern foxhound, and none of those of the Massy buckhound or of Dr. Collyns's majestic

---

[1] The date ascribed by Mr. Baring Gould to 'Arscott of Tedcott' and to his famous fox-hunt in the West country is 1652.

heroes. Very often the artist is not satisfactory, nor the hound, but the type is a foxhound type and not a staghound type. Indeed, as against Mr. Fitt's 'Windsor' theory, in the picture at Cumberland Lodge, by Chalon, of Sharpe with the King's hounds, the hounds are more like the modern foxhound-harrier than the redoubtable ' Ultimus Romanorum ' of the ' Sporting Magazine.'

The Duke of Richmond gave me the other day the contemporary account of the great Charlton run, when twenty-three 'glorious' hounds ran into a bitch fox after having run her from 7.45 A.M. till 5.50 P.M., on January 26, 1738, fifty-seven miles, two furlongs, ten yards by measurement as hounds run. No wonder Charles Davis declared there was nothing like the old Goodwood sort, and stuck to them. These were foxhounds,[1] of course, and the chronicler tells us with unction that after crossing Halnaker Hill to Sebbige Farm, the Master of the King's (George II.) Staghounds, Mr. Jenison, had had enough of it: 'thoroughly satisfied ' is the way he puts it.[2]

But to return for a moment to Merkin and her owner. Colonel Thornton thought such great things of Merkin that he backed her to run any hound of her year on a drag or train scent five miles over Newmarket, giving 220 yards start, for 10,000 guineas.[3] Merkin's time trial— incredible as it sounds—was four miles in seven and a half minutes. The match does not appear to have come

[1] William III. took the Grand Duke of Tuscany to hunt with the Charlton foxhounds.

[2] The inference is that neither he nor his horse was accustomed to such runs with the slow and heavy staghounds.

[3] These contests were very fashionable at this period. In the match for 500*l*. between a couple of Mr. Barry's and a couple of Mr. Meynell's hounds, sixty horses started, and only twelve got to the end. Seven to four was bet on Mr. Meynell's hounds, who were badly beaten. The course was from the rubbing-house at the town end to the starting-post of the B. C., and the distance was covered in a little over eight minutes. The last horse was Rib, ridden by Will Crane, and he was a King's Plate winner.

off, and the Colonel sold Merkin for four hogsheads of after-dinner claret. He appears to have liked bringing wine into a deal, and he sold Dash, a celebrated pointer—painted, I think, by Stubbs—to Sir R. Symons for 160*l*., to be taken out in champagne or burgundy, a hogshead of claret, an 'elegant' gun, and another pointer. Dash was half a foxhound, and a celebrated French Vendée hound called Greffier was half a pointer.

It would be worse than the evolution of the northern and the southern hound if I delved into the action and reaction of foxhound and pointer blood, but I remember well that, as a boy, I used to go and shoot at a very good grouse moor called Strathavon, near Tomintoul, with Colonel Legendre Starkie, who had a great kennel of pointers and Gordon setters. I remember the particular style and excellence of a black and white pointer; he used to stand to birds with his stern straight up in the air. This was not quite right, but Colonel Starkie liked him especially from his striking likeness in appearance and ways to a foxhound. On this subject he writes to me: 'Shot, like many of my pointers, had three crosses of foxhound in him from three different kennels, Osbaldistone, Sir Harry Goodrich and Captain J. White. All these men had a famous breed of pointers, and each one of them had used the foxhound cross. This gave to their progeny endurance, and good legs and feet and pace.'

Mr. Mellish's hounds were lemon pyes,[1] and hunted wild fallow deer in Epping Forest up till 1805. As far as I can make out, they were the foundation of the old Devon and Somerset staghounds. In 1825 the Devon and Somerset were sold by Mr. Lucas to Mr. Shard to hunt carted deer in Hampshire. 'Nimrod' paid Mr. Shard a visit at Little Somborne

[1] Mr. Darby described the old Epping Forest staghounds as 'pointer fleshed, with a stalliony look about them.'

in December 1825, and professed himself highly satisfied with his equipment. ' Whatever Mr. Shard does, he does with spirit ' —a prime requisite, I concur, in carted deer-hunting—and the turn-out generally appears to have been on the Windsor model, as two good-natured friends of Mr. Shard's acted as yeomen prickers, which, says 'Nimrod,' 'gave the whole a very classical effect,' Mr. Shard's own person being adorned and enlivened by a handsome belt to which a bugle was suspended. They had not much of a hunt over a fenceless and featureless country; and the deer went for three miles with a couple close at his haunches. The deer after being taken was blooded in the tail, Sangrado's treatment, or this half of it, being in vogue at that time with stag-hunters; and he was in such fine fighting form by the evening that he seriously injured the first whipper-in. Speaking of these big North Devon hounds, 'Nimrod' observes, 'I should not suspect the Hampshire flints agreed with hounds of this great size '; nor did the Buckinghamshire flints and hills agree with the coarse, heavy-shouldered, so-called staghound of the Ascot kennels of thirty years ago.

But the old Devon and Somerset hounds cannot have been as slow as the Royal hounds in George III.'s time. The Rev. Mr. Russell writes of a celebrated trencher-fed pack and of this blood: 'I hunted, as many days in every week as my duties would permit, with John Froude, the well-known vicar of Knowstone, with whom I was then on very intimate terms. His hounds were something out of the common, bred from the old staghounds, light in their colour, and sharp as needles; plenty of tongue, but would drive like furies. I have never seen a better or more killing pack in all my long life. He couldn't bear to see a hound put his nose to the ground and "twiddle his tail." "Hang the brute!" he would say to the owner of the hound, "and get those that can wind their game when they are thrown off." ' Mr. Russell's reverend compeer was an excellent judge of what a staghound should not do.

I alluded just now to Mr. Nevill's hounds. Mr. Thomas Nevill was the younger brother of Mr. Benjamin Nevill, of Chilland, between Winchester and Alresford. These gentlemen were Hampshire yeomen, of old and honourable descent, and were possessed of considerable means. Mr. T. Nevill rented Chilland House from his brother, and kept a famous pack of St. Hubert staghounds from 1853 until his death in 1878. In spite of his infirmities, he was an enthusiastic stag-hunter, and was very constantly out with the Queen's Hounds when they went into the New Forest. He was obliged to use a saddle of a peculiar make, in consequence of having injured his hip-joint when a boy. It was supposed that he would never be able to ride again. The saddle which he invented, however, enabled him, though enduring much pain, to hunt his hounds, standing quite upright in the stirrups. 'I cannot,' he writes, 'describe the pain I went through at first, and still sometimes feel, or the narrow escapes I have had from many falls from losing my balance; but, thank God! I made my saddle answer sufficiently to enjoy riding to my hounds. I once rode from Chilland to the New Forest to hunt with the Queen's Hounds, and had a magnificent run from one end of the Forest to the other, a distance calculated by my friend when I returned in the evening to Chilland at 100 miles. My Dartmoor carried me through the chase and half-way back; then I took a forest horse which brought me home.' Dartmoor was nearly thoroughbred, but only 14¾ hands high. He is buried in a meadow near the house, with a deer and many bloodhounds near him.

Two or three days after I joined the dépôt at Winchester, the sale of Mr. Nevill's effects was announced by his executors.

I went up to Chilland to see what was to be seen : a small and poor house on the roadside ; three or four lean paddocks, with black tarred palings adjoined it ; some shaggy thatched stabling, and two or three ricks of hay. The hounds had already been disposed of, but there were two or three horses and I think two or three deer; but in those days I cared nothing for deer. Inside the house there was nothing, or next to nothing, of interest, but I remember in a glass case a stuffed rat which had stood up for twenty minutes before the Talbots in a twenty-acre turnip-field. However, they stuck to him like leeches and killed him handsomely. It was said that latterly they got so wayward and headstrong—for a bloodhound is never wild in the foxhound sense of the term—that they would run anything from a red-legged partridge to a turkey-stealer. But in their case it could hardly be called wayward-ness, for Mr. Nevill encouraged them to hunt anything and everything. In a letter to 'Æsop,' Mr. Nevill writes in 1861 : ' I now state to you the different animals the bloodhounds hunt. I often kill fourteen rats a day with them in turnips and hedges, and their cry is equal to their chasing the deer, and with the same energy as when after the stag. Badgers and foxes turned out, and drags, even as far as man, as I have recovered with them stolen goods from a thief. Water-fowl in sedge I occasionally hunt in the meadows for amuse-ment, and sometimes take them. One day I chased a swan for a quarter of a mile in the main river, and to see the hounds swim after him and come again to the bank and rest themselves for a moment, and then gallop away again, was astounding for a sportsman who would hardly believe such a thing. This shows the breed of the magnificent St. Hubert hound.' [1]

I never saw these hounds in the field, or indeed, strictly speaking, in kennel, but Mr. Nevill had presented my old

[1] *Sporting Reminiscences of Hampshire.*

friend, Mr. John Tubb, the eminent Winchester horse-dealer, who is still enjoying an honourable and esteemed retirement from affairs in that city, with a fine representative of his breed. When I knew this dog he was as blind as Homer, and no great company, but he was a favourite in the yard, and Mr. Tubb used often to sing his praises and exploits to the disparagement of a fine muscovy drake, also well stricken in years, which I believe he originally acquired as a bad debt, and to which he had never taken kindly. I forget the bloodhound's name, but I think it was Conqueror or Rufus. It had a Norman smack about it, certainly. He was a reddish dog; indeed, from age and grisliness he might have been called roan, with only a saddle of rusty black. Mr. Nevill bred them to black and tan, and to the richest of both colours; he drafted them hard for colour, and never used a faint-coloured dog. This one, I rather fancy, was drafted on this account, as I believe, although he had nasty flat feet and ineligible fore-legs, he was a good-looking hound of his sort. It was difficult to judge of his intelligence—a quality claimed for the St. Huberts—as he was not only afflicted, but passed his time always on the chain. He would, however, sometimes set up a noble bay of recognition on his master's approach, and upon one of these exhibitions of instinct and good-feeling I remember John Tubb quoting the first verse of 'Old Dog Tray' with visible emotion. He also fetched some plumcake for him, of which Rufus was very fond. Upon one occasion Rufus was all but settled by the dépôt coach getting hung up on his chain and kennel, which was located at the entrance to the yard. He was extricated with difficulty and half throttled by over-close relations with a soft wheeler we called Delilah, whose numbness was the 'causa mali'—at least, so the coachman declared. But I must not be led away into reminiscences of 'Our yard,' as Mr. Tubb always styled it in the converse we daily held together, and when he was speaking to any rifleman. It was with Mr. Nevill's hounds that Captain Henry Ward of the 60th Rifles was riding a recent purchase of John Tubb's which stopped halfway through the run, and, as Mr. Tubb described it himself, ' went and died,' thus irretrievably disgracing himself. The horse had been most fairly ridden, and the run was in no sense classical, rather the reverse ; but Ward was in a sad way, and at once volunteered to help John Tubb over the loss with something over and above the owner's risk, two guineas, backing up his declarations by an instantaneous tenner. This John Tubb gratefully accepted, but refused to take a shilling more, and ever afterwards cited Henry Ward as the mirror of dépôt chivalry. It turned out that he had only given 7l. 15s. for the horse the day before, so everybody was pleased.

Lord Wolverton's hounds, with very different conditions of mastership and economics, were much the same as Mr. Nevill's. I was only out with them twice—once with Lord Wolverton, who hunted them himself in Dorsetshire, and once with Lord Carrington, who, I think, also hunted them himself from Wycombe. But I remember both days pretty well, especially the Dorsetshire day. We drove to meet them somewhere in his best country, from Sherborne, a largish party. It was a glorious day late on in the season, and I shall not forget seeing those handsome hounds half swim and half ford a stream and shake themselves dry in the Riviera sunshine. The sky and stream were all blue, the rich grazing lands near the water all emerald, the margins all gold with kingcups.

> And then my heart with pleasure fills,
> And dances with the daffodils,

or the kingcups and the bloodhounds, and Lord Wolverton in his green coat on a milk-white horse, which all do quite as well as daffodils. But from a hunting point of view everything went wrong. There was little or no scent, unusually little for a deer, and the hounds were either very stale or slack or very much out of humour. Lord Wolverton had warned us not to seem to take any notice of them, or under any provocation crack a whip or speak to a hound, and he invited our particular attention to one old dog who, if trifled with, or if he imagined himself trifled with, came straight at your boot ; we noted his terribly uniform markings as well as we were able with reverent respect.

As far as I recollect we never ran a yard, and the hounds acquiesced in every difficulty. But we enjoyed our day. We were in a fine country, and at the end of the season this sticky vale rides well. A yellow bay horse I was riding, called the Stag, sprang on and off the roomy banks with all the airs of a dancing-master. At one moment Lord Wolverton seemed to contemplate buying him at 300*l*. I did all I could to encourage him ; unsuccessfully, however. The black and tan strain survives in Dorsetshire in the kennel of a spirited lady. Their nose and perseverance are tested by drag-hunting after a fleet page-boy. The other day Buttons only just got home in time, and slammed the door of a friendly outhouse in the very jaws of his pursuers, who were in quite an ' Uncle Tom's Cabin ' humour. ' The hounds,' said Mr. Merthyr Guest, when he heard of it, ' richly deserved the boy.'

The day we hunted from Wycombe the St. Huberts ran pretty well for the first twenty minutes in an orderly string, but with persistence and a sonorous, if rather intermittent, cry. There was nothing extraordinary, however, in the way of music, but this may have been partly due to the line taking us over dry café-au-lait-coloured fallows and ploughs. Just as in the Vale of Blackmoor, the chorus was loudest at the fences ; to my mind a detestable trick. It was said of the

North Devon lemon pyes that with the wind right you could hear them four miles off on a good scenting day. At one or two rough hairy places that day the noise was tremendous, and the black and tans would certainly have been heard a long way off. Every hound moused and waited his turn, throwing his tongue freely. In his 'Riding Recollections' Whyte Melville speaks of Lord Wolverton's hounds running at a great and sustained pace; of their charging the fences like a squadron of heavy dragoons, and so on. Now an all but solitary experience counts for nothing, but certainly nothing of this sort appeared either in the Vale of Blackmoor or on the Wycombe day. Nor, I confess, on the former day did they 'turn like a pack of harriers' to their huntsman, in spite of his marked and unwearying deference to all their humours and susceptibilities. Whyte Melville knew a great deal about hunting. Like Kingsley, whom he admired so cordially, he knew all about it instinctively. Added to this intuitive knowledge he had diversified his ideas by the test of countless experiences of hounds, horses, and countries. But in this appreciation of the Talbot as a stag-hunter, setting aside the observations he makes on the umbrageousness of his disposition, his natural wish to please an old friend, and to commemorate the pleasures of bygone days must have led him a little further than he really intended to go. However, most people would quite as soon be wrong with Whyte Melville as be right with any other writer on sporting subjects. Mr. John Roden, who bred eight couple of Lord Wolverton's hounds when first he started his pack, writes of them in a letter to the 'Sporting Gazette,' May 2, 1874: 'They will not be driven or stand cracking a whip; they get sulky or cross; they must be let alone, and the slower they go the more beautiful the hunting. . . . In work they do not cast like other hounds; each hound goes alone and never watches for another dog; in fact, they never take their nose

K

off the ground, and only one deer was killed by them in Dorsetshire. Even in the same field they never get a view, so all the deer have been saved without difficulty.' As no man ever hated his own flesh, we may assume that Mr. Roden is writing sympathetically of the St. Huberts; but it is clear that they are not adapted by their 'ingenium' to hunt in a pack, admirable as individuals may be on the line of a page-boy or a turkey. One of the many lovely and pleasant things about a pack of foxhounds is an almost over-alertness to each other's possibilities. At the shyest suggestion of a note, five out of six hounds fly to the scene of the discovery, bent upon confirming and wresting it from the discoverer. In a sense, a foxhound is apt to prefer his neighbour to himself—often too much so, indeed, in drawing. The bloodhound looks upon his neighbour either as a nuisance or a superfluity.

So much, then, for the two main varieties of the authentic staghound as known to more or less contemporary history. That is to say, first, the lemon pye, magpye, and badger pye, like George III.'s hounds which Colonel Thornton took to France, and like the Epping Forest hounds which went to North Devon; and, secondly, the black and tan St. Huberts or Talbots of Mr. Nevill and Lord Wolverton. It is as well, both for their own sakes and for that of their admirers, that they have either gone abroad or disappeared. They would have been sadly ridden over in these days, when riding is the avowed principle of so much hunting, and especially of stag-hunting. Whatever their qualities may have been of nose and patience, it is certain that the value of these was largely modified by characteristics requiring exceptional conditions, which 'these mixed times,' as 'Nimrod' called the democratic expansion of hunting even in his day, can no longer be expected to afford.

And now I have done with ancient history and tradition,

and I come to the stag-hunter of the present day. I will narrow him down to the hounds which have come within my own experience—the Queen's. Give me, to hunt the Swinley deer over the wide and varied district known as the Queen's country, a foxhound of the highest mettle and courage to be got. It is only with the foxhound that true joys are to be found. But here I may fairly be asked to state my general proposition more precisely. In foxhounds, granted the same spirit, there is as everybody knows a diversity of gifts. If, then, such a question be put—and for the sake of answering it, let me assume that it is put—I should say, after the experience of three seasons' stag-hunting, that both for appearance and style I would breed and draft a pack of staghounds to the standard of two particular packs—the Blankney bitches at the time Lord Lonsdale hunted them from Brigstock, the largest of the Hursley bitches during Colonel Nicholls's Mastership, say in the early seventies ; or, if we are to come nearer to the present day, to the model and fashion of a lemon pye strain which go straight back to Blankney blood, of which there are now a few individuals in Mr. Butt-Miller's kennels at Cricklade. Very likely it might be objected by some that the Hursley bitches would, at the time I am speaking of, have been on the small side for the heath and the Queen's forest country, but I do not believe a word of it. For one thing, except in some of the lower sweeps of the Chobham ridges, there is very little of the high sinewy heather which the Devon and Somerset have to contend with ; but, even if there were, they would have streaked through it on a scent as if it were paper. Besides, the Berkshire side of the Queen's country in Davis's best time, say in the forties, was a much more stubborn country than it is at present. There was more heath, less reclamation, great fuel fences as close and thick as haystacks, and yet Bartlett his old feeder declares that Davis's hounds were bred much smaller and finer than ours of to-day, and yet ran quite as hard.

> England's green pastures are grazed in security,
> Thanks to the Saxon who spared us our flocks ;
> He who, reserving the sport for futurity,
> Sweeping the wolves away left us the fox ;

and the pastoral as against the woodland characteristics of England have given us the foxhound and obliterated the staghound. He is the result of the country he hunts in and of the horses ridden to him, not of the animal he hunts. M. de Ligniville declares in his book that the speed and drive of the English hounds of his day were due to their being ridden to by gentry mounted on barbs and Turks in condition.

Put him where you will, at home or abroad, there is nothing like the foxhound. At times—as, for example, when he should be getting out of the way of a carriage—he certainly seems to think very little for himself. At other times—as, for instance, when in defiance of horn-blowing and remonstrance he flies on a heel line like a pigeon—he seems to think too much. But given the most untoward and unfamiliar conditions of climate, diet, management and huntsman, a foxhound will always have a try. Anywhere and everywhere, although he may not always persevere, a well-bred foxhound cannot help trying.

An illogical willingness to spend himself for the smallest wages adapts him, moreover, particularly to stag-hunting. Whyte Melville somewhere or other in one of his pleasing and unpretentious excursions into ethics tells a story of a foxhound which, as a puppy at walk, had once caught a swallow with a broken wing. It ruined his prospects in life. The prisoner of hope, 'cette éternelle espérance qui ment si bien qu'on la croit toujours,' he ran himself out chasing swallows.

To a certain extent the Queen's Hounds have to hunt their deer in the same spirit. It is true that Mr. Assheton Smith declared that blood was not a necessity to finely bred hounds. He cited, in proof of this, a week of most extraordinary sport to which his hounds once treated him, after they had been out for nine days in succession without blood. Besides, I quite admit that a bulky havier and a sound swallow are not comparable pursuits. After coursing him in view, Rhetoric and Rhapsody have the constant satisfaction of running up to striking distance of their old ally and baying respectful defiance at him. Honours, so far, are quite easy. But now the deer and his safety and comfort become everybody's business. Their part in the transaction is only acknowledged by loud and threatening rates of the whips, or, worse still, by the stinging thong of some well-intentioned amateur saviour of venison in distress. This must be galling and disagreeable. I should have been sadly sorry—so would every member of my field—to see a deer hurt by a hound. Yet I could not but be a little sorry too sometimes for the hounds, and regret the ungracious rebuffs which had to be administered to these faithful subjects of the Queen.

The average stag-hunter no doubt admits that the hounds are necessaries. He would not like not to find them at the meet, and during the pursuit they are a sort of legal tender that he is really having a day's hunting; but here his interest in them ceases, and I can quite understand his point of view. Even fox-hunters settled down in hunting quarters to all the rigour of the game will notice fifty things about horses, bits and bridles, boots and breeches, habits and pretty faces, for one thing they will notice about the hounds. In every hunt of course there are exceptions, who are understood to frequent the flags in the dog-days, and who ask to be allowed to sample the young entry at inconvenient times. But I am generalising, or rather averaging. Besides, even these exceptions rely for their reputation chiefly upon two or three couple of easily recognised hounds. One season, years ago, I hunted a little from Brackley, and a ruddy whole-coloured Grafton bitch called Glory was in constant request. Someone was always cheering or chiding her. I even knew her by sight myself. On November 12, 1872, the Queen's Hounds ran a deer called Highlander from Uxbridge Common through Lord Ebury's park, and took him after a fine run. Frank Goodall, who then hunted them, enters in his journal : 'I shall never forget poor old Garland cutting the herd of deer asunder in Moor Park, and carrying the line across the park all by herself; it was, indeed, most beautiful.' I wonder if anybody else, out of I dare say 100 or 150 persons, except Lord Cork and the whips even noticed Garland's distinguished services on this occasion. Fortunately there is always a per contra in most human affairs, and although it is the fashion to pity the Queen's Hounds for all kinds of humiliating indignities to which they are subjected by their followers, they enjoy some advantages which do not fall to the lot of foxhounds. Indeed, most of the stock accusations of unfair riding made against the Queen's field are unjust and as apocryphal as travellers' tales. If the turn-out is properly selected and the laying-on properly managed—and a little foresight on the part of the Master and hunt-servants should always be able to compass this— the pack should get away all together, and thus, though they may of course be over-ridden, individual hounds are not liable to be cut off and carried off the line, as constantly happens when only three or four couple get away with the fox, when the field is eager, and the first fence away from the covert looks made to jump. In such cases, unless you suffer from a huntsman who waits for his hounds to get together, the body of the pack scattered about in the thriving hazels of a big wood have to make up their leeway as best they can ; they do not get the 'all start fair' chance which staghounds get. Besides, owing to the ill-hung, patched-up nature of the gates in Buckinghamshire and Berkshire, and to the good-natured character of most of the fences making it easier to jump the fence rather than have to fumble and perhaps get off to open the gate, the Queen's Hounds do not get so much squeezed out at gateways as often happens in strongly enclosed and well-gated fashionable countries, when the huntsman, with any few hounds he can get together at the moment, has gone on as quickly as he can either to a holloa or at the best of that mocking spirit, information.

A Master of hounds of my acquaintance, who hunts his own pack in a wild and strong country, and who takes a lot of catching if he gets away on anything like terms over what William Goodall used to call the 'big old grasses,' writes to me : 'My experience is that few who have their two horses out for a day's hunting, a pair to drive them to covert, and a hack to gallop home on, care about the hounds which have given the day's sport, or observed the way in which they hunted during the day, the way they drew for their fox, the head they carried over the grass, the way they stuck to it over the fallows, or the old hound which took it down the road when the body of the pack was at fault, so long as they were able to tire their horses, dirty their boots, and have a good gallop over a negotiable country ' ; and he goes on to say : ' I have been asked most pertinent questions about hounds by people whom one would have thought were the most unlikely to have interested themselves in such matters, and I have picked up many a wrinkle from the criticism of a man who was riding the horse that had taken the milk to the station, when most of us were still folded in the arms of Morpheus. This, perhaps, is not very remarkable, as the probability is the dairy farmer walks a puppy and rides to hunt, whereas the other hunts to ride, and has a garden and a gardener which dispense very readily with the companionship of a foxhound puppy.' No doubt this is all absolutely true; but, like most matters of fact, it must be made the best of. The hound—as I shall have occasion to say later on—is paramount in France; the horse here.

But the over-riding, or rather the being ridden over contingency, is one which largely determines the selection, the career, and the future of a Queen's buckhound. Every now and then Goodall notes in his diary how poor old this or dear old that have got a little too close to some cut-me-down captain, whose name he always contrives to get hold of. Military rank is invariably given to the equestrian in these semi-obituary notices. Possibly the neighbourhood of Aldershot and Windsor, and the fact that unmanageable horses seem to be an inseparable element in the society of large garrison towns, account for this. But the question of over-riding brings me to one or two of the more particular reasons which justify my original and—setting aside harriers, otterhounds, and beagles—self-evident proposition, that a foxhound is now the only possible staghound. Nose is hardly the first consideration with a stag-hunter. The scent of a deer lies so high and sweet, that most days there is enough scent to carry them all along with their sterns as straight as tobacco pipes—as Mr. Tom Smith liked to see them—a rare thing with foxhounds. Nor do the Queen's Hounds profess, like the St. Huberts, to take a line along the bottom of a stream, that is, under water, as tunefully as along its soggy margin. A well-watered road is more likely to be

EASTER MONDAY. A VIEW NEAR EPPING.

THE HEROES OF THE DAY, MEN OF DETERMINED COURAGE, RIDING HARD—UP TO THE HOUNDS

the scene of any signal exploit in the neighbourhood of
Windsor. But still we have always had a Garland or two
about the place, and a thick-shouldered, throaty hound called
Cardigan twice gained a reprieve from transportation to
France by hitting off a cold line on the hard high road. It
is worth remarking here that such a lover of a good-looking
hound as the late Mr. Smith, who not only knew how to hunt
hounds but also how to draw a hound, rather agrees with the
French critics I shall refer to later on, who think that in
our rage for pace and shape we sacrificed nose. 'A throaty
hound,' says Mr. Smith, 'is now rarely seen in a pack,
although very common some years ago, when men thought
more of hunting than of riding; but by getting rid of the
throat the nose has gone with it, for a throaty hound
has invariably a good nose; and that hounds were so until
the end of the last century, nearly all sporting pictures of
hounds will prove.' This reminds me of a story told me
of George Carter, for many years huntsman of the Fitz-
william, and a famous hound-breeder. Hounds could
scarcely feel a line on some dusty fallows when a throaty
hound called Remus opened with decision, and held the
line across the furrows. Carter cheered him to the echo.
'Yooi Remus, I'll give you a bitch for that!'

Speed and drive are the first things to think about in
a hound to hunt the carted deer. These are all-important.
It is true that draft as you may, and draft as I did for speed
and dash, every hound cannot go in front. In the nature of
things that is impossible. Even running at a strong head,
hounds make their little mistakes and suffer their little ill
fortunes which are constantly changing their order in the
pack. But in a pack of twelve couple—in my opinion the
right sort of number for stag-hunting with a large field of
horsemen—every hound should be fast enough to stay in

front if he gets there, thanks to a good start or to some little
accident in his favour.

A strong deer nearly always involves a certain period of
pursuit about which there are few pleasurable agitations.

> The fastest are failing, the truest are tailing,
> The Lord of the Valley is over the hill.

He always is, or seems to be. It is an idiosyncrasy of stag-
hunting, and these dull bits must be relieved by racing pace
contrasts. Everyone knows a particular sort of hound—he is
as ubiquitous a type as the pug-fox,[1] who always will get himself headed somehow. The hound I am thinking of seems to
be always behind, though always galloping. Incessantly you
pass him, repass him, and yet overtake him again. Yes, there
he is again, staunchly pursuing, usually with his ears back.
He catches your eye each time out of the corner of his own
with an amiable 'Here-we-are-again' twinkle. Fox-hunting,
he may often have many fair—or at all events plausible—
excuses to offer, and we may be certain he would state them
admirably. Even stag-hunting he might have something to
say in his defence, and complain of the wagonettes and
lighter vehicles which keep up wonderfully well. But in stag-
hunting excuses cannot be accepted. The first year I had the
hounds, we had one or two of the sort. With a couple or two
more unprofitable servants they found their way to the boards
of a great London theatre—a box for the men being a part of
the consideration very properly insisted upon by Harvey—
and nightly enlivened the vicissitudes of a hunting party and
the echoes of an enchanted forest in a most lifelike manner.
I was told that the way they strained upon the leash
after some offal ingeniously displayed in the opposite wings,
brought out in much admired relief the well-turned limbs

[1] Our fox-hunting ancestors of the seventeenth and eighteenth centuries
divided foxes into two classes the greyhound and the pug. The pug was only
hunted if no greyhound was forthcoming.

and proportions of two or three beauties becomingly attired as yeomen prickers..

But, passing from their successes on the stage, drafts from the Queen's pack distinguished themselves in many ways during my time. Falkland (the hound I have already mentioned) was a weakish ill-coupled dog, but had the blood of all the best kennels in his veins, and covered himself with wounds and glory worthy of his namesake.

> In thee alone, fair land of liberty,
> Is bred the perfect hound, in scent and speed
> As yet unrivalled, while in other climes
> Their virtue fails—a weak, degenerate race.

Somerville is quite right, and it may here be pointed out that only English blood answers with boarhounds, and that a pack of boarhounds must be constantly recruited from England. It is admitted by French authorities, notably by the late Duc d'Aumale, who told me so himself, that even the produce of English hounds mated in France will not do as well, climate and conditions apparently having a detrimental effect upon their fire and courage. A pied hound called Woodman, which I drafted for rather lumpy shoulders and a suspicious tendency to the kennel lameness once so dreaded at Ascot, was sent by Harvey to Captain Peacocke, who was at that time hunting his old country, the Isle of Wight, and Captain Peacocke wrote to me afterwards that Woodman was invaluable on a road, although not distinguished for drawing. And a bitch named Nellie, which was too small for us, went to Prince Murat, and entered so well at roedeer—a most difficult animal to hunt—that he told me last year that he was breeding from her.

Up in my part of the world there is a celebrated pack of blue-mottled harriers known to a wide circle of admirers and friends as the Rossendale. They are ridden to by the subscribers, but have always been hunted on foot by two men in scarlet coats, knee breeches and gaiters, and tall beaver hats with gold bands. 'Hey! stick, stick,' is the only caution and encouragement they get, both in and out of season. This is the converse to the stag-hunter's cheer. With us 'Get away on, hanging about there!' is the counsel of all perfection. It must not, however, be supposed that, like Sir Walter Scott's hero, the rush and fury of the chase was all we cared for at Ascot. Quite the contrary. Staghounds should be able to race like Persimmon, but I would have them hunt like what Mr. Smith calls 'ploughholders'; and with this object in view I used to meet in the heather districts oftener, I think, than some of my hard-riding field liked. What I disliked of all things was a hound which bayed at its fences; in the early part of the season the young entry were a little apt to do this. It is hereditary, I believe, but I think it was often due to a sort of shyness and bewilderment at the stampede which a Hawthorn Hill or Wokingham field means, and if not the result of heredity they often come right. How well I remember a bitch called Nemesis, which was actually sentenced to transportation to the boar-hunting baron aforesaid. I can see her now hanging in a sort of cluster with another first-season hunter whose name I have forgotten, on a little bank on Mr. Auckland's farm. I stopped the impetuous 'William' almost in his take-off, and sacrificed my start to give myself the satisfaction of helping them over, my opinion of the delinquents not being improved by my catching the thong of my whip round a powerful bramble. Meanwhile, there they sat, eyeing me deferentially, but making little or no effort to get over. However, Comins begged Nemesis off on the score of her youth and noble collaterals, and she fully justified his clemency and judgment.

Staghounds do not have to draw. Lord Henry Bentinck, when he hunted the Burton country, used often on a gloomy

December evening to throw his hounds into a big woodland on their way home after a long day's hunting. The hounds which drew well were the hounds he bred from, for drawing under these circumstances was his great criterion of stoutness. But although the Queen's Hounds have not to draw, they must be stout and tireless, for they are never vanned, and on the Buckinghamshire sides, hounds go twenty miles to some of the meets by road, and then have to hunt all day in hills and flints and get home again.

In conclusion then: speed, dash, stoutness, and nose are the four things to go for and insist upon in the modern staghound. I know that I have not assigned the same importance to nose in what I have said as to the other qualities —perhaps I have not attached enough. But still, for the 'sweet' scented deer give me stoutness and speed first. Since I wrote the earlier portion of this chapter, I have come across some observations of Mr. Smith's, which are so wise that they shall finish it up for me. After laying stress upon the supreme importance of nose and stoutness, he says: 'The two qualities often go together; for it is the stoutness which makes a hound willing to try to hunt and make use of his nose, which a slack hound would not try to do.'

CHAPTER VII

THE HARROW COUNTRY

*After years of life together,
After fair and stormy weather
Will it evermore be thus
Spirits still impervious
Are the bounds eternal set
To retain us—strangers yet?*

ALE, in the Harrow country, was Charles Davis's favourite meet. How often, during my own Mastership, have I been congratulated upon being the hunting suzerain of those elysian fields! Nor is this to be wondered at. Few people fond of hunting can travel northwards by any of our great railways without for a few moments thinking a little less affectionately of their own country; without contrasting its uninviting ploughs, its bleak moorlands or its cramped enclosures with the smooth sea of emerald, and the virgin enclosures which Harrow spire commands.

Alas! the glory has departed. The Harrow country survives as a tradition. It has long ceased to be a fact in the everyday life of the Royal pack. The hunt horses used to go on to Uxbridge or Hillingdon the night before hunting, but the stabling they occupied knows the welcome invaders no more. Whyte Melville, I think, breaks Satanella's neck and her rider's back in a newly drained pasture somewhere out Pinner way. It would be a breach of the unities to do so now. If the Queen's country is ever to be the scene of the same sort of euthanasia, the novelist must have recourse to an oubliette in the heath or to a Buckinghamshire wattle.

I do not know the beginnings of our ending as regards the Harrow country. Nominally, of course, the country is still by way of being hunted over by the Queen's Hounds. Even in my time the Middlesex farmers still received and expected paddock tickets for Ascot races. But for many years past there has existed an uncomfortable sort of judicial separation tantamount to a divorce. Possibly at some time or other there may have been some little unintentional neglect of the diplomacy of hunting, upon which we hunting folk must learn to rely in these days quite as much as upon the science of our huntsmen or the good gifts of an open season. Possibly the reduction in the £ s. d. allowances to the Master of the Buckhounds during Lord Bessborough's Mastership, and the consequent reduction in the number of hunting days from three to two, may have had something to do with it. But be all that as it may, it is certain the conditions of this part of Middlesex can never have been favourable to the stability of hunting. Graced conspicuously with all the most attractive features of a hunting country, the corresponding mind and disposition have always been lacking. There are not, and never have been, any large estates with resident owners to help hunting. Much of the land is owned by non-residents, and occupied by tenants with no direct or personal interest in it. Nearness to a great city gives every acre an accommodation value. Much of the pasture is let for summer grazing to cattle-dealers. Hay for the insatiable London market is the staple and most remunerative industry. Lord Cork told me that when first he hunted in the Harrow country he was struck by the manure which had almost expropriated stock. In the better times rents were run up to a very high figure. Even in these days they have kept up. To pay them the meadowland must be wound up to the highest pitch of production by heavy manuring from the London mews and dust-bins. These spécialité conditions of agriculture did not agree very well with the Queen's Hounds and their following, and I am free to say that very rich permanent meadowland does suffer from a huge field of horsemen in wet seasons. But it must be borne in mind that the Queen's Hounds never, even in the palmiest days, hunted the Harrow country—except for an odd day by arrangement —after Christmas, and with a travelling deer probably did less harm than a pack of foxhounds, or even harriers on a twisty fox or catchy scent.

All about Harrow the grass has always been a sensitive plant. One of the favourite amusements in the Easter term when I first went to Harrow was going out jumping on a half-holiday. It was never a general practice, but a certain set were much addicted to it. A great friend of mine at Harrow, 'Budge' Arnold—a son of Mr. Matthew Arnold's—was a great organiser of these parties of six to eight boys. You jumped, as you hunt in France, by invitation. The success of the party depended to some extent upon a sort of jumping jester, who was expected to do something amusing, or which we thought amusing. As far as I recollect, this usually took the form of jumping into a muddy pond. It sounds a simple and not very exhilarating pleasantry, but, like many other things, all depended on how it was done. I have seen it quite fail in its object, and in that case the drenched and shivering jester was called an ass. The crack jester in my time was Elliot Neeld, in Butler's house. He always came off.

The jumping parties were capital exercise, and gave us a famous appetite for muffins and hare soup of a most noble liver-chestnut colour at Winkley's. I have never met with hare soup of that exact colour or consistency since. As somebody may always be trusted to say at a shooting-party luncheon, it was not the worst part of the day. The nearest I ever get to it is in the commercial room of a country inn : a good place to make for, both for fare and company. Exclusive, no doubt, but we can all travel in small courtesies.

But there was a hazardous as well as a gay side to a jumping party. There was always the chance of being chivied, caught, and haled before some rural Jeffreys by the angry occupiers of the soil. Embalmed in the oral history of the school were noble legends of stand-up fights and desperate mêlées, in which brave Harrow boys of the past had successfully engaged a savage but courageous peasantry. In my time no one was ever caught, and there were no fights or mêlées of this Homeric kind, but I remember Arnold [1] and myself being chased. The farmer's men, encouraged by their employer's curses and liberal promises of beer, until he was beaten off by want of condition, ran well over a fine line of country on the Pinner side, and the palisade of the Philathletic field, which was our point, is not the sort of obstacle you can take in your stride. However, we shinned over it somehow by a short head, and they did not follow us into the school territories. The episode lost nothing in the telling at 'Four Bill.' I recall these reminiscences in evidence of an almost morbid consciousness of the preciousness of grass which animated the occupiers of land all about Harrow as far back as 1868–9.

Lord Cork became Master of the Buckhounds for the first time in 1866. But long before that the Harrow country was a sort of hunting Eastern Question. For several years prior to 1866 his predecessors had been discouraged, if not actually prevented, from taking the hounds into the best of

[1] To my sorrow, Arnold died the following year, in the middle of the term, quite suddenly, and after a few days' illness. I missed him very much. For a long time we had inhabited the same forms ; our progress up the school being very temperate.

it. In theory the Queen's Hounds hunted it; in practice, however, it was in an uncomfortable way. No one knew what he was writing about better than the late Mr. Higgins, and nothing could be better or more amusingly done than his account of a day with the Queen's Hounds written early in the forties, and during Lord Rosslyn's Mastership. I must not spoil it by a paraphrase. The road which Mr. Higgins (a fine horseman) would have us believe he has been sticking

THE COUNTRY FAR AND WIDE IS UP IN ARMS AGAINST US

to, no longer serves: 'In a fit of frenzy we deviate into a green lane; becoming still more excited we open a gate into a field, and adventure upon a cart track. The track ends in a heap of manure; we desperately crawl through a weak place in a fence, and, our blood being up, jump a couple of rotten hurdles; and then we are entangled in the heart of the Harrow country. The deer and hounds may be gone to York for all we know or care; for on collecting our scattered senses we find that we have objects of major import to attend to. We are in the enemy's camp; the country far and wide is up in arms against us. No man will tell us the way to the nearest road; insidious clods only pretend to open gates, that they may get a grab at our reins as we pass through; and others, infuriated, flourish pitchforks in gaps and accost us in terms "peu flatteurs." We bestir ourselves like men, to extricate ourselves from the unhandsome fix, and ride as we never rode before or intend to ride again. Some get falls, and are led away into captivity by the lords of the soil; but the survivors, of whom I have the fortune to be one, after escapes of a perfectly Afghan character, manage to gain the high road from Uxbridge to London, when they hail the seventh milestone with joy, not, I trust, unmixed with gratitude.'[1]

This little instantaneous photograph may also be interesting, even at this distance of time, as signalling the 'lucida sidera' of those days: 'King sticks to them; about five or six other men do likewise. On the left, Dicky Vyse, Beauchamp Proctor, and Billy Baillie of the Blues lie well alongside the leading hounds. Stout Makepeace follows gallantly in their wake, as well as his weight will permit. On the right, Davis glides smoothly along, whilst Jem Mason and Allan Macdonough are racing with one another, looking out eagerly for the big places to jump.'

During Lord Cork's short tenure of office in 1866—he was only in a month or two—hints were freely given him that the difficulties were not insuperable, and that if the tenant farmers were properly approached their objections could be got over. This was actually effected by Lord Colville's tact and urbanity, the best of all sesames for locked gates. This is what Lord Colville writes to me about it himself: 'I cannot tell you under what circumstances the Queen's Hounds were banished from the Harrow country. But one

[1] *Wild Sports of Middlesex.*

day during my first season, Harry King—the then huntsman, and who had recently succeeded Charles Davis—said that a gentleman from the Harrow country wished to speak to me: it was, I think, Mr. Sherborn. He [Mr. Sherborn]

Harry King, Huntsman to the Queen's Hounds, July 1866 to December 1871

said he thought there was a feeling among the farmers that, under certain conditions, I might take the hounds back there. Some time later he told me that the farmers and owners consented. We might have a day or two in the Harrow country, but the hounds were not to go there if the ground was wet. The first run we had over the Harrow country was on December 23, 1867. We met at Denham Court, and had an excellent gallop over the grass, an hour and twenty minutes, and took at Willesden. I well remember how well poor Harry King rode to his hounds, over a stiff country which had not been hunted over for nine years, and where gaps were scarce.

'On March 2, 1868, we had a meet at Denham Court. It was late in the season, but the country was dry. The Prince of Wales was out, and we had a remarkable run. From Denham Court we ran past Pinner to the foot of Harrow Hill. The deer went right up to the top of the hill, I believe, passed through the churchyard, and down the other side of the hill into what are called "Duckpuddle Fields," and thence to Wormwood Scrubbs, where I well remember seeing the Duc de Chartres, his horse bogged, with a wire fence twisted round his legs. We took the deer at Paddington Goods Station, and accompanied the Prince of Wales to Marlborough House, riding through Hyde Park and down Constitution Hill in hunting dress.'

Lord Cork came back to the Buckhounds in January 1869. As the Harrow country was always forbidden fruit after Christmas, it was not until the autumn of the same year that Lord Cork was able to form an opinion of its boasted merits from personal experience. He and Frank Goodall had some capital fun over it, as the following letters from Lord Cork, and a few extracts from Goodall's well-kept journal, which he most kindly placed at my disposal, will show. They have the value of being the testimonies and experiences of riding men in a riding country. Goodall was quite undefeated over the biggest country in England. When huntsman to Mr. Tailby he held the position, in the estimation of those most competent to form an opinion in his day, equivalent to that held by Firr now. His style of riding compared favourably with that of Charles Davis and Jem Mason in their best days. He rode over a country with the same ease which characterised those two fine horsemen. The flying fences, the jumping from grass

FRANK GOODALL ON CRUSADER. HUNTSMAN TO THE QUEEN'S HOUNDS, APRIL 1872 TO MAY 1888

to grass, the fair take-off of the Harrow country, were entirely to his mind when he was riding Cardinal or Crusader, and showing the field how the thing should be done. He never really took to the sticky bank and ditch business, but enjoyed some fine runs over it.[1]

[1] Goodall writes to me from Lyndale, Southall, where he is now living:—
In reply to your letter, I have much pleasure in giving you my opinion of the country hunted by the Queen's Staghounds, and may add that I consider you have paid me a great compliment in asking for it. The Harrow country I liked exceedingly, and it reminded me very much of Leicestershire. It

Now for Lord Cork; in Goodall's journal there are constant references to his riding. He is always there to keep the field in order, help to take a deer, and to show them how to ride in any and every sort of country. So his opinion of the Harrow Vale is worth having.

'A good many short and some long runs,' he writes me, 'soon convinced me that on a good horse, and with one's heart in the right place, there were few greater enjoyments than a turn-out at Bull's Farm, at Down Barn, at North Holt, and at Wiltshire's Farm, near Hayes, or a take near Harrow or Pinner. During 1869 the 9th Lancers were quartered at Hounslow, and a cheery hard-riding lot they were. Headed by Lord Bill Beresford, they were always to the front over both the Bracknell and Harrow country, and—may I be forgiven for saying it—sometimes nearer the stag than the hounds.

'I remember well a run at the end of December, when, in consequence of King's illness, I had to hunt the hounds myself, a difficult task at any time, particularly when personally the hounds know little about one. The meet was at Uxbridge Common, the field large, consisting of some of the hardest riders from London and adjoining neighbourhood, and my 9th Lancers. My friend, Mr. F. Cox, in his day one of the finest horsemen in England, and still with a seat which

was nearly all grass, with flying fences, plenty of water to get over, but less room between the fences than Leicestershire. To negotiate this country a horse must not only be able to jump, but both race and stay—the only drawback to this country being that there was not enough of it, and the meets were long distances from the kennels, the nearest being Hayes, sixteen miles away. My favourite horses for this country were 'Cardinal,' chestnut, very plain looking, but good; 'Norman,' a chestnut purchased by Lord Hardwicke, whom I rode for ten seasons, and who only gave me one fall, which I may say was a very bad one, and laid me up for the rest of the season. 'Crusader,' a grey horse purchased by Lord Cork, was a very great favourite of mine, and I think the best I ever rode during my long hunting career. He was a big upstanding horse, standing 16.2, full of quality, no fence too big, no water too wide, and no day too long.

many younger riders might well have imitated, was there as usual to welcome the pack with which he had hunted all his life, and to give his kindly and most useful advice to the master. The deer on being turned out went straight away in the Windmill Hill near Ruislip, then over some large fields rather deep in places, the fences being strong but mostly negotiable, in the direction of Pinner, crossing the London and North-Western Railway between Pinner and Harrow stations. Here, to the best of my recollection, we had our first check; distance, about seven miles. The deer appeared to have been headed soon after crossing the line, and to have amused itself in running up and down some of the high fences. The hounds after some little delay, having caught sight of him, the deer again put his head straight across the vale, leaving the hospitable roof of Mr. Brown at Hinton on the right, under the Midland Railway between Edgware and Mill Hill stations. Up High Wood Hill (a good pull up with a tired horse) by Totteridge Park to Chipping Barnet, where he went into a pond and was quickly captured.

'At this distance of time, twenty-five years, I cannot well recollect the names of those who went through the run, but I know they were very few. Shirley of Twickenham, who possessed, after Jem Mason,[1] perhaps, the finest hands in England, and was a good all-round sportsman, was certainly there. As I often told him, he was a bad man to follow, as whatever the fence might be, he never hustled his horse nor seemed to increase his pace, which on this occasion I found out to my discomfiture, as at the last fence but one he brought me down in consequence of this wonderful art, over a brook with a cut-away bank on the landing side. Fortu-

---

[1] A story is told of Jem Mason riding the line of hounds over a stake and bound country without a mistake when the ditches were full of snow, and in many cases on the take-off side, the take-off itself thus being a matter of guesswork. This is a dazzling illustration of 'hands' and of what can be done.

nately the ditch was not deep. I was soon mounted again, and I think followed Shirley in a good second. Messrs. Talbot, Walter Colson, Sanders, and the whips soon followed close up. Distance from London and North-Western Railway, about eight miles; total, about fifteen miles.

'Another good run, the date of which I cannot remember, was from the back of Wiltshire's Farm, near Hayes. The first stag having proved a failure, and preferring the brickyards to giving a run, I ordered Goodall to take the animal as soon as possible. In the meanwhile I galloped back to where I had left the deer-cart, and ordering the driver to come on as quickly as possible, took it into a field with a brook for the first fence. The deer thus uncarted in the presence only of myself, had plenty of time to look about him and start off at his own pace. This it certainly did, for when Goodall and the field came back nearly fifteen minutes had elapsed. Yet on my telling Goodall to lay on the hounds, they seemed to fly. I don't think I ever saw hounds run faster. We all had to ride pretty hard to keep with them. Those who hesitated were soon out of it. The line taken was over West Hill Farm and straight up to Harrow School. There we had rather a long check, the deer dodging about the lanes. Goodall at last viewed the deer crossing the school cricket-ground. He put on the hounds. The scent seemed as good as in the morning, for the hounds again left us rising the hill to where Kingsbury Races used to take place. It was as much as the few who still remained could do to keep them in sight. Turning to the right of Kingsbury by Neasden to Willesden, the deer was eventually taken at Brondesbury in a yard belonging to the late Mr. Sheward, of Green Street. I consider this the best run I had with the hounds.'

Goodall's accounts of runs and incidents speak best for themselves. Of the excellence of a day when a hind named

Miss Headington gave them a very capital run, he says : 'This day I consider a most extraordinary good one. Out of a field of 400, thirty-eight showed their faces at the finish, including the noble master [Lord Hardwicke] on his good horse, White Boy, who carried him from start to finish in the front.' And he adds : ' My horse Cardinal carried me well, although he began to go at last very, very politely.' Goodall had ridden one horse all through. They left off thirty-two miles from kennels.[1] '*March* 22, 1875.—Meet—Denham Court. Uncarted in a field close to the fisheries, and had a most capital two hours and forty minutes, and took at Bushey, near Watford. I got a regular ducking riding over a wooden bridge [2] at Hamper Hill. My horse Rosslyn slipped on one side and came upon his back on the top of me, and in the struggle my spur got caught in the stirrup, and he dragged me down the brook for fifty yards, and luckily my spur leather broke and let me at large. Although I felt very much shaken I went on and did my duty, and rode home twenty-four miles in wet clothes.' He enters under date November 27, 1877 : ' The Prince Imperial was out to-day ; he rode my favourite mare, Countess, and I fed the hounds and left them at Lord Salisbury's, at Hatfield, for the night. I came home by train,

---

[1] The deer was taken three fields from Scratchwood. This was a celebrated fox-cover in the old Berkeley country in the beginning of the century. Lord Berkeley found a fox in Scratchwood and killed him in Kensington Gardens. Lord Berkeley's country extended from Scratchwood to Thornbury, in Gloucestershire, and he had a kennel at Gerrard's Cross, where the Queen's Hounds so often meet, as well as at four or five other places. ' The tawny coats ' hunted over 120 miles of country, and at one time thirty hunt horses were located in the village of Charing, now Charing Cross.

[2] The same thing happened to me some years ago with the Queen's Hounds. Lord Suffield, at that time Master, had mounted me. He led his horse, The Dunce, across. I stupidly thought I could ride across it. There was a little rail about two feet high at the far end, and when my horse—a very free but most intelligent animal by Bass Rock—saw The Dunce arch over, he began to trot. I shall never forget the disagreeable sensation of going off the planking. I was hardly hurt, and we got out the right side without the loss of a moment, but rather wet.

wet through to the skin.' This day they met at the 'Rose and Crown' inn, Harrow Weald, and ran through Cannons Park. Londoners may like to know, or doubtless do know, that the two inspiring stone-façaded houses on the north side of Cavendish Square were built from designs for the lodges of Cannons, built in the early years of the last century by the Duke of Chandos, the supposed 'Timon' of Pope's 'Essay on False Taste.'

I spoke just now of the services rendered to the Queen's field for many years past by the Great Western Railway. 'Hunting,' I remember Baron Ferdinand de Rothschild saying to me some years ago, in days when, if hounds really ran over a gentlemanlike country, he would go like a swallow, 'is a charming amusement, but a detestable occupation.' At the risk of a charge of heresy and schism I entirely agree. But if this be true of fox-hunting, it is trebly true of stag-hunting. Stag-hunting is essentially the professional or busy man's playground. The stag-hunter should have other occupations or interests sufficient to make his day with the stag a treat and the loss of it a disappointment. For this reason London is the best, and indeed the only, place to hunt the stag from. In 'The Noble Science' Mr. Delmé Radcliffe investigated the effect which railways would be likely to have upon the breed of horses and upon fox-hunting. He predicts that they will become 'the most oppressive monopoly ever inflicted on a free country.' The most narrow-spirited, he declares, will agree to this. And this is his conclusion of the whole matter: 'When we consider the magnitude of the convulsion which this mighty railroad delusion will effect, the fearful extent of its operations, the thousands of human beings thrown out of employ, the incalculable diminution in the number of horses and consequent deficiency in demand, we cannot but wonder at the blindness which has countenanced the growth of a monster which will rend the vitals of those by whom it has been fostered.' These prophecies need no comments. It may, however, be worth remarking that many fashionable hunting countries are finding it necessary to protect themselves by stringent and scaled regulations as to subscriptions, because of the immense expansion of hunting which train services organised *ad hoc* mean.

A short time ago the 'Field' newspaper took exception to the ratcatcher costume of the Queen's field, and it must be admitted that an intelligent foreigner, captivated, we will say, by Sir F. Grant's picture of Ascot Heath and its patricians, who hires a horse for a day with Lord Coventry, would be æsthetically disappointed. We can no longer boast of a d'Orsay, a Brummell, a Beaufort or an Alvanley. Blacking is no longer made of port wine and red currant jelly, or boot-top liquid of champagne and apricot jam. We feel the levelling tendency of the democratic tailor.

The Prince of Wales and the Duke of Connaught always wear scarlet out with the Queen's, and approve of the strictest tenue. Of course it is the counsel of perfection. But it must be remembered that the Queen's field has changed very much in the last thirty or forty years. The loss of the grass country, and the excellent sport shown by Baron Rothschild—a pack like the Queen's without the bondage of a subscription—over a fine country, essentially a riding country, and in many ways a stag-hunting country, have seduced the richer London contingent from Slough and Uxbridge to Leighton Buzzard. The field is now chiefly local and resident. Day in, day out, ten to twelve would now be a high average of horses boxed from Paddington, and comparatively few are kept at livery either at Slough, or Windsor, or Ascot. As a matter of fact most of the regular London gentlemen who hunt with the Queen's Hounds have stuck to the traditions of the past and to scarlet.

I hear that the *doyen* of the hunt, Mr. Bowen May, ordered a new red coat this very season, and it is the large and ever-increasing local field who are responsible for the relaxation in the morals of hunting dress. Far be it from me to speak lightly of these high things, but it may be pointed out that the large majority of those who hunt with the Queen's are not hunting in a large way: probably, if the staghounds were abolished, they would give it up altogether, and get their exercise from golf or cycling. I dare say a great many of them are not very rich, and are not in a position to undertake the serious responsibilities of leathers and top-boots, which in many ways mean a considerable tax upon the resources of a small establishment. *De rigueur* hunting dress must be very well done or not done at all. Some excellent servants never learn to do leathers properly. It is at once an art and a craft. Tops, too, want an eye for colour.

I am a stickler for the tall hat. It looks the best, and in every way is the best for riding of all kinds, which includes falling. A tall hat gives a little finish to horsemanship which the wideawake can never hope to achieve. But given the tall hat, properly put on box-cloth breeches and well-cleaned butcher boots look a great deal better than the buckskins and tops of the single-handed or the parlour maid. My old friend, Mr. John Tubb, whose instinct in all these matters was unerring, always admitted a strong prepossession in favour of what he styled ' a man dressed serious.'

CHAPTER VIII

THE FOREST

Laudabunt alii claram Rhodon, aut Mitylenen,
Aut Epheson—

or Wokingham or Gerrard's Cross, but every Tuesday and Friday in October the Queen's Hounds meet on Ascot Heath at ten o'clock—not the Ascot Heath of Sir F. Grant's well-known picture, but on the grass immediately in front of the Royal Hotel. A brass band discourses here during the race week, but the hounds and hunt-servants look much nicer there than the band-stand. The field is small, unconventionally dressed, and uncertainly mounted. The hunt-servants wear their oldest coats, and, in my time at all events, did not ride their most precious horses.

The deer cart is sent either to Red Lodge, Gravel Hill, or South Hill Gate, which are within a couple of miles of Ascot. The First Whip rides on to uncart, and, after giving him (the Whip) a few minutes' law, hounds move off and are laid on in the usual way. Unless we were fortunate enough to have harboured an outlying deer, this accurately describes the routine preliminaries of a day's forest hunting.

Anybody who has hunted with many different packs of hounds must have observed that every hunt enjoys some native characteristic of its own which the stranger is invited to notice. There will always be something or other which the country claims as a more or less satisfactory distinction.

BUT YOU SQUELCH AND STAMBLE ON

These distinctions are often anything but reassuring: such, for instance, as drains—which, if you get into them, involve a stay for hours, and a sovereign to pay for a team of cart-horses—menacing stone-faced banks, or impervious doubles. On the other hand, you may be congratulated upon the first draw being in the centre of 'our vale,' or on the sporting indifference of the farmers about seeds and roots.

The forest and the forest hunting claim and deserve special consideration. To my mind, the forest is not enough appreciated by the gallants who ride to the Queen's Hounds. They think it dull. Some little time ago an article in the 'Spectator' declared that the ideal of modern hunting is 'to ride hard and straight,' and even went so far as to represent an accident as its pleasurable objective. What would Sir Roger de Coverley and the stone-grey horse have said to this? I shall admit over and over again in the course of these pages that staghounds are things to ride to. Agreed and agreed, that, tried by the æsthetic canons of a riding country, it is better fun to set a nice horse going after a Reading-bound deer from Hawthorn Hill than through the fir-trees and Spanish chestnuts of Swinley; but, still, much of the wide landscape stretching away from Ascot to Winchfield and Farnham and Guildford and Woking possesses a chief essential of any hunting country, and the very first essential of a carted-deer country—wildness. I do not mean to say that all this country is forest. A low margin of cultivation, the course of a stream, a kinder soil, have here and there invited enclosures and tillage, a farmhouse or two, and a few cottages. But this makes a little change. It is true that the sour grassland is boggy, that the banks are rotten, and that there is a good deal of untidy trailing wire. But you squelch and scramble on in the hope, which always animates the cross-country rider, of soon getting into a nicer bit of country.

Thus the forest and the heather make up for much which the encroachments of population have taken from the wide provinces over which Charles Davis hunted the Queen's Hounds thirty years ago. You cannot quite get rid of the deer cart, nor of the mysterious attraction this 'very pulse of the machine' has for a considerable public on wheels and on foot. Three large colleges, Mr. Waterer's extensive nurseries, and the Gordon Boys' Home are disenchanting occurrences; and I remember a humiliating pursuit in the grounds of the Royal Military College at Sandhurst, owing to our civilian horses not liking the look of the abattis and inundations, revetments and trous-de-loup which train our youth to arms. But you can still ride for miles in certain directions without meeting a soul or seeing a house. No cattle, no sheep, only sand and heather, birch and fir, and sweeps of yellow bog-grass. Red brick, tarred palisades, and residential amenity stop short at the Bracknell and Bagshot road.

I never dared to turn out on the sly, and, as it were, draw through the forest until we hit the line.[1] It would have disappointed so many people, and after all would only have been a distinction and not a difference. Besides, in the forest, at all events five minutes after hounds are laid on, given a little luck and a little imagination, you are hunting a wild animal in a country as wild as Uam Var.

No one knew this country I have outlined better than Charles Kingsley. He has described it in a way I can never hope to arrive at. The thrill of hunting things was in his blood. When I was a little boy, I was at a famous private school at Winchester, kept by the Rev. C. A. Johns. Mr.

---

[1] This is undoubtedly the right and ideal way to manage the uncarting. Davis, I am told, always uncarted quite away from the crowd, and only put a couple of old hounds on to keep the deer moving, thus saving him (the deer) from being mobbed and bewildered and letting him get his bearings and make his point. But in these days it would be very unpopular and almost impossible to carry into effect.

A HUMILIATING PURSUIT IN THE GROUNDS OF THE ROYAL MILITARY COLLEGE AT SANDHURST

Kingsley, as he was then, and Mr. Johns were old friends and brother naturalists. I remember, one July afternoon, Mr. Kingsley taking our class in Xenophon. We felt flattered, but nervous. In the first three or four sentences we came to ἦν δὲ μέγας παράδεισος. He forgot all about the rest of the lesson, and went off into a ringing description of hunting cheetahs and Persian greyhounds, and bustard and florican, and antelope. And then, having made us see the παράδεισος, he told us about the Chase at Bramshill, and its Scotch and silver firs, and the bishop who shot the forester by mistake and built the almshouses at Guildford to his memory.

One of the happiest days of the year at that happy school was when we all went down to Lyndhurst to hunt white admirals and fritillaries. Twice, I think, Mr. Kingsley came with us. I can see him now, with his trousers turned up high over famous lace-boots and a butterfly-net and collecting-box, coursing a purple hair-streak over an intricate country, in the hope of catching it before it spired—which is the way of purple hair-streaks—into the high oak-tops. But I remember something better than that. I can hear him viewing away a fox we put out of a snug patch of whitethorn. His scream was as 'remarkable and susceptible' as Jack Raven's.

At three-and-twenty, Kingsley tells us, his brains were full of bison and grizzly bear, mustang, bighorn, and adventure; but, fortunately for us, these things were not for him. Had it been otherwise, 'Westward Ho!' and 'Hypatia' might never have been written. His lines fell in quiet places, amongst quiet people. Eversley is close to Bramshill, on the skirts of the Hampshire moorlands. It is not in the forest proper, which, I suppose, is confined to Windsor and Swinley Forests; but the country round Eversley and Bramshill is still rougher and wilder. The

Queen's Hounds ran over it several times in my day. I remember one particular day hunting a deer on a cold but fairly holding scent across Hartford Bridge flats. As they hunted like beagles, and chanted their Gregorian, and now and again spread like a sky-rocket, the men and I—to use a West Riding expression—were 'rarely suited.' One season we had an outlying hind about Bramshill; we never caught her, but she came back of her own accord one day to the Paddocks, and in at the Paddock gate, which Groves, the deer-keeper, propped open for her. She was so difficult to harbour that we called her Hide-and-Seek. Like an enchanted deer in a German fairy tale, she seemed to know what we were about. Once she had been harboured in a small wood below Bramshill House for several days, and used to go out and feed every night on some turnips. The very day the Queen's Hounds met at Bramshill to try to catch her, they seemed to hit a line on their way to the meet over Hartford Bridge Flats. Of course, we never found Hide-and-Seek, and the very same afternoon she was seen hanging about Swinley Paddocks. As far as I remember, she again worked her way back to Bramshill, and eventually came home to her friends and the old beans and clover hay at Swinley.

When 'Nimrod' made his tour of inspection of the reputable hunts of his day, he dismissed Sir John Cope's country, as it was then, in a very cursory way. My boy was at a capital school just against Eversley Green, under Bramshill, and I remember his saying in a rather homesick letter, 'The fir-trees are very dismal.' 'Nimrod' was of the same opinion. 'It [Sir John Cope's country] partakes,' he says, 'of a sort of Cimmerian darkness in November,' and he warns the hunting aristocracy, whose society he affected, against its clays and sands, bogs and heath, immense fuel hedges, deep, blind ditches, and bad foxes.

But Mr. Kingsley never tired of the firs and their 'sawedge' against the red sunsets, and all their belongings and incidents.

Mr. Garth in his scarlet and Mr. Cordery in his green coat were ever welcome sights, the hounds and hunt-servants his chosen brethren and companions. And so one afternoon, he tells us how, after visiting his sick people, he rides the old mare away through the fir woods, under the dome of buff and grey cloud, and comes right across Mr. Garth's hunted fox. Shall he halloa as he did in the New Forest? It is needless. Louder and louder, nearer and nearer, swells up the chorus music of hounds running in woodland.

Perhaps he may have written the 'Ode to the North-East Wind' when he got home that day.

> Through the black fir forest
> Thunder harsh and dry,
> Shattering down the snowflakes
> Off the curdled sky.
> Hark the brave north-easter!
> Breast-high lies the scent,
> On by holt and headland,
> Over heath and bent.
> Chime, ye dappled darlings,
> Through the sleet and snow,
> Who can override you?
> Let the horses go!
> Chime, ye dappled darlings,
> Down the roaring blast,
> You shall see a fox die
> Ere an hour be past.
> Go! and rest to-morrow,
> Hunting in your dreams,
> While our skates are ringing
> O'er the frozen streams.

Somerville never wrote anything like that. There you have the life and character of the well-bred foxhound in verse.

This is what he says of the foxhound in prose: 'The old

savage ideal of beauty was the lion, type of mere massive force. That was succeeded by an over-civilised ideal—say the fawn—type of delicate grace. By cunning breeding and choosing, through long centuries, man has combined both, and has created the fox-hound, lion and fawn in one; just as he might create noble human beings, did he take half as much trouble about politics (in the true old sense of the word) as he does about fowls. Look at that old hound, who stands doubtful, looking up at his master for advice. Look at the severity, delicacy, lightness of every curve. His head is finer than a deer's; his hind-legs tense as steel springs; his fore-legs straight as arrows; and yet see the depth of chest, the sweep of loin, the breadth of paw, the mass of arm and thigh; and, if you have an eye for form, look at the absolute majesty of his attitude at this moment. Majesty is the only word for it. If he were six feet high instead of twenty-three inches, with what animal on earth could you compare him? Is it not a joy to see such a thing alive? It is to me at least. I should like to have one in my study all day along, as I would have a statue or a picture; and when Mr. Morrell gave (as they say) two hundred guineas for Hercules alone, I believe the dog was well worth the money, only to look at.' The last sentence would have delighted Captain Cook, a great authority in his day. In his book published in 1826, the Captain complained that, while people thought nothing of giving three hundred guineas for a hunter, they would not give money enough for hounds; 'whereas,' says the Captain, excited into italics, '*everything depends upon a pack of hounds.*' I do not like the prose so much as the verse. It is a little excessive, and the 'breadth of paw' will not do for Peterborough.

But old Virginal has hit it off, and Kingsley turns the mare's head homewards. This is a capital description of forest-riding: 'So homeward I go through a labyrinth of fir-stems, and, what is worse, fir-stumps, which need both my eyes and my horse's at every moment. . . . Now I plunge into a gloomy dell wherein is no tinkling rivulet ever pure; but, instead, a bog hewn out into a chessboard of squares parted by narrow ditches some twenty feet apart. Blundering among the stems I go fetlock deep in peat, and jumping at every third stride one of the said uncanny grips half hidden in long hassock grass . . . out of it we shall be soon. I see daylight ahead at last, bright between the dark stems. Up a steep slope and over a bank which is not very big, but, being composed of loose gravel and peat-mould, gives down with me, nearly sending me head over heels in the heather, and leaving me a sheer gap to scramble through and out into the open moor.'

I said just now that the forest was unpopular with the riding men. They dislike the unfairness of its emergencies and the certainty of its vicissitudes. A Jem Mason may be cast in a pot-hole, a Jock Trotter flounder into a gobble-cow bog, and the hidden prehistoric ruts, made nobody knows how, leading nobody knows where, may at any moment discountenance a Gambado.

'It is these plaguy holes on the heath throw a horse down,' observed Mr. Garth to a dear friend of mine,[1] after watching him recover from one of those long-drawn-out blunders that seem a lifetime to the rider. This is danger unredeemed by distinction. Yet, assuming you escape all the untoward possibilities of a forest run, it is a great mistake to think that it is an easy thing to ride to. In hunting jargon you must keep right at the tail of hounds. A deer will hardly run the present fast foxhound pack

[1] The late Mr. John Hargreaves of Maiden Early, for many years Master of the South Berks. Mr. Hargreaves was in his real element amongst the banks and ditches of the Hawthorn Hill country, and often came out with us on a Friday.

out of scent on a good scenting day. He does not go much faster at one time than another, but he goes no slower, and he keeps going on. So do the hounds. Under the fir-trees, and even among the birch and Spanish chestnut, there is no undergrowth to stop them. On a really good scenting day hounds can carry a head through a great deal of the woodland, and there are none of the high palisaded enclosures which the economics of forestry have recommended in the New Forest. The forest banks and

THE HIDDEN PREHISTORIC RUTS

grips mean nothing to the necks and shoulders and the dash which their inheritance of the best blood in England gives the Queen's Hounds, and outside on the open moorland, the heather, except here and there in the deeper hollows, is not high enough or strong enough to make hounds go appreciably slower. It makes them string, and individual hounds single themselves out. A rather long-backed hound named Hotspur, which Harvey brought with him from the Isle of Wight—a great favourite of mine—always led through the really thick heather. Thus, when hounds really run, and the man really rides to them wherever they go—following the rides on such occasion is a mere hope-for-the-best affair — a really fast forest run is in some ways a greater test of horsemanship than crossing the obvious enclosures of a fairly fenced hunting country; I think Comins, the Queen's Huntsman—a most dashing forest rider—will agree with me. In the latter case on a free and experienced horse the rider need only be a passenger, but in the forest the man must *ride* his horse, he cannot be merely carried.

In the forest, as anywhere else, it is an advantage to be on a fast horse; but, whatever you are on, you have often got to ride him fast, under circumstances peculiarly unfavourable to fast riding, and which are often irritating to the temperament of a high-couraged and sensitive animal.

I remember hunting for a few days with Lord Lonsdale some years ago when he hunted the Woodland Pytchley. One afternoon, latish on in the season, we literally rode into an old dog-fox in Boughton woods. He jumped up between us. The hounds got away right on the back of the fox. We both started on the back of hounds. I was riding a handy, quick horse by Berserker, and those stately woodlands have been well administered and thinned. But Lord Lonsdale lost me in three minutes—not so much because he was riding a faster horse, although I dare say he was, but because of his superior horsemanship and his knowledge of *manège* riding, which, to my mind, especially distinguishes him from other celebrated riders to hounds. It is your legs, and not your hands, which take a horse through trees. Since then circumstances have given me plenty of opportunities of learning to ride quickly through woodlands; but I am no good at it. Perhaps on that account I may be overrating its difficulty.

But whatever the forest may be for the rider, it is a

famous place for hounds No huntsman with Swinley Forest within five hundred yards of his kennels can find an excuse for not having hounds in condition, almost at any season of the year. It is a mere platitude to say that there is nothing like big woodlands to teach a pack of hounds to run together and hunt together. We all know that. But the anomalous and inevitable conditions of hunting the carted deer give to forest hunting a quite particular value. Thanks to the forest, or the forest country, the Queen's Hounds enjoy advantages without compare, and which should be turned to the fullest account.

Once forest hunting begins, the young entry get their chance. They begin to realise themselves. Life is not to be made up of snubbings from the surly old hounds, of dull constitutionals, of quarrels with Splendour and Streamer, of the unbroken monotony of regular hours, regular meals, and of kennel-life generally, with not nearly so much to do as there was in and about the pleasant farmyard near Wokingham or Slough.

During the first two or three days' forest hunting it is advisable to check hounds every now and then; Charles Davis always did this, and his hounds in the forest were said to be as perfect in close hunting as harriers, although he was in the habit of taking out over thirty couple, and a large proportion of unentered hounds. It gives the stragglers a chance to get up. But towards the end of October these artificial checks should not be necessary. A hound hates being lost in a great lonely wood with no familiar sights or sounds for miles, and a hound which is always getting lost is either peevish, faint-hearted, or slow, and not worth Scotch oatmeal at 13*l.* a ton. The open heather country is a capital test of drive and action. I like to see hounds lay themselves right down over the rough ground or the patches of burnt heather as if it were permanent pasture. Some hounds,

JOHN COMINS

HUNTSMAN TO THE QUEEN'S HOUNDS. APPOINTED APRIL 1, 1891

good ones too, have a sort of high, romping action at these times which I never approved of. On a scent a hound should streak along.

And now as to horses in the forest. The horses, I think, are cleverer than the men. I have seen wild, light-headed horses never put a foot wrong. They make their riders and themselves hot, cross and uncomfortable; but, in apparently constant jeopardy, they seem to enjoy the same sort of protection which Providence is said to accord to drunken men in railway accidents. But it is difficult to say how a horse will carry you in the forest. I had a black horse called William which I rode for three seasons with the Queen's Hounds, and which I always rode a good deal during the forest hunting. William, now the favourite of a friend of mine, is a very free horse in the open, childishly fond of galloping and jumping, and indeed, unless ridden in front, he 'pleasantly tightens the rein,' to quote a dealer's euphemism; but in the more gloomy and mysterious parts of the forest, or in deep, suspicious-looking heather, William would always go behind his bridle, ringing a sort of tune on his bit at an extravagantly actioned trot. At such times he seemed to have laid upon himself a self-denying ordinance, neither to catch hold nor to gallop until things were more like what he was used to. This kind of pace has two objections: it does not get you on very fast, and it gives you a tremendous cropper if anything goes wrong. I have a lively recollection of William, when conscientiously escalading an ineligible bit of riding ground near Minley, being betrayed in a thicket of rhododendrons; even his shoulders could not save us—to use an expression of that noted horseman, Dick Christian, he fell 'like a clot.'

I had another horse called Agitator, by Republican; he was own brother to Doneraile, and had won one or two steeplechases himself. Agitator was a charming hunter, with fascinating ways and style about him; but the swish of branches used to excite him, and he would bound about in a most foolish way at times if I rode him through the stuff. He was 16.3, and not at all the sort of horse which you would pick for the forest; but however close the grips came together, you could not make him put a foot wrong, and you could not have filled an hour-glass from the damage he did to the crumbly little banks you occasionally have to cross. This instinct some horses have of putting in a short one has always seemed to me like the instinct of time which some people possess in a greater degree than others. There is no better test of an active, resourceful horse than to canter him along the grass siding to a high road, with different-sized grips at short intervals. If he times them all without disturbing the smoothness of your seat, or making you involuntarily job him in the mouth, you may be sure it is all right. It is not a trial an intellectual dealer will often recommend to you.

I always liked the forest as a school of morals for excitable, fractious-mouthed horses, which are often treated with greater consideration than they deserve. Nine times out of ten, so far from being humoured, they should not even be consulted. 'He wants very light hands' is an implied compliment to a horse's courage and to his owner's riding, but it usually only means that this undesirable animal has always had his own way about his neck and head and mouth. Light hands are not the same thing as good hands. Very often light hands only mean that the rider has a good seat, and is consequently undisturbed by a rough uncomfortable ride, and independent of his reins. The late Mr. Chapman, one of the hunting horsemen of the century, once told me that you should think of your horse's mouth as a piece of delicate pie-crust. It is a pleasant fancy, but, like pie-crust, a mouth wants making, and depends on the cook. Mr.

Chapman himself always rode on strong bridles and asserted his prerogatives. He would never put up with the various liberties a light bridle permits a horse to take with his rider. A long cheeked sliding-bar double bridle, a Cheshire martingale, a leather strap instead of a curb chain, turnings here, twistings there, plenty of fir-trees, and the discontents and surprises of the forest are the best things in the world to make your Rupert and Lady Clara Vere de Vere lose the self-consciousness which so often renders them a nuisance to themselves and their riders.

And so farewell to the forest and the heather, to the lean cultivation, the ineffectual turnips, to the commons and the geese, the jays and the unfashionable side of the Queen's country. Let all stag-hunters remember that Charles Davis, the great tradition of the royal pack, was devoted to the forest. One October, on the last day of forest hunting years ago, he said to Dr. Croft, of Bracknell, who knew him well, and to whom I am indebted for a great deal of help and information, 'Now my fun is over—on Tuesday my troubles begin.'

CHAPTER IX

BANKS AND DITCHES

Make me feel the wild pulsation I have often felt before,
When my horse went on before me and my hack was at the door,
Yearning for the large excitement that the coming sport should yield,
And rejoicing in the cropper that I got the second field.
Ha, ha, ha! was that an oxer? What, old Rambler, is he dead?
What of that? pick up the pieces, he was mortal, go ahead

THERE is very little to be said about the Buckinghamshire side of the Queen's country. It is a land of large undulations, light-coloured plough, beech-woods, and flints. Here and there in the valleys a narrow tract of permanent pasture cheers you up, and fills another corner in the sketch-book of memory. I saw the body of the pack carry a rare head up the emerald stream line of the Amersham Valley one day, with a hound called Splendour three hundred yards in front of them all—we could never make out where or how he had got such a lead. But it cannot be considered a good hunting country from a riding point of view. In old days the Queen's Hounds used sometimes to run down into the Vale of Aylesbury from Gerrard's Cross—at least, so the late William Bartlett, for many years second whip, used to tell me. One or other of our Nestors used always to remark to me—it was the veteran commonplace of this particular meet—that the wind, whatever its quarter, was right for taking us thither. But, alas! it never did so in my time. At the same time, all about Gerrard's Cross and Beaconsfield is not by any means a bad stag-hunting country. At all events there is lots of room, and we had some capital gallops in that part of the world. When there had been plenty of rain these pale ploughs and the high beech-woods carried a capital scent, and the configuration of the country wanted a galloping horse ; indeed a better bred one than Berkshire.

The best thing I remember was fifty minutes from Chalfont Park with an outlying deer, named Bramshill. We found him in a large patch of broom, just above Captain Penton's house, where he had been treated for two or three weeks as an honoured guest. Harvey drew up to him very quietly and slowly, and the hounds had owned a line for three hundred yards before the deer jumped up. This was a very pretty find ; the deer jumped with such gay bounds through the broom. I was riding a mare called Milkmaid, not up to my weight, but she was all but cleanbred and fast, and carried me well. I don't think I ever remember going for so long at top speed. Comparatively few people really lived through it or saw it. As there was nothing to jump all the way, there is no harm in saying so ; it was more like a flat race. Bramshill took to the reservoir at Chalfont St. Giles, and we had to leave him there. This deer was a great water lover. We had taken him in a pond at Elvetham the first day he was ever hunted. The following year I took him down to the Vine, where we hunted one day by invitation, thinking we were safe in that dry and waterless country, but he found his way straight to the only ornamental piece of water for miles, Ewhurst Park, and he again refused to come out.

There were several good riders who used to come out on the Bucks side of the river, most notably Mr. Drake, the rector of Amersham, who joined us once or twice. Except for the Rev. Mr. Fowle, whom George III., on a public occasion, declared to be one of the best cavalry officers (Mr. Fowle having at the time of the French Wars raised a corps of Berkshire

Yeomanry), one of the best riders, and also one of the best preachers of his acquaintance, and whom he much wished to make a bishop, the Royal Hounds do not appear to have ever been distinguished for any of the hard-riding parsons who adorn the sporting literature of fifty years ago. A writer of authority in the early years of this century declares that he would back the bench of Bishops against the Judges any day over a country or on the flat, and the pages of 'Nimrod' teem with the exploits of resolute clergymen, who seem to have been especial favourites, and to have often attracted distinguished and particular notice. Thus, 'the Rev. J. M.,' writes the Duke of Cleveland in his diary, 'shone as conspicuously on his grey mare as in the pulpit, and was alone with hounds over Ainderby Moors.' Again, 'The Vicar of P. is no humbug,' writes 'Nimrod.' This satisfactory conclusion was due to the Vicar's love of hunting, and to the sporting character of his invitation to the writer and Sir Bellingham Graham to drink more claret. 'If you drink enough. it will make your eyes look like boiled gooseberries.' The first time I saw Mr. Drake out we happened to run fast over half a dozen old grass fields with rough, old-fashioned fences. This was quite at the beginning of the run, and we were all full of go. As I watched the 'seriously dressed' horseman smoothly cutting out the work for us on a well-bred old chestnut horse, I knew at once we were entertaining an angel unawares. Perhaps Mr. Drake would have come out oftener, had he known the pleasure and interest his style of riding gave us all.

Whether hounds run fast over it or slow, Bucks is not at all a bad country to give a horse confidence; the neat wattles are encouraging to a degree, and here and there a sort of fringe of young and innocent hazel, with no ditch, teaches a horse to get up. As far as I remember, the only time I saw a *bona fide* upstanding gate jumped by one of the Queen's field was on the Bucks side. Mr. Shackle of Redleaf was the hero of this incident, on a well-bred black horse he owned in 1892. It was charmingly done, and the black horse landed noiselessly on his hind legs on to a rough service roadway leading into some farm buildings. I nearly Absalomised myself by jumping the fence alongside into an orchard with apple-trees of the most gnarled and deformed description. The gate, too, was new, painted black; the next worst colour to white.

The Slough country, with its once popular meets, I consider quite unsuitable to stag-hunting; it is distinguished by almost every characteristic you don't want—population, wire, a river, a canal, a railway, cabbages, strong wheat land, and soggy grass with a black subsoil. The opening meet at Salt Hill is one of those institutions which can no longer be defended in practice. In 1893, I remember, we spent the whole of our time—it seemed very long—crossing and recrossing the river by Maidenhead Bridge, finally taking the deer in Weston's yard before a large assembly of Eton boys and maidservants. It was stag-hunting at its very worst. Indeed, I have often thought the best thing about these teeming flats between Bray and Windsor—which I admit sometimes carried a scent--were the varying prospects of Windsor, rising like an enchanted castle into the clearer sky out of the lilac-blue haze which broods upon the low horizons of the Thames Valley. Often and often I have thanked Windsor with loyal satisfaction for that stately outline of towers and terraces, and felt compensated for a stupid hunt.

But now let me take my readers to the banks and ditches of Berkshire. Most of the glad emotions so pleasantly recalled to us by Mr. Bromley-Davenport in the couplets quoted at the head of this chapter, are to be had for the asking by the stag-hunter; indeed, if there is a scent and the

Queen's field are in the humour—which, to do them justice, they invariably are—and if the deer goes the right way from Hawthorn Hill, it is very possible to rejoice in your cropper at the first fence which happens to be a very typical example of the Queen's bank and ditch country.

There are no oxers—nor need this be a matter of inextinguishable regret—and very little timber. Mr. Van de Weyer's fine grass land around New Lodge was fenced with rood upon rood of uniform post and railings, but I do not think I can remember seeing them jumped. One day when we nearly ran straight over this bit of country, I thought of doing it, but there it ended. The rails are not very high, but they are painted black, and they stand up out of the level fields with horrid integrity without a suspicion of a lean from you. The geometry of their alignments gives the whole affair a building-plot look; and in bold relief several hunting gates are painted a staring white, and open easily and quickly. It requires moral as well as physical courage to resist such a conspiracy. A sporting doctor was the only conspicuous exponent in my time of timber jumping. He had a white horse and a bay horse, which like himself were both highly versed in the art, but he literally had to hunt for opportunities of exhibiting their talents.

There is no water either in the Berkshire side of the Queen's country; that is, no jumpable water. The not-to-be denied stag-hunter will have frequent opportunities of swimming if so minded, but very few of pounding the field over a bumping brook. Take them all through, the fences are mostly of the deferential breed; you seldom come to the sort of place which Jem Mason described as comprising eternal misery on one side and certain death on the other; or of the character so neatly suggested by a hard-riding nobleman to his huntsman: 'What's the other side, my Lord?' 'Thank God, I am.'

But the best part of it—all about Wokingham and Hawthorn Hill and Warren House—is quite a nice country to ride over on an active horse, who goes up to his bank with a flippant one, two, three, four, and his ears pricked and jumps on and off it quick. And the banks are not big and wide like some of the Blackmore Vale banks which constitute quite a regular operation. When all goes well, you do not get quite the same emotion as you do in a stake and bound country, on a free horse. They are not to be had in any on and off country. But, on the other hand, when all goes wrong, you are not liable to the imperial crowners which Mr. Sawyer watches his friends take in Market Harboro', and which are so capitally rendered on the yellow back of that most admirable and inspiring novel. You are much more likely to sprain your ankle than to smash your hat; the very few falls I had were all of this latter sort, and I cannot remember having ever been shot handsomely into the middle of next week. Indeed, with the exception of the railway gates of an occasional level crossing, and a fair choice of well-protected deep cuttings, Bucks and Berks only present average opportunities either for falls, or for conspicuous exploits. Jack Mytton and men of his kidney would find little to satisfy their ambition in the Queen's country.

Some few examples of punishment cheerfully taken by the men of old time and of their ethics may serve to edify the present and rising generation of horsemen.

'No sympathy was like his,' says Mr. Mytton's biographer.[1] It certainly found vent in unusual ways, for we read of his knocking down his tutor and putting an eminent horse-dealer to bed with two bulldogs and a bear, to say

---

[1] He might have added his digestion. On one occasion he and a friend consumed eighteen pounds of filbert nuts. At the close of the séance they were 'up to their knees in nut-shells.'

nothing of larger traits of a generous nature. Nature, however, cannot be expected to be prodigal of her Myttons, and it might not be easy to string together a long chaplet of true Mytton lustred pearls. Here, however, are two or three merely average selections.

'Nimrod' relates how a Mr. Stanhope who was staying at the time with Sir Bellingham Graham, being already in a more or less maimed condition from previous exploits, was stretched for dead early in the day. He was taken to Bosworth and blooded; three ribs being found to be broken. Mr. Stanhope, however, resisted these insinuations of the faculty, and came out again two days later. The field were hindered by some high rails which were being pulled down, when Mr. Stanhope insisted on 'having a try,' with the result of another heavy fall. 'You are a good one, by G——!' exclaimed his host; but as he probably did not wish to have him laid up in his house all the season, he added, 'You shall ride again no more,' and Mr. Stanhope, to his great annoyance, was sent in a post-chaise to Leicester. This fall accounted for two more ribs and his breast bone. 'Not a bad sort to breed from,' is the chronicler's appreciative comment.

Upon another occasion, a Cheshire whipper-in pleases 'Nimrod' very much by this account of his injuries: 'Three ribs broken one side, two on tother, both collar bones, and been scalped.' It further appeared that his horse 'Valentine,' whom, it is true, he calls a 'dunghill brute' for lying on him half an hour, when he did get up, kicked him on the head till the skin hung down all over his eyes and face. 'And do you know, sir'—this was the part of the story which appealed most to 'Nimrod's' best feelings—'When I gets to Wrexham, I faints from loss of blood!' Only a Blackburn Rover could stand this sort of thing in these days. As a pendant to this undefeated hunt-servant may be cited the gay stoicism of a man of fashion. This was a Mr. Williamson, who fell from a height before a large company into a deep road. 'There was something very frightful in the motions of Mr. Williamson.' It turned out that, in addition to more important injuries, this gentleman's jaw was broken, and most of his teeth

CHARLES HOARE, SECOND WHIPPER-IN TO THE QUEEN'S HOUNDS,
APPOINTED JULY 1, 1894

knocked down his throat. Mr. Williamson was young and good-looking. He declared he would not have taken a thousand guineas for his teeth, but with true sportsmanlike feeling said he regretted them less than the run he had missed. It is true that Mr. Henry Kingscote's feat in getting to the end of a fine run in spite of eleven bad falls, owing to having blinded his horse, is recorded as a somewhat rare example of grim resolution. Such incidents were taken in perfect good part, and in an 'all in the day's work' spirit which would cause something like alarm and even unpleasantness in these more narrow-minded days. What for instance should we say to this? Mr. Assheton Smith and Mr. J. White always rode very jealous of each other. On one occasion they came to a great bullfinch with only one possible place in it. Mr. White got at it first, but stuck fast in the middle of it, to Mr. Smith's great annoyance. 'Ram the spurs in, and pray get out of my way,' says Mr. Smith after a decent interval. 'If you're in such a d——d hurry, why don't you charge me?' was the rejoinder. Mr. Smith took him at his word, and on they went as if nothing had happened. Or, to the generous sang-froid of one of the many hunting Dukes of Grafton? The Duke had been thrown into a ditch; a young curate who was following him stick for stick shouted out, 'Lie still, your Grace,' and cleared him handsomely. The Duke, we are told, on being extricated from his predicament by his attendants, declared himself highly satisfied with such an exhibition of presence of mind, and upon rejoining the hounds promised the young divine his first vacant living. This he carried into effect, remarking to his friends, when he told the story, that if he (the curate) had stopped to help him out, he should never have patronised him. Whilst we are considering the mighty deeds of the past, and in a day of magnum-like flasks and trunk-like sandwich cases, it may here be noted that Mr. Meynell—the hero of the great Billesden Coplow[1] run and the 'Hunting Jupiter' of his day—always breakfasted on a tea-cup of veal tea, and

---

[1] Feb. 24, 1800. From the Coplow by Tilton, Skeffington earths, to Enderby Warren, crossing the Soar below Whitstone. Twenty-eight miles in 2 hours, 15 minutes.

depended during the day upon a flask of tincture of rhubarb, the only refreshment he carried.

But passing from the chivalry and stomachs of our forbears, it may here be observed without disrespect to their memory that a note of the many more clement and intelligent conceptions of manners and taste, which have fruitfully multiplied during the inspiring reign of Queen Victoria, is the changed standard of riding to hounds. Little or no credit is now awarded to a Mr. Stanhope. A man who overfaces a generous horse and is always taking heavy falls, is looked upon as a fool—all but as a knave. That So-and-so is always 'on the floor' is as much as saying that So-and-so is a poor performer. He is spoken of in accents of pity, not of admiration; and you are given to understand that though his heart may be in the right place, his hands and another part of his person are elsewhere.

Every now and then, of course, some great necessity arises, and a gallant pair pound the field. A fall is inevitable, but fine shoulders, fine hands, and a fine seat bring the staunch partners out of the crisis handsomely. I have seen both the late Mr. Chapman and Mr. Corbett Holland fall in a way which was a lesson in the arts of horsemanship. But to ride your horse fairly, to get to the end of many runs with few falls, and to finish a season with a soundish stud, is now the criterion of artistic riding to hounds, not the bravo-like adventures of the Mytton type, which entitled the foxhunter to a place in the sporting anthologies of sixty years ago.

And now as to the sort of horse to ride with the Queen's Hounds. 'Whoever rides Radical should be as quiet as a mouse, as bold as a lion, and as strong as a horse.' So said Mr. Assheton Smith, which is the same thing as saying that Radical was not everybody's horse. At the same time horses of his class, for he was one of the best-bred hunters which ever went over Leicestershire, are the best anywhere and everywhere. All who have hunted in a bank and ditch country have met the victim of an uncomfortable conviction that the animal he happens to be riding is out of his proper country; that he exults in big flying fences, and disdains to lay a foot to a bank. Nine times out of ten, however, you would find the same individual—say if you met him in Mr. Fernie's country—paralysed by the self-same animal's supposed preference for banks and doubles. Here and there, perhaps, a Leicestershire horse is not at his best in a bank country. Radical, for instance, ridden by anybody but Mr. Smith, might not have done himself justice in the Bracknell country; and it is undeniable that many good horses are not quite Leicestershire horses. But for my own riding anywhere I like a horse which has been obliged to jump high, and wide, and strong; and in the whole of my hunting experience I only remember owning one horse which could not be trusted to kick back at a bank.

One of the finest exhibitions of hunting riding I ever saw was in the Cattistock country some years ago. The late Lord Guilford was at that time hunting the country. We found a fox in Briarswood, and ran for twenty minutes very fast over the best of the country. All banks and doubles. Lord Guilford was riding a horse which had only arrived the night before, and had been sold out of Leicestershire because he took off too soon from courage and over-jumped the fences and himself. A horseman such as Lord Guilford was—I put him in the first half-dozen of my acquaintance—can to some extent govern accidents; but I cite this as an illustration of the steadying effects big banks have upon the most extravagant high-flyers.

There is a picture, by Byron Webb, of Mr. Tattersall on a thoroughbred mare named Black Bess, with the Queen's Hounds in an alluring middle distance, in the little room facing the office at Albert Gate, which he has given me leave

MR. EDMUND TATTERSALL ON "BLACK BESS"

FROM THE PICTURE BY BYRON WEBB IN MR. TATTERSALL'S POSSESSION

to reproduce. The man and the mare are just what stag-hunters should be, and equally good-looking. I delight in the green coat and the careful ease of the abundant cravat. But this mare is the very model of a stag-hunter. All blood, fore-legs right under the points of her shoulders, long deep ribs, no lumber, and I will wager you would hardly hear her on the hardest high road—a great point in a stag-hunter. Road work, and fast road work, is inevitable, and a noisy hackney-actioned horse knocks his legs to pieces in no time, to say nothing of getting upon his rider's nerves.

Quadrupedante putrem sonitu quatit ungula campum.

That is right enough on the permanent pasture or in an hexameter, but it is a desolating sound on the Wokingham and Reading road.

Thoroughbred horses, Dick Christian told the 'Druid,' make the very best of hunters. 'I never heard,' he declared, ' of a great thing but it was done by a thoroughbred horse.' They certainly make the best stag-hunters, for only blood, and quality legs and feet, can stand the long distances, the long runs, and the road work. Bucks is hilly, Berks is deep. A slow or underbred horse is soon blown, if not actually outpaced by staghounds, and the more confidence you have in his jumping and his courage, the greater the disaster when it comes. After twenty minutes you would not know the horse; poor devil! as he rolls and slobbers along he would not know himself. Is this the animal that devoured the first four fields like a tiger, and jumped like an india-rubber ball? With the thoroughbred horse it is just the other way. He is often a bad beginner, but the farther he goes the better he goes. The first fence he all but fell from getting too near it, the second fence not liking the look of some straggling thorns he came round, the third fence he left his hind legs ; but though annoyed or disappointed with him, you know he does not mean falling, and you wait his own good time. Now you have been going for the best part of an hour, the claims of high descent have asserted themselves, the best blood of a century is coursing and mantling through his veins, he swells the muscles of his neck, and cracks his nostrils in patrician disdain of every difficulty; he is jumping bigger and bigger, galloping with the force of a steam-engine, collecting himself with the balance of a rope dancer. You know what it is to be really carried.

You know what it is to be Really Carried

However, I must not gallop my Pegasus to death, and restrain myself from any further description of an animal we most of us desire, all deserve, but never find. Suffice it to say that a horse must have his veins full of winning-post blood to carry you safely after the everlasting Swinley deer and over the inevitable miles home.

A sentence in one of Lord Cork's descriptions of a good run in the Harrow country suggests a few further observa-

tions on mere riding to staghounds. 'To hesitate,' he says, 'meant that you were out of it.' Of course this is in a measure true of all riding to hounds when they run fast, but it is especially true of staghounds. Given favourable conditions,

CHARLES STRICKLAND, FIRST WHIPPER-IN TO THE QUEEN'S HOUNDS,
APPOINTED JULY 1, 1894

pace with staghounds is epidemic—you keep on going fast, going on.

A good deer, although he may not run a straight point,

always gives that impression. It is a question whether he can be headed, once he has made up his mind; and this accounts, to some extent, for the extraordinary places he will run into. If he had meant crossing it, I do not think Epsom Hill on a Derby day would have turned Guy Fawkes. Thus staghounds, once they get settled, run on at a pertinacious sort of speed, which most people must find rather tiresome after a bit. There are none of the lightning changes of temperature which illuminate a run with foxhounds. Staghounds, for instance, would seldom inspire a ' Thirty quick minutes from Ranksborough Gorse,' written, I believe, between dressing time and dinner in the congenial atmosphere of stained leathers and a hot bath. But there are exceptions to every rule, and there can be no question that every now and then the Queen's Hounds, not only in pace, but in their drive and fling, give you all the ' vital feelings of delight ' of the foxhound.

It is a question whether you can ride ' cunning ' with staghounds. In all kinds of hunting a really high post and rail or a sullen brook are apt to develop the guile of the Red Indian. Very often this does not matter much when fox-hunting. Horrible injustices often occur, and the battle is often rather to the wary or the swift than to the brook- and rail-jumpers. But with staghounds the event seldom transforms hesitation into judgment. Once you begin to hesitate, it is a hundred to one you see no more of the gallop. One has to account for one's failure somehow, of course ; you acted, for instance, upon a theory that the deer would not go here or was making for there. I have occasionally practised this self-deception upon others, but rarely with any success upon myself.

I remember especially missing the end of one of our more or less classical runs from Shinfield, close to Reading. We ran for a great number of miles under a needlessly

splendid sun, the deer being ultimately taken in Fleet Pond
after a great display of aquatics. In this case a deep river
with a boggy bottom, a high bank, a mere apology for a ford,
and an impetuous horse with a great taste for 'taking off' on
the slightest provocation, suggested a theory as to the run of
the deer. Satan in boots and breeches, who is always at hand
on these occasions, whispered something about a bridge, just

The First Whip's Horse subsided with only his Head out of Water

as Valesman, the first whip's horse, subsided with only his
head out of water under our startled eyes. At the head of the
divisions of caution which quickly form on such occasions
I led the way at a confident pace to the nearest high
road. We kept bolstering ourselves up by saying, 'He
is hanging our way.' 'This is his line!' and no doubt
I pressed into our service something about a side wind,

which is always supposed to woo the affections of the hunted red-deer. Not a bit of it. We never got to hounds again, and I had twenty miles home to Reading, suffering from a hot red coat, a spring headache, and that intolerable sense of injustice which always accompanies well-merited misfortune.

A writer of some note of George III.'s day declared that were the king once to see a fox well found and handsomely killed he would give up the staghounds. He condemns stag-hunting for its lack of 'ecstasy,' and the glorious uncertainty which should distinguish hunting; the sulky or generous temper of the deer being the sole variety the stag-hunter can count upon. It is true the stag-hunter recks nothing of the hazards of a doubtful find, a wild night, a chain of woodlands, and a main earth. But to say there is no uncertainty is to say you have never ridden over the banks and ditches of Berkshire after Bartlett or Guy Fawkes.

LORD RIBBLESDALE
M.B.H. 1892 to 1895

CHAPTER X

BLACK AND WHITE

Ille potens sui
Lætusque deget, cui licet in diem
Dixisse, Vixi: cras vel atra
Nube pelum Pater occupato
Vel sole puro.

SPORTING literature often suffers from a surfeit of success. In the jungle, on the river or the hill, and especially in the hunting-field, the reader's mouth is over-satisfied with good things. As an antidote I will cite one of my own personal experiences of the Harrow country. For the most part these are dismal and ineffectual to a degree. With the exception of one day, when we met at Harefield, and ran into a detestable country—'the wrong way,' with which all beasts of the chase are so conversant—we only met once in the Harrow country of famous tradition during my Mastership, so I remember this occasion very distinctly. Like my more fortunate predecessors, I too had received several assurances from individuals of welcome and goodwill. It was a dry time, and an experiment seemed worth trying. I am horribly afraid of wire; not on account of the horsemen, who, in the well-laid-out environs of London, may be trusted to take remarkably good care of themselves, but on account of the deer and the hounds. The latter can of course be stopped, but there is nothing more sickening than the sight of a good deer doing his generous best in a wired country; and the Master of a pack of staghounds who knowingly exposes and condemns a deer to what this means, is a criminal in boots and breeches. However, the farm upon which we were to turn out, at all events, was not wired. If, as I expected, we ran at once into a wired country, I meant to stop the hounds and trust to luck, which had often befriended me, as regards the deer. In the event, however, these resolutions were not tested, as it was impossible to hunt owing to a cotton-wool fog which never lifted.

Never shall I forget the depressing accompaniments of that day. Just as we grumble more at our mishaps than we give thanks for our benefits, bad days have always impressed themselves more upon me than the good days. Only one of my stalwarts, the London gentlemen, turned up at Paddington with a friend from the North. The pea-soup fog would certainly not have kept the rest at home; and as my eye swept the platform for my missing divisions with all the heart-searchings of Deborah and Barak, I realised that their absence could only be due to the Quixotic nature of the enterprise. Neither the veteran scarlet of Mr. Bowen-May nor the dreadnought outlines of Mr. Noble Smith were to be seen. On the other hand I discerned a respectful pity in the demeanour of the courteous staff of the Great Western Railway, who contribute so materially to the comfort of hunting with the Queen's Hounds. However, after our locomotive had wheezed and creaked like some monster in distress, off we went in an all but empty train. London's yellow-brick girdle always depresses me. But on this particular morning the row upon row of crowded loneliness, the symmetrical monotony broken only by the pre-eminence of some public-house, the panorama of neutral tints, were quite in harmony with my spirits. Circumstances seemed to be too much for me, just as they must be for those who have to live in those endless yellow-brick houses.

There is a great deal about the look of a platform when

you hunt by train. Some look like the job, some do not.
This particular one did not. The fog seemed thicker than

CHARLES SAMWAYS, SECOND GROOM TO THE QUEEN'S HOUNDS[1]

ever, which was consoling at all events. Like Watchhorn
before Sir Harry Scattercash had given him the second

[1] Samways entered Her Majesty's service in 1875 as rough-rider; he was appointed second horseman to the Master of the Buckhounds in May 1880, and promoted in 1894 to be second groom, vice Reuben Matthews.

glass of port wine, I was by this time longing not to hunt. The hounds and hunt horses had slept at Hillingdon, and my second horseman met me at the station with a depressing account of a dull evening, chilly stabling, and languid feeders. It was all very different to the cheerful days of yore he remembered. Samways is a man of perception, resource, and counsel. A good second horseman, like a good valet, should guess what his master is thinking about, and I saw ' the day's disasters in his morning face ' ; he now declared the fog would never lift, suggested the next train back to Paddington, and that he should ride one of my horses on to the meet and send the hounds home.

But by this time the two London gentlemen had coaxed their shrouded favourites out of the horse-boxes, and were asking their way to the hotel. Evidently they were all for a ride of some sort. For the matter of that, so was I. The bare mention of Agitator had cheered me up. ' Post equitem sedet atra cura.' This, as Major Whyte Melville has pointed out, is one of the very few mistakes Horace has made. In the shape of an awkward stile downhill, ' cura ' may for a moment be embodied in front of you, but there is no room for him behind really superlative shoulders, and these consolations were waiting for me only a hundred yards away.

The railway hotel, implacable yellow brick of course, was as little like hunting as the platform. We were looked upon as peculiar animals by an indolent landlord and an incredulous barmaid, Samways in his gold-laced hat being taken, I imagine, for some mounted janissary of the London County Council. However, the cherry brandy—a great incentive to stag-hunting—was pronounced all but up to the Slough sample by my companions. That being the case, there was nothing irretrievably rotten in the state of Denmark. Whilst I was writing a letter—in itself an outrage on a hunting morning—an old gentleman in a peajacket drew a confused picture of what things used to be before Lord John Russell's Reform Bill, in a manner which would have delighted Lord Marney. Those, it appeared, were the days to go hunting in. 'Things,' as he rather vaguely kept declaring, 'were something like.' What with the plush furniture, the oleographs and Japanese grasses of the parlour, and the damaged reminiscences of the peajacket, the icy fingers of depression began clawing at me again. No time was to be lost in mounting. There was nothing for it but the elaborate freedom of Agitator's action. Agitator in the meanwhile had created a diversion, though hardly in our favour, by planting one neatly on the potboy's posterior, whom, failing an ostler, Samways had commandeered from the security of the bottle and jug department, and who was now being lectured for his folly in getting near a long-tailed blood horse. 'You'll know better another time,' Samways was sternly saying as we came into the yard, an assurance which did not seem altogether to comfort the potboy. Five shillings, however, did wonders for the injured part and off we set for the meet. But the mist grew worse every yard of our way. I divined wire everywhere, which is much worse than actually seeing it. The kindest of welcomes awaited us, and a most hospitable host had all sorts of good things to eat and drink laid out for our benefit, but there could be only one opinion about the fog. As to the wire, the hunt-servants who had come a different way, and one or two unenthusiastic local sportsmen, confirmed the opinion I had already formed. Even Comins, the keenest and hardest of stag-hunters, thought it would not do. For once I was glad that the weather made it impossible to hunt, and glad to order the hounds home.

So much for a *dies atra*. And now let me refresh myself with the recollections of a much more amusing day, when we met by invitation in the old Berkshire country, which I jotted down at the time.

March 2, 1893. Posted from Swindon to Kitemore. Orr-Ewing put up hounds, horses, and men at the kennels; self, horses and Samways at Kitemore. A very wet night. However, it had faired up by the time we started. Water out all over the place. Forded the redoubtable Rosey Brook on our way to the meet, a lively but not inviting stream. Van de Weyer, who I suppose has often been in it in old days, had prepared me for its peculiarities. This morning it was running bank-high and out over the banks. Took a mental but futile note of the look of the ford we crossed by. A great concourse at the turn-out. Foot-people for miles round. I was told many had started at 4 A.M. to get there. Waggons, musicianers and cock-shies. Might have been a country race-meeting by the look of things. Serried ranks of spectators drawn up on neighbouring high grounds commanding the Rosey. We were all hospitably entertained by several capital farmers,[1] living at Baulking; my host had very pretty daughters. Sloe gin, I think it was—very good, and fashionable heliotrope colour. Found the Beaufort contingent all landed up, well-mounted, and ready for anything.[2] Joe Moore had managed their journey arrangements capitally. Turned out Blackback soon after twelve o'clock, amidst great and general confusion. Fast-asleep, who was very fresh, nearly threw me off by shying at the Aunt Sallies, just as I was going to address the foot-people on the situation. By the time I had recovered one stirrup and my hat, Blackback was out of the cart. After going two fields parallel to the brook the hill-folk turned him

---

[1] Mr. George Reade, Mr. Robert Whitfield, and Mr. Thomas Matthews.
[2] Messrs. J. Hibbard, James, Charles, and William Rich, Joseph Moore, Joseph Large, and the late Mr. Frank Hiscock, all came up from the Duke of Beaufort's country.

THE WILLOWS PRESENTED A SCENE OF WILD CONFUSION

down over the Rosey, which he crossed at some conventional
willows—a nasty, flooded-looking place from where we
were. The knowing ones now made off for the ford. However, the heliotrope kept a good many in the path of
glory. The country being very deep and much water out, I
gave him very little law—also on the principle of 'For God's
sake start us, captain, before the whiskey is out of us!'

The willows presented a scene of wild confusion. For a
hundred yards each side of where the hounds crossed there was
no reasonably fair take-off, the water being out over banks. I
think all the hunt-servants more or less got in. The fact is,
we are more accustomed to boating than water-jumping. Mr.
Harvey, on Romeo, appeared to make a sort of duck and drake
job of it, but did not part, greatly to his credit. The spluttering
about was tremendous. Waterspouts filled the startled air.
Everybody got in. Charles Rich, according to his own account, climbed up one of the willows after driving Moore's old
grey that he was riding into the water up to his neck. I could
not understand what he did next, but they got over somehow
on right side together, Charlie being wet up to his middle. 'A
d——d good performance, I call it,' he said to me afterwards,
which, as he weighs nineteen stone and is no climber, I
think it was. Self, and Goldsmith on a well-bred white
horse, and one or two more rode up the brook. Goldsmith
found a place with a little rise to it, good take-off and friendly
bush. It was really no width anywhere, so we got over.
Luckily, hounds had gone no pace meanwhile, and dragged
along into the wrong country, of course, Lechlade way out
of the Vale. The chase now led us to the Thames, running
strong and high, only to be crossed by an unholy white spar-
bridge near a weir. For once the men and hounds managed
to get over first; then came Jim Rich and one or two of my
Wiltshire friends, burning to distinguish themselves. Jim
Rich's fool of a horse slipped and got cast on the bridge.

Hind leg hitched through the spars; all passage blocked.
A nice predicament for me and large and brilliant field!
At first we gave the usual advice. 'Take care! Look
out! Mind where you're going to!' His brother Charlie
again on the right side, urging him to shove the blooming
horse into the river and let him swim for it. Jim seemed to
think it a good joke; and if it had to happen, it was as well
it should happen to a Rich. They have a talent for rescues
and emergencies, and are the sort of Deal fishermen of the
Beaufort Hunt. Meanwhile, there we all were. After hoping against hope, I started *magna comitante caterva* for the
nearest bridge, four miles off. By this time I was on William,
and directly we got to the high road we set off at a strong pace.
The high road had all the requisites—hard, wide, well-kept,
and no grass siding to lure one off it. After galloping for fifteen bright minutes or so, we at last saw scarlet specks bobbing
along about a mile away from us, half right. Thank Heaven!
hounds looked as if they were only just running. After
some difficulty in persuading William of my good intentions
—for he fancied by this time that he was taking the good
news from Bruges to Ghent—I turned out of the road with
Sturges on his white horse and two of the second horsemen
who had kept 'follering on' with their usual dash; the rest
of our party being beaten off by our superior disregard for
our horses' legs. We made straight for them over quite a
nice line of hunting country. To my surprise, or rather not
to my surprise, there were both Charlie and James Rich.
Just as they were resolved on putting Charlie's first counsel
of perfection into effect, the animal had recovered the leg
which was over the edge of the bridge. Not liking the look
of the swirling starchy water, he made a great effort, ably
assisted by Charlie, who had hold of the root of his tail,
the others meanwhile hauling at other coigns of vantage.
Up to this point I think they had enjoyed this more than any-

thing. We had to go back over the spar-bridge, and another horse did just the same thing. This time the body servant of a young lady with a deep silver lace band hat, and the old drab Zouave gaiter. However I was the right side, having exerted my prerogative of 'Master, please!' and bidden Jim sternly to the rear. Charlie was with difficulty restrained from staying to see if he could not get this one in, and lustily roared the same advice to Hatband. After dragging on a mile or two we had a long check, the floods and our ignorance of fords and bridges having played the dickens with us. Just as we were settling down into the doldrums of stag-hunting a baker's cart brought up tidings of great joy. The baker had met the deer at some cross roads about two miles away. Harvey at once subjected him to a severe cross-examination as to his acquaintance with the look of a deer, perhaps remembering the story of the yokel who took a squirrel for the fox—'He wor but a little one, and he run up a tree.' The baker stood it well, and offered to go with us as a sort of hostage, declaring he would chance it, which I suppose referred to the afternoon delivery.

Harvey having satisfied himself of the baker's *bona fides* and natural history, started off at a hard-held gallop, blowing his horn. We wanted a little enlivening. The baker's roan pony leading us to such purpose that his loaves kept being jerked out from time to time. The baker must have forgotten the cross road, for when he came to it on he went. 'Hold hard!' we all shouted, like one man, whilst I added the conventional 'You're all over the line!' On this he pulled up so short that one wheel went into the ditch, and a large wicker basket flew out. However, it was all right, and that thick-shouldered Cardigan hit it off and took it down the road at least two hundred yards; none of the others seemed to own it. We slotted him out of the road, and then hunted up to him rather nicely over a fair country, through the park and young plantations of a gentleman's seat to a large piece of water (Buscott Reservoir), in which Blackback was swimming serenely about. In went the hounds, and I began to feel nervous. Bartlett's [1] fine tenor of entreaty and remonstrance now rent the air—it is always one of his great moments—though I never saw any effect produced on the hounds.

Harvey, meanwhile, blew his horn, trotting promi-

IT WAS ALL I COULD DO TO GET 'WILLIAM' HOME

nently up and down the bank, whilst all who knew how cracked their whips. My Wiltshire friends were quite entranced with the spectacle, and declared with one accord they would have come miles to see it alone. Blackback, meanwhile, was veering unconcernedly about in the middle, very little in front of Notion, who, ever since she once got a

[1] For many years second whipper-in, retired on pension in 1894, and died the same year (see footnote to p. 93).

nip at a deer in the Loddon, has much improved in her swimming. There was no boat-house, and I was beginning to be really uncomfortable, when, greatly to my surprise and satisfaction, out went Blackback on the far side. We ran into him in a deep ditch three or four fields further on. Jim Rich had an arm round his neck in a trice, as if he had been at it all his life. There can have been only twenty or thirty people up with us at the end. All my Beaufort guests were there, I am glad to say. William had had quite enough of it. He tires himself from his implacable energy. I gruelled him at Farringdon, where I had some poached eggs. Inn full of talkative and happy hunters. We all thought Joe Moore's horse was going to die when we got him into the stable. A stiff brew of hot ale and whiskey was being administered when I left. It was as much as I could do to get William home the two or three miles I had to go to Kitemore. He dwelt like lead upon his own footsteps. We were both very glad to see Samways. Only a couple short, I think, and the men's horses did pretty well, in spite of their moderate performances at the Rosey Brook. They are not quite what they should be. Rocksavage out, and preserved a knowing air of mystery throughout. It is a pleasure to see him ride over a country. Ease and power combined. His horse always gets the best possible chance, and always seems to take it. He said he thought the hounds were fat. I dare say they are. They certainly are good ones to eat.

Not a very brilliant point, but we circumvented a lot of country, and I think the people of the district all enjoyed it. We were treated with great hospitality and kindness. Brown, who hunts the old Berkshire, and Orr-Ewing, the Master, had thought of everything possible to help us in every way. The Queen's Hounds had not been in this part of the world for seventeen years when Lord Cork brought them down.

CHAPTER XI

KENNELS AND STABLES

'There can be no more important kind of information than the exact knowledge of a man's own country ; and for this, as well as for more general reasons of pleasure and advantage, hunting with dogs and other kinds of sports should be pursued by the young.'—PLATO, *Laws* (JOWETT), vol. v. p. 334.

QUEEN ANNE established the kennels on their present site at Ascot. She inherited her father's love of hunting, who, as Duke of York, was if anything over-fond of it. Pepys more than once complains of the routine Admiralty business falling into arrears owing to the Lord High Admiral being out hunting. Swift speaks of her hunting in burning July weather in a calash—a sort of gig—for she did not ride much latterly, and in order to get about and see the hunt she was always having new rides cut and bogs drained. We horsemen owe much of the pleasure of the October forest hunting about Swinley and Bagshot to Queen Anne.

Kennel lameness was the great scourge of the Ascot kennel in the earlier years of this century. Sharpe and the whips, described rather mildly as 'kind and civil' men by a writer in the 'Sporting Magazine' of 1814, appear to have acknowledged themselves powerless to deal with it.[1]

George IV. thought otherwise. Brighton, in his opinion, was the panacea for all things hurtful, and for a year or two he sent Sharpe there with the hounds for sea-bathing, their

---

[1] The central figure in the plate opposite is G. Sharpe, huntsman ; the others are C. Davis, J. Mandeville, and J. Freeman.

departure for the sea-side being formally announced in the
'Gazette.' Brighton failed, and Davis appears to have
thought, like Sharpe, that there was nothing to be done, and
that five or six couple at the least must always be down
with it. He speaks of the lameness like a man who has lost
his sense of proportion and possibility. 'No artificial means,'
he writes to Mr. Vyner, the author of 'Notitia Venatica,'
'can make a lame kennel a sound one. You may build it
with marble and alabaster and heat it with fire; all won't

THE OLD KENNEL AT SWINLEY

do,' and in 1838 he sends Sir John Halkett the best dog in
the kennel, Ganymede.

'I should be pleased,' he writes, 'to give you one of the
best and stoutest I ever bred. He was never known to
tire, but he is now afflicted with our *cursed torment*, kennel
lameness, of which he may recover in a fresh place, but
never would here.'

This taking them to a fresh place seems to have been
the only remedy practised with any success. Bartlett, his

feeder, whom I have quoted so often in the course of these pages, declares to me that he has seen hounds taken away in the kennel cart, unable to move, to farmhouses where their kennel might be a pigsty, but in about three weeks they would return, permanently and effectually cured. A curious fact which Bartlett also brings to my notice is this. The same lameness was rife at Cumberland Lodge in the harrier kennels ; the suffering harriers, brought to the Ascot kennels, got well in about three weeks, and the change to Cumberland Lodge had the same effect upon the impotent staghounds. Bartlett sticks to it that the cure was permanent. But it is difficult to reconcile these statements with the Sharpe and Davis view of the malady.

Under Harry King, things were no better; he had to some extent imbibed the paralysing conviction of his chief that there was nothing to be done. But thanks to Lord Cork, the Ascot kennel is now free from 'the cursed torment.' When he took over in 1866, the lameness was very prevalent. He had all the kennel yards and houses laid with concrete over a thick layer of dry rubbish, and on the top a layer of asphalte. These practical means succeeded, a further improvement being made by Goodall, who, when he was appointed huntsman, raised the benches nearly two feet.

There was no symptom of kennel lameness during my Mastership, and I imagine—although on this point my opinion is not worth much, seeing that I was not brought up to hounds—the plan and general arrangements of the kennels and premises are favourable to health. The drainage is excellent, all sewage being carried on to a small sewage farm by a well-planned and rigorously inspected system of pipes and sympathetic manholes. The water supply is pure and abundant, and the kennels and whelping houses face southeast by east, which I understand is a desirable aspect. Large grass yards inside the precincts make famous play·

grounds for the young entry, and the hunt-servants and feeders have a bit of garden ground attached to their cottages. There is ample and excellent storage for meal and coal, so that the Master, if so inclined, can take advantage of low prices. The average establishment has always been forty couple, say thirty-five couple of working hounds. It sounds a good many for two days a week, but the Queen's Hounds are never vanned, and the flints on the Buckinghamshire side and the five-and-twenty miles journey home, which is a constant experience, must be taken into account.

Harvey instituted a capital practice, although I do not know whether it has been continued. The hunting pack after being fed were always turned into a big loose box filled seven or eight feet high with wheat straw, and he did not disturb them till well on in the next morning.

There is no difficulty about getting walks, and in my time we entered six or seven couple out of the five-and-twenty walked in the district; but it is not a country for good walks, as there is not enough grass land or milk, and too much residential amenity. The two plans of the kennels are not quite up to date, but they give a good general idea of the premises and distribution. But enough of technicalities. When the thorns and daisies are out, and the whelps about, and the sun is shining, no pleasanter place than the kennel green can be imagined.

In 1875 the Queen honoured the kennels by a visit.

'And now,' Goodall notes in his journal on the 23rd of March, 'a red-letter day. Her Majesty went all over the kennels, taking great interest in the hounds and in every detail.' This was indeed an honour. Not even the fact he records of being very 'unpresentable' from a black eye and contused face, due to his fall with 'Rosslyn' off the wooden bridge, could diminish Goodall's pride and pleasure.

But Chance, the most sensible and companionable of

kennel hacks, is waiting on the pillar reins of the hack stable, and I must canter over to Cumberland Lodge, by the pleasant

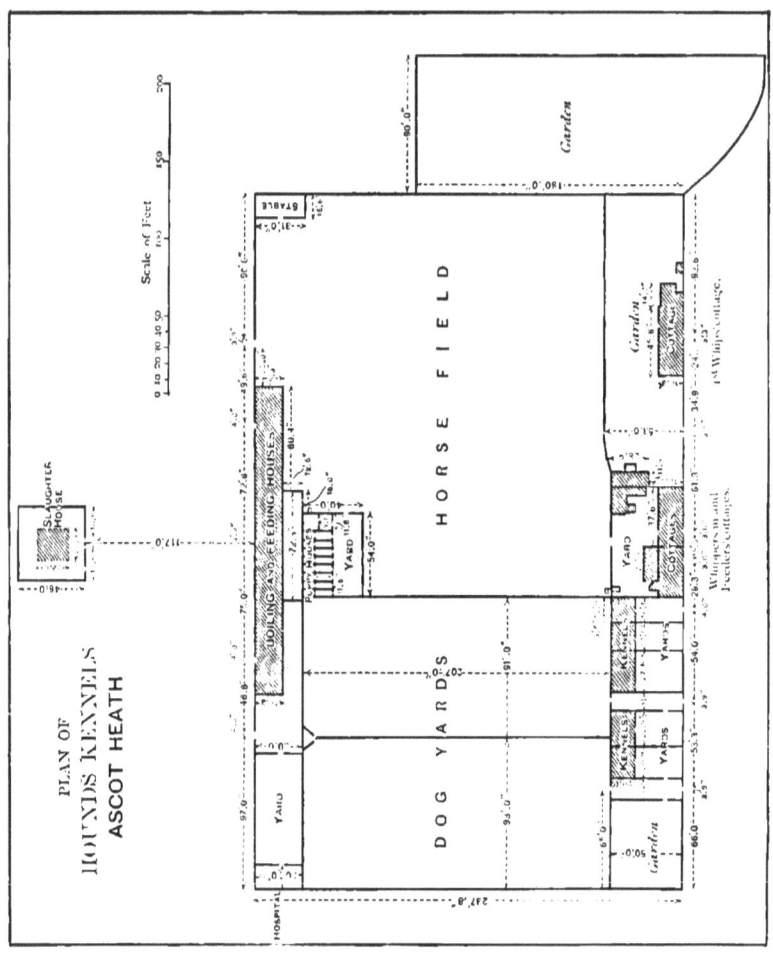

grass rides we both know so well. The situation of Cumberland Lodge is fairly central, and the place has great advantages of good air, famous all-the-year-round exercising ground, and plenty of things for the horses to look at—deer,

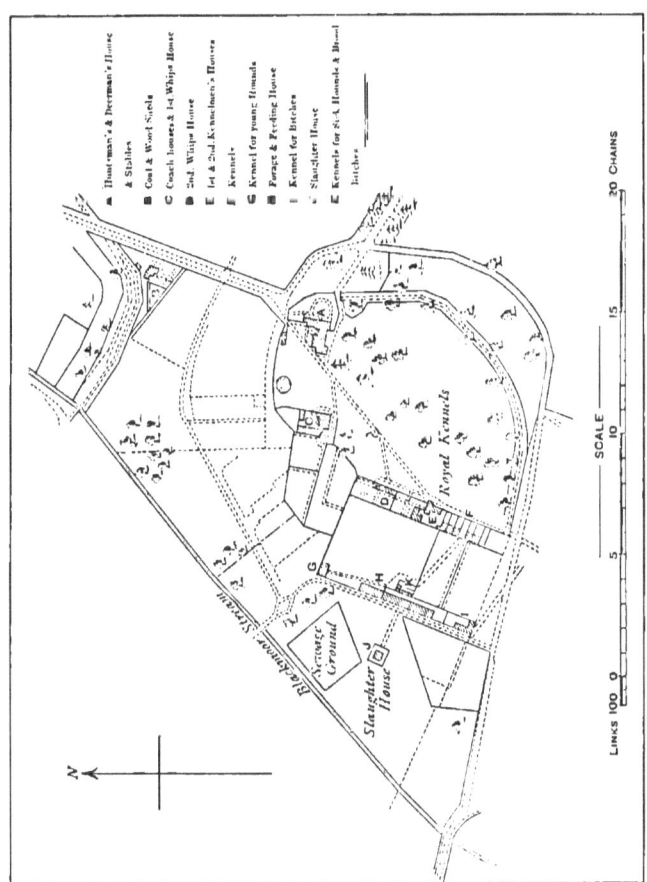

and cock pheasants and rabbits, and fern and fine trees. They make a little variety for them at exercise.

The present buildings stand on the site of an old keeper's cottage described in Norden's Survey (1607) as Hayman's

Lodge; a comfortable range of warm-toned red brick, with a high-pitched gable roof, and all sorts of proper and sympathetic things about it—wide lawns, spreading trees, a cricket ground, and at the back a very remarkable kitchen garden. The stabling has all the dignity and character of a royal and ancient establishment, and the refined look which only belongs to the older-fashioned stabling of people of quality. They were built by Charles II., like his father, a fine schoolhorseman, who delighted and surprised the Duke of Newcastle by the gay shrewdness of his sayings about horses, and also by the integrity of his equestrian principles. Sarah, Duchess of Marlborough, added to and improved Cumberland Lodge during her rangership of Windsor Great Park, and Sir Jeffry Wyattville carried out some further additions whilst he was playing the very deuce at Windsor. Mercifully, however, he did not think it worth 'Gothicising.' I forget how much stabling there is, but we always had a lot of horses there, twenty-five or thirty, and yet there always seemed to be plenty of room, and plenty of work for more. Most of it is stall stabling, but of the wide, long, generous sort, with old oak divisions and posts. Horses do here just as well as in boxes, and a shy feeder put next a greedy one very soon gets into the spirit of feeding time. The summer boxes are very good, the best I think I ever saw: every two boxes has an open yard the full size of both, and the horses take turns in going out, one all night and the other all day. Given the right sort of land with shade and water, spareish for grass, with a sweet bite here and there, I like turning horses out myself. Here and there an individual horse is better summered in a box; but most horses gain in every way by the contrast and the freedom of the out-door life. It puts nature into them and makes them more independent and sensible. At Cumberland Lodge we had no grazing land. However, this I think is the only weak point; and many

people would not agree with me as to the benefit of the out-door life, and the change from a box, where a horse can neither see nor even hear his companions, to a sort of club life.

The Prince of Wales summers his hunters at Cumberland Lodge, and in the days when H.R.H. kept harriers (which he afterwards gave to the farmers of the Queen's country) the harriers were kept there. In the good time when H.R.H. hunted frequently with the Queen's Hounds, that is, in from about 1864 into the beginning of the seventies, he saw some excellent runs and owned some capital horses. Lord Colville has already told us of one great run. I believe only three really saw the end of that one—Colonel, now Sir Nigel, Kingscote, King the huntsman, and Mr. Sowter, the well-known Haymarket saddler; but the Prince, Sir Nigel tells me, went at the top of the hunt as far as Harrow, when with the majority of the field he made a bad turn in the lanes. On this occasion the horses were sent home by train to Windsor, and the Prince's horse, a very favourite mare named Firefly, caught cold and died within a day or two. Another run in which H.R.H. rode 'hard and well'—terms which are not always synonymous—and to the end, was from Taplow to St. Albans. Sir Nigel instances another, when the deer was taken near Tring—which must have been a long point—where they had mutton-chops and poached eggs so well served that they merited and received very special attention and commendation from the Prince. Some of his best horses were Firefly, Paddy, Thornton, Rural Dean, Q.C., Lockington, and Charlie, and they were all ridden regularly with the staghounds. Though all were well-bred high-couraged horses, Thornton, Firefly, and Paddy were perhaps the special favourites. Q.C. was a grey; the Prince was mounted on him by the Duke of Beaufort when he was staying at Badminton, and liked him so much that he persuaded the Duke to sell him. 'Paddy,' Sir

Nigel writes me, 'a chestnut horse which I bought out of sale of the present Duke of Westminster (then Lord Grosvenor), was, take him all in all, the horse H.R.H. liked the best for many years; and once when staying at Badminton we had quite a good run over the Dodington Vale up on to the high country toward Badminton. I well remember the Prince riding Paddy over a stile first, that, with horses having come so far and so fast, very few indeed would have looked at.'

It is a common saying that a moderate horse really fit will beat a first-rater that is not fit, and the importance of condition in a stag-hunting stud cannot be overrated. Average condition will not do. A horse must be wound up, and never allowed to get stale, otherwise the effects of a severe day's hunting take a long time passing off. Propitious antecedents play a great part in conditioning a hunter. Personally, I should never buy young horses for the stag-hunting work: it is not so much that a well-bred young horse may not carry the huntsman or whip to the very end, and come home apparently fresh, but it takes the steel out of him, and his constitution is apt to resent it. A stag-hunter must be a seasoned animal. I like them eight or nine years old, out of a crack stud, with three or four years of some one else's oats in them, plus the elbow grease some Meltonian Mr. Tiptop's subordinates have devoted to muscle and sinew.

I referred just now with grateful recollection to Chance. And it may here be noticed, that good kennel hacks are most valuable servants in the Royal establishment. They are like the odd man in a large house, who always does most of the work. The hunt horses are sent on direct to the Buckinghamshire side meets, and the men ride their hacks on with the hounds, the hacks being sent back to Windsor, and waiting there till the hounds arrive, or meeting them elsewhere on intelligence, or the chance of the hounds coming home that way. This saves the Cumberland Lodge stud many a mile, and gets them into their own quarters a good two hours earlier. But given the alliance of the hacks, mounting the establishment is a serious matter. To get on comfortably with the Queen's Hounds and the tireless Swinley deer, you really want two sets of horses, one for the Bucks side and one for the Berks. The furthest meet from Cumberland Lodge in the Friday county is Loddon Bridge, thirteen or fourteen miles; and most of the best Friday meets are within ten miles, but the Chalfonts, Holtspur Heath, Beaconsfield, all run into fourteen to twenty-five miles.

'I have been stag-hunting for between thirty and forty years, and I have come to the conclusion that the demand on the stud in the Royal Hunt is greater than that upon the stable of a master of foxhounds.' So writes Sir Henry Simpson, the widely known and respected Windsor veterinary surgeon, and he goes on to say, speaking from professional experience of the Cumberland Lodge stud, ' No one in my time can say the horses have been overworked, which must have been the case if the Master for the time being had attempted to horse the hunt in the same ratio as would amply suffice for a fox-hunting establishment.' As I have said elsewhere, you want a very well bred one for the far side ; even thoroughbred is not too good to stand the long hours, the hills, and the ever-lengthening miles home which a good run means. To my mind it is an economy to have two horses out for all the men, and I usually had an extra horse out in case of a casualty—this with two for myself meant nine out daily, and five-and-twenty miles home was quite an every-day occurrence. Unfortunately, too, in stag-hunting the second horses do not always mean any very great saving to the first horses ; often and often we could not get them at the right moment to make a difference and in any case the

P

second horses have had an average day's hunting before they are requisitioned for active service, having been obliged to keep going. Nicks and points serve them very little. However, I do not wish to further load this page with 'the gibberish of hunting studs,' to borrow a phrase from a puzzled Quarterly Reviewer of the Delmé-Radcliffe day.

I will only again quote Sir Henry Simpson on the very

JOSIAH MILES, STUD GROOM TO THE QUEEN'S HOUNDS,
OCTOBER 1843 TO MARCH 1894

point which led to a deliverance from the Archbishop, that is, the cruel strain upon the horses. It is always an advantage to hear both sides, however unevenly matched from the point of view of knowledge of the subject. It is in no sense a rejoinder, as it was written in October, long before the Archbishop came to the front. This is what the layman has to say: 'As regards hunting casualties or illness, the result of a hard day. I think I may say with safety of the Royal Hunt, as I may say of other well-ordered hunting establishments, that, in proportion to the risks run, the casualties are not high. Casualties, of course, will always occur, but if a hunter is in condition and fairly ridden, the effect of a severe day's hunting soon passes off.'

As I have said a little about hunt horses in this and in other chapters, I must not close it without a few grateful and affectionate words to the memory of one of the Queen's most faithful and affectionate servants, Josiah Miles, for very many years stud-groom at Cumberland Lodge. He died in the Queen's service after a mercifully short illness in the second year of my Mastership, greatly regretted and respected by all who had ever known him. I know my predecessors felt his loss and appreciated his ability and devotion to his charges quite as much as I did. Duty was ever his first thought, and his daughter writes me that almost his last conscious words to her were to remind my second horseman of a particular bridle which I had desired should be used next hunting day. Miles started in the Queen's service on his wedding day, October 4, 1843, as second groom under Charles Bryant, and was appointed first groom on Bryant's death in 1867. In the summer of 1893 the Queen presented him with a medal in honour of his fifty years' service. I rode over to Cumberland Lodge the same evening to see and congratulate Mr. and Mrs. Miles, tea and a talk with Mrs. Miles being one of the many pleasant things which came with the Mastership of the Queen's Hounds. They had driven over to Windsor together, and the Queen had given Miles his medal with her own hands. It was a most happy tea.

The present stud groom, Reuben Matthews, succeeded Miles. He has been at Cumberland Lodge for a great many years; having been appointed second groom when Miles succeeded Bryant. Thanks to Lord Coventry's kindness, I hunted two or three times last season with the Queen's Hounds, and greatly enjoyed myself with my old friends. I never saw hunt horses looking bigger and better. They did both the stud groom and the master credit.

REUBEN MATTHEWS

CHAPTER XII

ASCOT AFFAIRS

Excussus propriis aliena negotia curat

EVERY Master of the Buckhounds, I fancy, is urged on his appointment by some of his racing friends to deal in a statesmanlike way with the stands.

Several people spoke to me seriously on the subject, and of course they all had ideas of their own as to what should be done. Some of these were a little difficult to follow. But one and all had espoused great principles, and separated themselves—judicially—from all questions of detail. Any and every objection—such as interference with the high road, the local authorities, private ownership, the configuration of the ground, the convenience of the resident population—were brushed aside. A large outlook was the thing, and all these puny points would work themselves out. However, during the time I lived at Ascot I came to the conclusion that, in principle and indeed in fact, which is a very different thing, there was quite enough to be said in favour of setting the stands at an angle to the Straight Mile course to make it worth careful consideration.

But how was it to be done? After looking over and over again at the ground, and the villas, and the high road, and the possibilities of space, I decided that, for many reasons—economic and utilitarian—the mountain, that is the stands, could not go to Mahomet. Mahomet, that is, the course, must come to the mountain. The accompanying plan shows how I thought it could be managed. Some explanatory notes drafted at the time this plan was submitted to the Jockey Club cited the general grounds upon which I made the proposal and the particular advantages claimed for the alteration. I have nothing to add to these notes, so I give the exact text: 'For some years it has been very generally objected that the occupants of the stands and enclosures[1] on the present alignment are unable to see the races run over the New Mile course until the horses are nearly home; for instance, the line *marked A on the plan* is drawn parallel with the front of the Royal stand. It will be seen that the starting point and the greater part of the present New Mile course are actually behind the front of the Royal and other stands and enclosures.

'The Master of the Buckhounds is of opinion that this objection may be successfully dealt with by an alteration in the direction of the present New Mile course, and he would suggest laying out a new Straight Mile as shown on the annexed plan.

'The whole course would thus be thrown considerably in front of the stands and enclosures, and their occupants would literally see each race run out from start to finish.

'Another consideration disposes the Master of the Buckhounds to recommend this alteration. The present New Mile course is just under a mile, and cannot be lengthened on account of the high road. There is thus no room for fractious animals to be quieted in, and a consequently increased risk of false starts. The new course, on the other hand, is exactly a mile in length, amply sufficient space being provided behind the starting post to enable a large field of horses to be conveniently marshalled. This is a very practical

[1] Royal Stand; Master of the Buckhounds' Stand; Jockey Club Stand; Iron Stand; Grand Stand.

PROPOSED NEW MILE COURSE, ASCOT, BERKS.

advantage, in view of the fact that the rich stakes at Ascot attract large fields of horses.

'It is, however, obvious that, if this new course is carried out, the turn from the present Old Mile course on to the new course would be an impossible one, and would require to be altered as shown by the line *marked* B *on the plan*.

'The effect of this alteration would be to shorten the course run over in certain races [1] by about fourteen yards, but this will be easily rectified by throwing back the starting posts that distance.'

Upon the whole the plan found favour, but it was of a philosophic, not a practical kind. The stewards of the Jockey Club took up a safe position. 'You offer us, at least so you tell us, a course where everybody will be able to see instead of a course where hardly anybody sees. That will be charming. Pray do so, and we shall all be happy and grateful; but it is for you to act in the matter. It is not our business, and we do not propose to make it our business.'

Then, as always happens when all changes from the known to the unknown are concerned, the *quieta non movere* instinct in human nature came to the alert. It was further pointed out, and with some force, by my predecessor in office, that even at Newmarket, in the very heart of the racing world, fifty per cent. of the people, including most of the finest judges, will not trouble themselves to leave the July stand and go down to the first winning post to see a race, and H.R.H. Prince Christian, a true lover and judge of racing, objected that any plan by which the horses would be seen coming all the way would rob him and other racing idealists of that precious psychological moment when the first cap comes into sight out of the dip of the straight mile.

[1] Gold Vase; Ascot Stakes; Visitors' Plate; Coronation Stakes; Ascot Derby; 36th Ascot Biennial Stakes; Gold Cup; St. James's Palace Stakes; 31st New Biennial Stakes; Ascot High Weight Plate; Hardwicke Stakes.

On the other hand, individuals of unimpeachable authority whom I consulted gave the plan their careful attention, and wished the alteration might be carried into effect. However, the writing was already on the wall. It would have been manifestly unfair to pledge my successor to a large undertaking and heavy expenditure, in his view of questionable advantage and necessity, and the Friday of Ascot week, 1895, terminated my connection with Ascot affairs and power, for good or evil. If the change is ever carried out, it is clearly one of those departures which must be taken by mutual and cordial consent of both the ins and the outs.

Here let me add that I had no personal prepossessions in the matter. Assuming the terms of the problem to have been correctly stated, I merely advanced my proposals as a practical and feasible solution. A fair composition could have been made—at that time—with the owner of Sunningdale Park for the acquisition of the additional land required for a new Straight Mile course, and for carrying out the plan in all its details. There were no difficulties in the way as to gradients, nor as to the laying of the course, which, assuming the work to have been begun, say, in October 1895, should, so I was informed by expert opinion, have been in order for the Ascot races this year, or at all events for next year. In the meanwhile, whilst the new course was consolidating and getting a good face of grass, all could have gone on just as at present. Many people took a kind interest in the matter from first to last, and I was especially pleased by the hearty encouragement of Captain Machell, who came down to Ascot with me one day, and went over the ground with the plans most carefully. Even those who did not agree with me listened courteously, if with a wandering eye, to all I had to say on a subject which my readers will agree is not particularly entertaining. 'The Captain,' I remember, said a very characteristic thing the day he came down. I said that I was disinclined to ask So-and-So's advice. 'Oh!' he said, 'I should; I always ask for advice. One need never take it.'

From time to time great fault is found with the state of the course at the time of the meeting, and I should like to say a word or two here about the difficulties which have to be met.

The soil is sand and gravel; rain silts away through it like a filter. Thus racing Ascot is in constant jeopardy from the dryness and the drying qualities which are the boast of residential Ascot. Only the deep-rooted grasses can withstand the zest of a spring sun, its escort of parching easterly winds, the dewless nights, the spiteful frosts, and the unhandsome pranks, from a farmer's point of view, our climate often plays upon us in April and May. Ascot Heath has no natural advantages but beauty. The course is regenerated common land, and the grass, and especially the New Mile, is peevish haggard stuff and hardly honest. No better illustration can be given of its hostility to the best intentions than the fact that sheep have been tried both on the course and on the lawns, but owing to thinness of the turf soil and the dry and thirsty subsoil, they did so little good and stained the land so unbecomingly that much had to be re-turfed. The fact is that unless you have a wet spring you cannot expect a really good course, and April and May are critical and anxious months for Major Clement, who for many years past has spared himself no trouble to make each Ascot meeting better and more convenient than its immediate predecessor. He watches the weather with the strained attention of the prophet Elijah. But Major Clement is only an experienced and faithful steward of the many things committed to his charge; he is not, as some of the newspapers seem to think, either a magician or a Jehovah, and he has ungrateful conditions to deal with, which I am glad to have had the opportunity of stating.

And now I come to a terrible responsibility of the Master of the Buckhounds. I use the word responsibility advisedly, for he is annually held accountable not merely for the enjoyment and safe conduct of fashionable society, but also for the satisfaction of its progressive desires.[1] Far be it from me to lift the veil which shrouds the excellent mysteries of the Royal Enclosure. Suffice it to say that the most well-intentioned and upright Master of the Buckhounds must be guilty of injustice. Clearly, unless he gave his life to it, he cannot be expected to know everybody; but setting this aside, allowance must be made for the pressure of a Frankenstein-like society, for the wear and tear of his nerves, for the eccentricities of his digestion. Added to these comes the strain of a seemingly four-fold multiplication of posts, a locust horde of telegrams, devoted powdered footmen who refuse to quit your premises, however uncomfortable, without an answer, and all the other irritants of his everyday life from say April 1 till about midday on the Wednesday in Ascot week, when the well-directed dropping fire of applications begins to slacken. Nor is this the place to record the elegant anguish of Worth- and Paquin-dressed disconsolates, the dignified remonstrances of their more influential

---

[1] The following figures, which Major Clement has kindly sent me, may amuse the curious and serve to indicate the present scale of the demands of an Ascot week.

On the Gold Cup day there were sent from the Ascot offices in 1896, 12,753 telegrams and 46,000 words of Press matter; and in 1897, 10,500 telegrams and 45,000 words; the diminution in the latter case was due to the fact that betting on the lawn of the Grand Stand was this year prohibited. For the Grand Stand luncheons alone, exclusive of the more solid viands, there were cooked —1,800 fowls, 1,200 pigeons, 1,700 lbs. of salmon, 1,500 lobsters and 500 quails. Of such figures as these Pantagruel himself would not have been ashamed.

relations, and the despair of their admirers. These things are pitiful, but inevitable, and the Master of the Buckhounds is often the unconscious executioner of all kinds of agreeable plans and stimulating hopes. Of course he is abused: if he happens to be a Liberal any rod is good enough for his back; if he happens to be a Tory, he at once becomes a noble of the type which justified the French Revolution. But for the most part he is forgiven freely. Besides, the 'all against all' character of· the scramble comes to his rescue. Lucretia's many friends have got a little wearied with her account of her preparations and Paris tryings-on. She cannot, like Constance, 'instruct her sorrows to be proud,' and they naturally cannot help being amused at her failure to get her ticket. There is a general sense of relief that the tiresome Gracchi have been refused.

In my time one incident occurred of a probably unique kind, which may here be recorded. I received a message which demanded very instant attention. It appeared that an individual with a kodak was loose in the enclosure. He had commenced operations by several snaps at the Royal party, and when last seen was actively engaged upon a group of duchesses. Needless to say that he was described to me as a complete radical in appearance. Hoping for my own sake, as well as for that of the Newcastle programme, that he might not turn out to be an Irish member, I portrayed him to my green-plush-clad myrmidons, who, assisted by some good-natured volunteers, at once set off in pursuit. Owing to the congested state of the enclosure, progress was difficult, and the chase for some little time eluded them like a will-o'-the-wisp. He had been seen here, suspected there, noticed *flagrante delicto* somewhere else. At last, however, he was delivered into our hands, and haled into my presence. It ended rather tamely, for he turned out to be a distinguished visitor to our shores, accredited by the embassy of one of the great Powers, and a relative of an ex-crowned head. However, I administered a wordy reprimand or rather lecture on the trite thesis of 'autres pays,' &c., and made him promise to banish the partner of his guilt to the boot of a distant drag. To this he sadly but courteously consented, and the incident closed. I only hope I invited him to luncheon.

CHAPTER XIII

PREDECESSORS

They shall not be ashamed when they speak with their enemies in the gate

HAVING regard to the antiquity of our office, it must be admitted that, with a few distinguished exceptions, Masters of the Buckhounds have not left a very marked or consecutive impression upon the pages of constitutional history or the roll of constructive legislation. The office belongs to the livery of politics. Its duties and opportunities lie outside the walls of Parliament. We cannot, for instance, boast that a Cromwell, or a Pitt, or a Gladstone ever dignified the couples: at the same time, tried by the most rigorous tests of proportional representation, we stand out very fairly well. We can hardly be said to be an insignificant order when we remember that two of us have been beheaded for high State reasons—Sir Bernard Brocas, whom Mr. Burrows has told us all about in his valuable introduction, and Lord Rochford, Anne Boleyn's gifted brother. Nor can we justly be said to be undistinguished. Lord Leicester in Queen Elizabeth's, Sir William Wyndham in Queen Anne's, and Lord Granville in Queen Victoria's reign, all held high offices of State. And we can point to a long succession of booted and spurred, gentle and noble men who have done their duty more or less picturesquely in the saddles to which

Royal favour or party politics have called them. Upon the other hand, we have at times been treated with little respect. In the 'Infernal Marriage' Pluto promises Cerberus the Buckhounds in the event of a change of the Ministry—I am bound to say his antecedents qualified him to deal with the Royal enclosure. It was the post Lord Marney most coveted ; and I was told a story the other day which, as it is wounding to my self-esteem, I shall degrade to a footnote.[1]

I cannot pretend to having made any exhaustive inquiry into the subject, but it has occurred to me that with the exception perhaps of William III. the greatest men have not been the best riders. As all Masters of the Buckhounds are presumably first-rate horsemen, this may have something to do with it ; we may be the victims of our aptitudes.

A distinguished Frenchman—a lover of belles lettres and a student of Napoleonics—told me the other day that Napoleon rode 'affreusement mal,' and the slouching seat Meissonier always gives him is doubtless historically accurate. It is the seat of a round and short-legged heavy-stomached man, and the artist hits off exactly the restless poise of the paunch upon the pummel of the saddle. One 'Nim South' formed an equally poor opinion of the Duke of Wellington's horsemanship, as well as of his get-up, when he saw him out with Sir John Cope's hounds at Hartley Row Gate in 1831. As everything about the Duke of Wellington is worth remembering, and as he hunted regularly on the heather and Hampshire side of the Queen's and Mr. Garth's country, some of Mr. Nim South's appreciations may here be cited. After telling the readers of the 'Sporting Magazine' how he has to wait in a drizzling rain for some little time at the

---

[1] 'Ben' Stanley, the celebrated Whig Whip, was walking one day with Lords Bessborough and Granville, both of whom had been Master of the Buckhounds. A new Administration was in process of formation and one of them asked Mr. Stanley what Lord So-and-So was likely to have. 'Oh, the Buckhounds, of course ; the only place for a fellow like that.'

turnpike, Mr. South says : ' I saw a red coat winding along at a snail's pace, the wearer evidently disregarding the sprinkling. " He is a sportsman," thought I, " and see, he wears drab breeches—a sure sign of one ! " '[1]

As the wearer draws nearer, Mr. South finds to his surprise that he had mistaken drab fustian trousers for kerseymere breeches, the horseman's ' grave and thoughtful countenance ' making but poor amends for such a shock. The rest of his costume was disquieting in the extreme. ' His dress consisted of a plain scarlet frock-coat, a lilac silk waistcoat, kid gloves, the aforesaid fustians, and boots which we call Wellingtons ; and certainly they were Wellingtons in every sense of the word, for the wearer was neither more nor less than the illustrious Arthur himself. As he advanced my red coat caught his eye, and at the same moment my eye caught his undeniable nose. There was no mistaking him, and I took off my hat to the greatest man of the day.' Needless to say that the Duke converses with Nim South with all the urbanity which the interviewer invariably experiences at the hands of the truly great. ' We had,' Nim goes on to say, ' just the sort of day's sport to please a man like the Duke of Wellington, who, though mighty in the field of war, cuts no great figure in the hunting field. Indeed, to do him all due justice, I have seldom seen a man with less idea of riding than he has. His seat is unsightly in the extreme, and few men get more falls in the course of a year than his

[1] In spite of Beau Brummell's instruction to his tailor, ' Keep continually sending leather breeches,' it would appear that at this time cords and not leathers were the vogue ; George IV., as we have seen, ordered cords for Dom Miguel's visit. When the Mr. Tomkinson of the day electrified the Meltonians with his uncompromising riding to hounds, he was at first classed by Nimrod as ' a slow one ' on account of his wearing leathers. They soon found out their mistake, and the Cheshire squire appears to have had much the same effect upon the mind of Leicestershire as that produced by his gallant descendant some few years ago on the occasion of his first visit to Melton. Lord Wilton's and Lord George Bentinck's distinguished appearance in buckskins at Croxton Park races some two or three years later is said to have brought them into fashion.

Grace. Nevertheless he seemed to enjoy the thing amazingly, and what with leading over occasionally and his groom's assistance, he did very well.' The Duke did not mind falls. He used to relate with evident pleasure how on one occasion he counted eight pairs of shoes flash over him as he lay cast in the landing side ditch. This was in England, but the Duke hunted regularly from Paris after the Peace.[1] On one occasion he rather annoyed Charles X. by saying when the stag, after ringing about for hours in the forest of Compiègne, took them out into the open, 'Ah! this is more the thing; it reminds me of the Vale of Aylesbury.' Judging from my own experiences of *les petits environs* and the French open, the stag must have picked a very exceptional bit of country. Perhaps it was the unusual look of things which made Charles X. a little nervous and consequently a little short. The Duke was a great supporter and a most generous subscriber both to the Vine and the Bramshill hounds. At one time he gave 400*l*. a year to the former, and on hearing that Sir John's hounds had drawn the Strathfieldsaye coverts blank, he warned all the keepers that a repetition of this would mean their discharge. One day a well-wisher advised him to take up his stirrups a couple of holes. Bad advice, which I hope he did not take, although he appears to have accepted it in good part. But a more striking example of his patience in the hunting field is given in the 'History of the Vyne in Hampshire.' Mr. Chute's hounds were never advertised, and one day in March, 1820, the Duke sent his horses to Clarken Green, as he had been told by the huntsman that the hounds were to meet there that day. They never turned up, and the Duke spent much time in trying to find them;

[1] A great many Englishmen were in Paris at this time. Lord Pembroke astonished Parisian society by his fine harness horses and turn-out generally. He asked his groom one day what he did about exercising horses. The man replied that he had been twenty times round Wyndham Place, as he called the Place Vendôme. He had evidently made himself thoroughly at home.

but he only writes to Mr. Chute, 'Not finding or hearing anything of you I have returned home. I regret this exceedingly, particularly as I feel you will have waited for me.' Only a strict disciplinarian would have put up so uncomplainingly with such an annoying misunderstanding. A five-pound subscriber in these days would have at once written to the papers and asked leave to publish the correspondence.

In spite of some very hunting-like and perceptive stanzas,[1] Lord Byron himself was no great horseman. Lady Blessington gives an amusing account of their first ride together and of his get-up. Accustomed to the irreproachable appointments of Count d'Orsay, who always went up to the front with the best of them in the Harrow country, she was amazed at the variety of his riding gear—' trappings, cavessons, martingales, and heaven knows what else,' overlaid the very moderate hack he rode, whose stumbles frequently discomposed his rider very much. His dress was quite as unusual as the Duke of Wellington's. A short-waisted nankeen jacket, much shrunk and very narrow in the back, embroidered with three rows of buttons; nankeen gaiters, a black very narrow stock, and a dark blue velvet cap with a rich gold braid and a tassel, and blue specs. He gave Lady Blessington the idea of being an exceedingly timid rider. Sometimes, she says, the nankeen jacket gave place to a green tartan tunic.

Although he writes to his sister from Southend in 1834

[1] He broke, 'tis true, some statutes of the laws
Of hunting : for the sagest youth is frail.
Rode o'er the hounds it may be now and then,
And once o'er several county gentlemen.

He also had a quality uncommon
To early risers after a long chace,
A quality agreeable to woman
When her soft liquid words run on apace ;
Who likes a listener, whether saint or sinner,
He did not fall asleep just after dinner.

of nearly killing an Arabian mare in a run of thirty miles, which is not to be wondered at, seeing that he adds, 'I stopped at nothing,' Lord Beaconsfield can hardly be said to have kept up his riding. Mr. Gladstone's riding was limited to the observances of the Liver Brigade in Rotten Row. Mr. Carlyle rode far and fast for pleasure and dyspepsia, but there is no reason to think that he was in any sense a horseman; like most Scotchmen he speaks and thinks of them as 'beasts,' although from time to time he handsomely acknowledges the good care which the 'very clever creatures' take of him. Sir Robert Peel was a clumsy and inelegant rider, and his death is attributed by most of his biographers to his weak seat, which prevented him recovering his horse's stumble. But enough of these inconsequences, I must get back to the title of this chapter.

As the first Master of the Privy or Household Pack, George Boleyn, Viscount Rochford, Henry VIII.'s Master of the Buckhounds (1528–1536) is the proper person to begin with. Lord Rochford had his full share of the prosperity of his family at Court. One way and another father, mother, sisters, brother, all made the most of good looks, shrewd heads, and slender scruples. Sir Thomas and Lady Boleyn could point with satisfaction to an earldom, the garter, a rebuilt country house, and fat acquisitions of property: Mary Boleyn for a time enjoyed the prestige of being the king's mistress: Anne became his lawful queen: George Boleyn was given the Buckhounds, and received many other pleasant and profitable marks of Royal favour. He is a favourite with most of his biographers. His personal gifts were of a kind which I hope will always command respect. He could ride, and shoot, and dance, and make love, and lead a masquerade better than his neighbours. But his intellectual attainments appear to have been considerable. 'Il a laissé chez ses contemporains,' says M. Bapst, 'une réputation de bon littérateur.' Although he said himself he could never write decent Latin prose, he had distinguished himself at Oxford, understood colloquial Latin and Italian, and spoke and wrote French with ease and correctness. Mr. Hepworth Dixon pays a high tribute to his elegant culture, and cites him as a notable member of a progressive Young England party, and an ardent partisan of liberal learning. 'Early in life he had begun to toy with verse, a fine accomplishment of a liberal age, and by his talents he was helping that revival of English poetry which his playmate Wyat and his cousin Surrey were to foster into vigorous life.'[1]

As we can hardly accord to Davis the rank of a poet, Lord Rochford is the only poet of our order.

> Farewell, my Lute, this is the last
> Labour that thou and I shall waste,
> For ended is what we began :
> Now is the song both sung and past,
> My Lute, be still, for I have done.

This 'farewell to his lute,' said to have been composed and sung by him the night before his execution, has the mother-of-pearl refinement which belongs especially to the poetry of that time.

These pages need have no concern with the truth or falseness of the charges brought against the brother and sister. They are matters of history ; but in no way affect the ethics of stag-hunting. On May 15, 1536, Lord Rochford was arrested on a complicated charge of treason to his king. He was tried next day by his peers. Long odds were laid upon his acquittal. He could not be shaken in cross-examination, and his defence was ably conducted ; ' he made answare,' we are told, ' so prudentlie and wisely to all articles layde against him, that marveil it was to heare.' But Henry VIII. had by this time persuaded himself that the masterful

[1] *Hist. of Two Queens*, vol. iii. p. 285.

Boleyn family compact had become a danger to the State, and that the public welfare pointed out his duty. Before all, the king was a man of conscience, and in the words Shakespeare puts into the mouth of the Duke of Suffolk, his conscience had again crept near another lady. The Boleyns must go. Lord Rochford was found guilty by a large majority. His friends were kept away; his enemies gathered together. Like his sister Anne, and in the fashion of the day, Rochford was versed in the controversies raised by the Reformation, and had identified himself actively with the new ideas.

The Catholic peers, led by his own kinsman, the Duke of Norfolk, who, it is said, had sworn to break him, voted solid. He was sentenced to be hanged, cut down alive, ripped up, drawn and quartered. Mindful, perhaps, of the rather dismal consideration shown by Henry IV. to Sir Bernard Brocas, who, though beheaded at Tyburn, was excused the preliminaries of being hanged and drawn, Henry VIII. commuted the more savage parts of the sentence, and he was executed by the headsman on Tower Hill on May 17, 1536.

Lord Leicester we all know a great deal about from 'Kenilworth.' But a letter of Castelnau's to Henry III. of France describes the sort of hunting which Queen Elizabeth and Lord Leicester enjoyed together.

After telling his sovereign that he had received a hospitable invitation from Lord Leicester, on behalf of the queen, to come and stay with him and have a hunt at Windsor, he goes on to relate the pleasures of the actual hunt, which appears to have consisted in driving a number of deer up and down inside a netted space in front of a well-screened butt (feuillade), in which Queen Elizabeth was stationed with her arblast. The sport then became varied by some coursing. 'Et tout le reste du jour jusques au soir, sortirent des thoilles (toils), ung, deux, trois, et à diverses fois, plusieurs grandz cerfs passant par la dicte feuillade, entreprenant deux et trois milles de course avec les lévriers les meilleurs de ce roiaulme, desquelz quelquefois ung, deux et trois portoient un grand cerf par terre¹' He concludes by a tribute to Lord Leicester's able management of everything, the satisfaction of the queen and the company, and the excellence both of the deer and of the hounds.

The 'lévriers,' I fancy, were not greyhounds as we understand the term, but of the same breed which were still preserved at Godmersham and Eastwell in Kent a few years ago. The keepers used them for deer-catching, and I was told that the strain could be traced back to Elizabethan times. A good one always pinned a deer by the ear, and this was a criterion of purity of strain. They were cream or fawn-coloured with dusky muzzles, with really greyhound speed, and half greyhound, half mastiff-like heads, long ridgy backs, loosely coupled, high on the leg and apt to be very crooked, resembling in appearance the boarhounds in Snyders' and Velasquez' pictures.

Lord Leicester gave Queen Elizabeth the first watch bracelet recorded in history; I suppose for her hunting days. Once, when she and he went to stay at Berkeley Castle, they had a day with the toils in the park in Lord Berkeley's absence, and killed twenty-seven prime stags, again having resort to screens and arblasts. When he came back and heard what they had done he was very much annoyed, and threatened to do away with his park and his deer altogether. It sounds rather an excessive straining of royal prerogative. I am sorry to say that one of Lord Leicester's first official activities after he was appointed Master of the Buckhounds in 1572 was to fall out with the Archbishop of Canterbury over some lands. But up to this time the See of Canterbury and the Queen's Hounds appear to have been on excellent terms. Under date September 4, 1564, Lord Leicester writes

[1] Chéruel, *Marie Stuart et Catherine de Médicis*, Appendix, p. 227.

to 'his singular good Lord' of Canterbury this considerate letter: 'The queen's majesty being abroad hunting yesterday in the forest, and having had very good hap, beside good sport, she had thought good to remember your grace with part of her prey, and so commanded me to send you a great fat stag, killed with *her own hand*; which, because the weather was wet, and the deer somewhat chafed and dangerous to be carried so far without some help, I caused him to be *parboiled for the better preservation of him*, which I doubt not will cause him to come unto you as I would he should. So, having no other matter at this present to trouble your grace withal, I will commit you to the Almighty, and with my most hearty commendation take my leave in haste.'

From the day when he rode down to Hatfield on a milk-white 'managed' horse to announce the death of Mary, the queen's partiality for her Master of the Horse—for Lord Leicester was a Pluralist and held both offices—seems to have been a 'secret de Polichinelle' at Court. When the Duchess of Suffolk engaged herself to her equerry, Adrian Stokes, the queen was surprised and indignant. 'What!' she said to Cecil, 'marry a horse-keeper?' 'Yea, madam,' he replied, 'and she says you would like to do the same with yours.' And Sir James Melvill and other contemporaries relate many public and private indiscretions; 'great liberties,' as he says, 'to be taken by a lady of thirty.'

With the people the Leicester alliance seems to have been popular enough : it was probably preferred to a foreign match. A contemporary writer,[1] after describing the Master of the Horse's good looks and fine manners, says : 'The queene had much of her father, for excepting some of her

---

[1] 'The Court of Queen Elizabeth, originally written by Sir Robert Naunton under the title of "Fragmenta Regalia." With considerable biographical additions by James Caulfield. London, 1814.

kindred and some few that had handsome wits in crooked
bodies; she alwaies tooke personages in the way of election,
for the people hath it to this day, King Henry loved a Man.'
As he advanced in years Lord Leicester lost his complexion;
became too high-coloured, and a little dull. Having made
away with his first wife, he is described in his latter days
as 'doting upon marriage with a strange fondness.'

In 1684 a Swinley deer led the Duke of York and his suite
a tremendous dance through Beaconsfield and Amersham
right away into Oxfordshire. Very few besides the Duke and
Colonel James Graham got to the end. Somewhere about
this time Colonel Graham, or Grahm, was appointed Master
of the Buckhounds and Lieutenant of Windsor Forest by
Charles II. There is a tablet in Charlton Church, near
Malmesbury, to his memory. He is set forth as 'a faithful
servant of King Charles and King James II., who lived and
died an unworthy but true member of the Church of England,
faithful to both his masters, and a sincere lover of monarchy.'
From many points of view Colonel Graham's career attracts
me more than any other Master of past days. The everyday facts of his life, collected by Colonel Josceline Bagot in
his charming little history of Levens, were worthy of Mr.
Stevenson's imagination. He was born in 1649, and married
Miss Dorothy Howard, a niece of the Lord Berkshire of the
day, after a romance in a slow stage coach. This young lady
was maid of honour to Catherine of Braganza. The year
1685 finds Colonel and Mrs. Graham living at Bagshot.
Evelyn stays with them on his way back from Portsmouth,
and describes their housekeeping and the park full of red-
deer, and how one of the children had the small-pox and
Mrs. Graham kept it with the others, because she thought
it better they should all have it at once.

But Colonel Graham's lasting reputation will rest rather
upon his gardens than his stag-hunting. Somewhere about

this time he purchased Levens, in Westmoreland, of Mr.
Bellingham, described as ' an ingenious but unfortunate young
gentleman,' who had run through all his money at a very
early age. Fortunately, the gardens which this Master of
the Buckhounds laid out have been preserved to us by the
piety of successive owners of Levens. 'They remain,' says
Lord Stanhope, 'a stately remnant of the old promenoirs
such as the Frenchmen taught our fathers rather, I would
say, to build than plant.' But although Colonel Graham
lived much in the North, pruning the perspective of his
terraces, mystifying his maze, putting annual touches to his
own glossy green silhouette, he also lived up to the very edge
of the ticklish times in which he played a dexterous part.
As well as being Master of the Buckhounds to James II. he
was also Privy Purse. He accompanied the king in his
flight to Rochester, and as one of his most trusted and
confidential agents he stayed on in England, watching and
reporting events. James II. wrote a long letter to the
versatile Chiffinch from Rochester. The letter is not remarkable for orthography, but it is characteristic of the careful-
ness for trifles which seems to beset the average individual in
a great crisis. The King had not quite lost his crown when
he wrote to Chiffinch; he had thrown the great seal into the
Thames, with the object of gaining time and delaying the
elections. The army was encamped at Salisbury, and so far
had not declared itself; 'Lillibullero' had not yet caught on.
There was still a chance. But his letter is all about trifles.
'Those things which you were a-putting up when I came
away'; his 'antickes' watch; his devotional books; his
shares in the East India and Guinea Company, and his
cash balances. All these were to be handed over to Colonel
Graham, and he ends up his letter by telling Chiffinch
to bid Graham not to forget to send him the usual returns
of 'the stablishment of my horse' and all the stable

news. A sustained cypher correspondence now set in between England and St. Germains. In this James II. is Mr. Banks, which was the name of the steward at Levens, Graham himself being sometimes Sir H. Paulsworth, sometimes Mr. Chapman. In spite, however, of the intrigues with which he was surrounded, the *ci-devant* Master of the Buckhounds was a cautious man, and appears to have kept his eye upon every shift of circumstances after the deposition of James. Without actually running with the fox and hunting with the hounds he so contrived his correspondence as to give as little handle to his enemies as information to his friends. Even in cypher his letters read all ways but a particular way. They were so involved and obscure that in a letter to Graham the Duke of Hamilton complains that they put him in mind of the Peace of Ryswick and the peace of God, in that they passed all understanding. It is true that in 1691 Luttrell speaks of Colonel Graham having 'got over' into France, evidently in a hurry, and that the next year two proclamations were out against him. And in 1696 he was thrown into the Fleet for complicity in the Fenwick plot. But still he succeeded marvellously well, in spite of several narrow escapes, in evading any serious trouble. I dare say through the good offices of Queen Mary, and very likely with the full assent of James, he made his peace with William III., and when things settled down after the Revolution of 1688 Graham returned to Bagshot and to office as Ranger. Thus, when 108 red-deer were sent from Germany to William III., the king orders his Master of the Buckhounds (Baron de Hompesch) to confer with Graham about the future of the deer; and we find him sending fruit and rabbits to Princess Anne from Bagshot, and promising to send her some char when he gets back to Levens. Colonel Graham was painted by Sir Peter Lely. Sir Peter Lely and the flowing wig of the day betwixt them were terrible levellers of individuality; but judging from the photograph this picture has a little more personal character about it than most of Lely's portraits. The picture is now at Levens. He was a tall, thin, dark man, and his conversation is commended by Horace Walpole for its dry humour. When living at Levens he was particularly fond of hunting an outlying buck and bringing him back into the park; beyond this, however, I know nothing of his hunting proclivities. His daughter Catherine married Lord Suffolk and Berkshire, and he died at beautiful Charlton, in the heart of wild Braydon, in 1730, in his eighty-first year. His last wishes are expressed in the strong Commonwealth English—pure as crystal. 'I hope when I die,' he had written to his daughter in 1729, ' your lord will allow me to be buried among my little ones at Charlton. If I die there send to Bath for a leaden coffin. I will have no hearse, but be carried by my own and your servants. All what is in my will observe and do it, which is not much. Thank you for all your goodness to me. God bless you and your lord and all the children.—Your affectionate father, J. GRAHME.' And he adds a postscript to this effect: ' Do what you can of kindness to my servants who have been careful of me.' Here, at all events, are none of the involutions of the non-committal letters. But now it was all plain enough sailing. He was very near the end of his voyage. There were no more earthly accounts to square.

In the last century the Master of the Buckhounds had a charming house[1] in Swinley Forest against the deer paddocks and he enjoyed, in right of his office, the use of about two hundred and thirty acres of arable, pasture, and woodland,

---

[1] A very complete and detailed history of Swinley Lodge, traced from the time when it is first specifically mentioned in Norden's *Survey of Windsor Forest* (1607) down to its final dismantling and sale by auction in 1831, is given by Mr. Hore in his History of the Buckhounds, chap. xviii.

which went with the Lodge. A faded outline of the pleasure grounds, the tangled vestiges of the shrubbery may still be traced. The Master cannot live in his stand on Ascot Heath, and I think he ought to have a habitation where he can take shelter after his inevitable sins of omission and commission as regards the Royal enclosure, that most thorny field of his later-day patronage. Swinley Lodge may have been a little shut-in and wanting in view in

SWINLEY LODGE, THE OLD RESIDENCE OF THE MASTER OF THE BUCKHOUNDS

winter-time, but the stately limes, the spangled thorns, the close companionship of the forest and forest sights and sounds must have made it a perfect summer house. A great deal of eating and drinking used to go on at Swinley, and every fourth of June the Master used to give a dinner to all the farmers and foresters. Twice or thrice the Royalty drove over from Windsor and watched the dancing on the green in front of the house. Hunting was expected to

be convivial. Mr. Jenison was honoured as a five-bottle man; Lord Cornwallis was a great host; but Lord Bateman, who held the appointment for twenty-five years, disgusted everybody by a 'penurious sterility' and 'personal pomposity.' Lord Jersey put things right again,[1] and the public got a Master to their mind at the fall of the Coalition, when Lord Sandwich, who used to take a dice-box out hunting with him and gamble with the Duke of Cumberland in the intervals of the chase, was appointed. We are told ' the exhilarating steams ' of roast sirloin and the ' vibrating echo of the cork ' once more inspired the stag-hunter's prowess, and awakened the long seclusion of Swinley.

And now to come to some of the Masters of more modern days, and a few odds and ends I have been able to pick up about them. Lord Maryborough, afterwards Lord Mornington, was William IV.'s Master of the Buckhounds, and had a very fine seat on a horse. He and the horse he rode were a great feature in the Royal procession, and I have seen an engraving of him leading it on a dappled grey horse which he bought from Mr. Shard, whose classical stag-hunting establishment I have already noticed, for 500 guineas. This is the way to do the thing.

Mr. Charles Greville does not give a good account of the morals of the Royal procession in William IV.'s time. ' His household is now so ill-managed,' he writes at the end of the Ascot week of 1833, ' that his grooms were drunk every day, and the only man of them who was sober was killed going home from the races!' However, he wrote this in one of his ' video meliora proboque ' moods, when he had been eating and drinking too much, sitting up too late, and not

---

[1] No sportsman now was to the mansion led,
No corks were drawn, no social tables spread,
'Twas blank and dull till Jersey's cheerful light
Dispersed the gloom of long incumbent night.

winning his money. Lord Lichfield, who was appointed Master of the Buckhounds in 1830, lived at Fernhill, and, as D'Orsay was a famous likeness-catcher, he must have been a very good-looking man. His tenure of office was marked by all the agreeable qualities accorded him by Mr. Greville. Upon the whole he comes out with flying colours from the trying ordeal of a special and detailed mention in those fascinating memoirs. 'He is a fine fellow with an excellent disposition, liberal, hospitable, frank and gay, quick and intelligent. Without cultivation, extravagant and imprudent, yet with considerable aptitude for business. Between spending and speculating, buying property in one place, selling in another, and declining to sell in a third, he has half-ruined a noble estate.' The writer of the article in 'Baily,' already referred to, says that Davis thought less about the horses than the hounds. Yet some letters of Davis to Lord Lichfield I have seen went into great detail about the horses which he himself and the men had ridden, and the way they had carried them. Lord Lichfield was a great favourite at the kennels, and he rode to hounds very well himself. On that account Davis probably made a point when writing to him of telling him a good deal about the horses.

We now come to some of the Masters of the present reign. Lord Chesterfield was Master at the time of the Queen's coronation. It was a sort of François 1er period of stag-hunting. He dressed himself and mounted his men and his friends sumptuously. He bought many of his horses of Shirley of Twickenham, the father of the Shirley whose riding Lord Cork commends in a good gallop in the Harrow country, and who at that time kept the Catherine Wheel at Egham. Quite a stud of Lord Chesterfield's horses were kept at the same place, and sent on from there to the meets for his many friends to ride. Dr. Croft writes me: 'I seem to remember a little about him and his appearance, though I

was quite a small boy at that time. I picture him as about the average height, rather thick in body, well got up, and so forth. I remember him coming to the meet at the Horse Shoes, Warfield, with Count d'Orsay and two others, four horses with postillions.' Captivated no doubt by Charles Davis's horsemanship, Lord Chesterfield became over-fond of standing up in his stirrups. But he overdid it, for it was said that if you were behind him you could see the ears of his horse between his legs. However, in one of the 'Songs of the Belvoir Hunt,' this Master plays a worthy part, and the bard compliments him upon his seat.

> See Chesterfield advance with steady hand,
> Swish at a rasper and in safety land;
> Who sits his horse so well? or at a race
> Drives four-in-hand with greater skill or grace?
> And when hounds really run, like him can show
> How fifteen stone should o'er the county go.

Lord Kinnaird comes into the great Quarterly Run and goes well all through it. It is he who ventures the observation that Dick Christian would be drowned in the Whissendine. 'But the pace was too good to inquire,' and on they all go. He was a noted Meltonian. Lord Kinnaird tried the experiment of giving the deer very little law and never stopping hounds, as against Davis's plan of sending a whip on for the first mile or so, to stop hounds at a moment's need. This did not answer; the runs were often over in a few minutes, and the deer being overpressed were often badly hurt. One very frosty season he hunted in the forest all through the frost and snow, and had some capital sport. He lived at Ascot, and was a great man in the kennel as well as a famous rider.

Lord Rosslyn hunted the Queen's Hounds from the stud house in Bushey Park; and he must often have looked at some of the pictures which have been reproduced in these pages, many of which were moved some few years ago from the Stud house to Cumberland Lodge. He was a fine horseman, and as great a judge of a horse, or indeed of any animal, as his greatly missed and lamented successor. In those days Harry King, who had just come from the Atherstone, was only second whip, Freeman, who came I think from Goodwood, being first whipper-in. Lord Rosslyn mounted the men admirably as far as appearance went, but the whips complained that they often had to do their duty on unmade horses, and that directly they had got them handy and accomplished they were sold. ' He [Lord Rosslyn] was,' says Dr. Croft, ' a bit of a dealer,' and his horse-book, which I have had before me, is full of valuations and sales of the hunt horses. I remember a capital picture of him at Dysart, in well-blacked butcher boots, and a blue bird's-eye old-fashioned neckcloth.'

' The best man of the Hunt ' at this time, 1841 and 1842, Colonel Anstruther Thomson writes me, ' was Dicky Vyse, a Captain in the Blues, and Fred Ponsonby, who used to ride like a demon. His boots and his breeches never met, and there was always a patch of bare leg between them.' Lord Clanricarde was another celebrated bruiser with the Queen's Hounds, but a very fine horseman, with long thin legs and a nice weight. Mr. Saxty of Windsor, the accomplished artist, told me that he once heard Bryant, the stud groom, tell Lord Clanricarde that the horse he was going to ride, belonging to Lord Bessborough, then Master of the Buckhounds, was not reliable at timber. The first thing Lord Clanricarde did—Mr. Saxty saw him do it—was to ride him at a white five-barred gate. They got over somehow.

The first time I ever saw Lord Granville out hunting was with the Pytchley. I remember the incident most distinctly, and it fully bears out the reputation he left behind him in the Queen's Country for resolute riding. It was a starving cold day. Lord Granville was looking ill and suffering from

gout, and he told me he had come out against his doctor's orders. He had on thick white duffel breeches, and the boots known, I think, as Napoleons, like those in which Mr. Herring's first-flight gentry lead the way. He and I had managed, with several others, to get thrown out, and we found ourselves with no visible means of getting to hounds, which were dragging along on a cold line two or three fields away. There was neither gate nor gap to help us, and a really high stake-and-bound fence of the type which John Leech drew so well, between us. A March day was just treating us to an interval of hail. I was riding a most ungenerous horse who made no allowance for one's mistakes, and took a serious view of jumping without hounds. 'I am afraid,' said Lord Granville with a pale smile, 'we shall have to go; will you try or shall I?' I felt that for once I should not be justified in following my leader. So I crammed Marsala at it, with a show of decision which did not take him in for a moment. Round he came, and our small party exchanged glances of discouragement. Lord Granville was riding an uncoupled rather Cleveland-bay-looking horse. He turned him suavely round at it, and over he went, and piloted his convoy to the haven where we would be; Marsala, who luckily did not like being left alone, at last climbing over somehow.

Eminent horse-dealers, like great painters, have their styles and manners, and Lord Granville knew and appreciated them all. I recollect his filling in with a few telling touches the portrait of the moralist who robs you of your wits by the integrity of his eye, and the almost sacred conviction of his utterances; the oracle who inspires you by the little he says and the much this little leads you to infer; the sophist who can turn an animal's defects to advantage. How he delighted too in those crude or delicate compliments —served to taste—to one's riding and judgment, which lead to so many deals.

Lord Granville's stories gained enormously, of course, by the telling restraint of his 'raconteur' style, which had a certain dryness and bouquet not to be surpassed, so it is perhaps as well that I only remember one of them. Lord Granville had bought a very expensive horse from Anderson. Some little time after he met Anderson and said to him, ' Well, you know the price was quite extravagant, but I am bound to say the horse is worth it.' Anderson made a little bow and said, ' I can assure you, my lord, your approval is our only profit in the transaction.'

In a speech which Lord Granville made many years ago at a farmers' dinner at Windsor, he went back to the pleasant days when he hunted the Queen's Hounds, and he told them that Mr. Disraeli had taunted Lord John Russell with having taken a young riding peer all boot and spur and pitched him into the prosaic office of the Board of Trade. His political services to his generation and to his party are in no danger of being forgotten. Speaking from recollection, I think one of the most persuasive speeches made on our side at the fever point of the first Home Rule crusade and cleavage was made by Lord Granville at Manchester. There he was amongst old friends and brave associations. In 1851, Lord Granville was sworn in as Secretary of State for Foreign Affairs, a rapid promotion. Madame de Lieven wrote ' in transports of joy ' of the appointment. ' Granville,' she writes, ' is very popular at Manchester and with the Free Traders, which is a great thing.' In 1855 he became the Leader of the Liberal Party in the House of Lords, a position which in the face of hopeless odds he felicitously held for thirty-six years without interruption. I can speak from grateful experience of the kindness and encouragement he knew how to bestow upon those who, like myself, succeeded very young, and knew very few people. Addison's Tory fox-hunter was of opinion that being able to talk French was prejudicial to a hunting seat. But he had never met a Lord Granville. At the Exhibition banquet at the Hôtel de Ville in 1851, England, owing to the ill-health of the Prince Consort, was represented by Lord Granville. On this occasion he charmed his hosts by responding for the Commissioners in a French speech free and flowing and full of telling points. 'Had he been Demosthenes himself,' Sir Theodore Martin tells us, 'speaking with the purest French accent, he could not have commanded more genuine applause.'

The late Lord Hardwicke's popular Mastership was marked by its debonnair magnificence. It was to some extent a sort of renaissance of the Chesterfieldian splendours. Nothing stopped him if it were a question of getting there to help a deer. Dr. Croft once saw him jump some high iron hurdles in an emergency of this kind. His recent death will be regretted by all who knew him in the Queen's Country.

Lord Suffield has the art of galloping like steam between his fences and yet jumping the place almost from a stand. He thus negotiates the trappiest obstacles with safety and despatch, without upsetting high-couraged and even fractious animals, and—for this is the real point—without giving spectators the faintest impression of sticky 'come-up' sort of riding. This means fine hands. The first time Lord Suffield went out with the Duhallow, a country which in the opinion of the natives is only practicable to those brought up within a few miles of Cork, they never could catch him for twenty minutes, a surprised top-sawyer of the Hunt being overheard thus to exhort his friend : ' For God's sake, Mike, ride at the man in the beard ! ' Unsurpassed as a judge of a horse or a hound, and one of the most undeniable cross-country riders of his day, Lord Coventry brings knowledge and experience to bear upon every practical detail of his office. The ancient honour and everyday welfare of the Royal Hunt are in safe keeping.

CHAPTER XIV

VÉNERIE AND THE VALOIS

Pour le plaisir des rois je suis donné,
De jour en jour les veneurs me pourchassent ;
Par les forests je suis abandonné
A tous les chiens qui sans cesse me chassent.
(Bouchet's *Complainte du Cerf*, 16th century.)

THE sixteenth century in France is the Velasquez period of stag-hunting. It formed the grand style. Woodcraft huggermuggered along with poverty and privilege in the provinces, but Vénerie, at once an art and a science, came to Court. Like some daughter of the gods visiting the sons of men, she disputed precedence with everybody and everything. Even the king's mistresses had to reckon with her. Diane de Poitiers, conscious of the attractions of an enchanting rival, spent large sums of money in building hunting stables and mews, and laid out her demesne at Anet to suit hunting. Meeting gallantry and intrigue on equal terms, hunting became the instrument of political ambition. It conducted and controlled the great affairs of state.[1] It challenged diplomacy and plenipotentiaries. The main current of politics, or what we should call politics in these days, streamed along the alleys of Fontainebleau and Compiègne and flooded the level plains of the Loiret and Seine-et-Marne.

François I., according to that eminent and polite Hellenist

[1] *Documents Inédits : Négociations avec la Toscane*, t. iii. p. 421.

Budé, did a great deal for hunting. In his Treatise on Vénerie,[1] Budé tells him in the dedication, 'Sire, vous avez tellement dressé et poli l'exercice de la vénerie, qu'elle semble estre parvenue à sa perfection.' At all events, he put all the gilding on just as he did to the doors and ceilings of Fontainebleau. Tornabuoni, the Tuscan ambassador, evidently 'un homme grave,' writes to the Grand Duke Cosmo I. de' Medicis: 'This Court is not as other Courts are; here they only think of hunting, pretty women, entertainments, and change of scene. The Court only stays in a place as long as the herons last. They hunt the stag twice, then one day's deer catching ('aux toiles'), and then on again somewhere else.'[2] Everyday life was one long hunting progress. This is how he describes the invasion of the country by the scarlet-clad locusts:

'Quelquefois le roi, outre ses cent pages, ses deux cents écuyers, piqueurs ou chevaucheurs, mène avec lui quatre ou cinq cents gentilshommes, quelquefois il est accompagné de la reine ou des reines, suivies de leurs nombreuses dames et filles d'honneur. Alors tous les appartements d'en haut, toutes les salles d'en bas, tous les étages, tout le château, toute la cour, toute à chevals, toute en habits rouges, semble au milieu de la campagne trotter, galoper à la suite du roi, aussi en habit rouge, courant le cerf ou le sanglier.'

This 'to-morrow to fresh woods and pastures new' way of going on quite upset all the Venetians.

> How swift we go, how softly, ah!
> Were life but as the gondola!

It certainly was not so at the Court of France to the homesick envoys and secretaries.

'Our embassy,' cries this indignant and saddle-sore am-

---

[1] *Traité de Vénerie de Budé*, translated from the Latin, Paris, 1864.
[2] *Documents Inédits: Négociations diplomatiques avec la Toscane*, t. iii. p. 17.

bassador, who was presumably little accustomed to horse-exercise, 'has lasted forty-five months; during that time we have never been a fortnight in the same place.' Cavalle, another Venetian diplomatist, informed his Government that François I.'s hunting expenses amounted to 150,000 écus a year. But even this unfriendly critic admitted he got value for his money. ' If,' he adds, ' you could see what the Court of France means, and what is done for the money, you wouldn't think it dear.'

Francis II.'s reign was in many ways anxious and uncomfortable. But the Tuscan ambassador Tornabuoni writes thus to the Grand Duke Cosmo I. in the thick of a storm centre:[1] ' In the midst of the most serious anxieties hunting goes on just the same. No one knows where it will all end, but stag-hunting is the great business of the Court; it is the only way apparently of getting things into motion ' ; and again he writes, ' It would appear that MM. de Guise force this poor devil of a prince into these amusements. They wish to see him entirely absorbed in them, as this will mean that they can keep the direction of affairs in their own hands.'[2]

Early in March 1560 the air was full of disquieting rumours. Privy conspiracy whispered in the corridors of Amboise. Any and every night one half of society at Court expected to wake up with its throat cut next morning by the other half. Yet nothing was allowed to stand in the way of hunting. In the middle of it all, when men's hearts were failing them for fear, both conspirators and conspired against set out for a week's hunting at Chenonceaux with a levity worthy of the chorus in ' Madame Angot.' Chantonnay, a keen observer, writes to his friend Cardinal de Granvelle :
' In three days these people seem to have got rid of all their

---

[1] *Documents Inédits : Négociations avec la Toscane*, t. iii. p. 421.
[2] *Documents Inédits : Négociations avec la France*, t. iii. p. 421.

fears. After having made a great fuss about holding the castle at all hazards with men at arms, and as many of the gentlemen of their party as they could get together, here is the King off hunting and hawking again, and with him as many of the Court as have got large horses to ride. As for his own suite, he has only two or three pages mounted on Spanish horses.'[1]

Moralists may admonish us of the vanity of human pleasures, but the composing and helpful influences of sheer amusement cannot be overrated. Years before Amboise, as Sir Walter Scott tells us, the strained relations between Charles the Bold and Louis XI. were eased, and the whole 'trame des affaires' changed, by the chevy after the Rouge Sanglier. As the false herald flew for his life in front of the Snyders-like 'Talbot' and 'Beaumont,' and doubled here and twisted there in a manner greatly approved by the spectators, both kings laughed till the cordial tears ran down their faces, and forgot all about their differences. I dare say that this is not founded on fact, but Sir Walter Scott always knows what would have happened, and it is quite as satisfactory to me as if it had happened.

Evidently from Chantonnay's letter, the Court was short of horses. Then, as now, hunting was dependent on the grim qualification, with which all who hunt are conversant, of having something to ride. In the preceding reign hardly any seasoned and mettled horses were to be had in France. In February 1557, a capital hunting month, and, I suppose, in open weather, the Connétable de Montmorency writes to M. d'Humières:[2] 'I've spoken to the King [Henri II.]

[1] *Archives de Vienne, Lettres de Chantonnay.*

[2] 'J'ay parlé au Roy [Henri II] pour vous donner ung cheval; il m'a dict qu'il vous donnera bien un poulain, mais de cheval fait il n'en a pas; mesmes des turcs que lui a amenés dernièrement Moranges il ne s'en est pas trouvé ung seul de service' (le 11 février 1557, *Biblioth. Imp., Fonds Clerambault* vol. 61).

about a horse for you. He said he would give you a foal with pleasure, but that he had not anything like a made horse to spare: even the barbs (Turcs) which Moranges brought over here last were a disappointment. There was not one worth having in the lot.'

Francis II. and Charles IX. inherited the love of hunting from both their parents. In spite of her fatness, Catherine de Medicis was very fond of hunting. Modern and progressive in many of her ideas, she had a soul above the numb Norman or Flemish 'haquenée,' the Gustave Doré squire, the brocaded leading rein, and the cushioned pad which wobbled about on their lusty backs. So she invented a side-saddle and started ladies riding to hounds. However, like most inventors, Catherine de Medicis had to put up with some early rebuffs.

On one occasion she fractured her thigh, and on another fell with such force on to her head that her skull had to be trepanned. Her daughter-in-law, Mary Queen of Scots, was also unfortunate. Feeling bound, I suppose, to adventure herself in the new saddle, she got a most disagreeable fall. Writing to Queen Elizabeth from Blois, December 27, 1559, our ambassador in Paris, Throckmorton, who was much esteemed at the French Court as a 'veneur émérite,' relates in graphic language and easy-going spelling how this lovely lady was swept off by the branch of a tree when out stag-hunting.

'The xix. of this present there happened a mervailous chance and escape to the Frenche Quene; who riding on hunting, and following the hart of force, was in her course cast of her gelding by a boughe of a tree, and with suddeines of the fall was not hable to call for helpe. And albeit there dyd followe her diverse gentlemen and ladyes of her chamber, yet three or foure of them passed over her before she was espied; and some of there horses rode so nere her as her hood was troden of. As sone as she was reised from the grounde, she spake and said that she felt not hurt ; and her self begaine to set her heare, and dresse up her head and so returned to Court ; where she kept her chamber till the King removed. She feleth no incommodite by her fall ; and yet she hath determined to chaunge that kind of exercise.' That the pace was too good to inquire would hardly, in those days, have constituted a sufficient excuse for such careless behaviour. The 'diverse' gentlemen and ladies of the household must have been too busy riding or perhaps flirting.

As against the magnificent and picturesque days of François I., Charles IX.'s reign was the literary and thoughtful period. I have already spoken of Du Fouilloux's book, and a host of grave treatises now formulated the definitions, postulates, and axioms of an exact science with all the French love of order and symmetry. Charles IX. himself was the author of a painstaking text-book. Not a single sentence, however, begins with I. Thus the want of the personal note makes it sadly dull. It has not the real spark about it. Unlike Henry IV., who wrote all about his day both to Gabrielle and to his Queen—how he got drenched to the skin, how he did not get back till one in the morning, but took his deer; how he is short of shirts, how he has the toothache, but hopes a day's hawking will put him right, and so on—Charles gives us nothing of himself except his theory.

However, Charles died before he had finished his book.

Pour aymer trop Diane et Cythérée aussi
L'une et l'autre m'ont mis en ce tombeau icy.

So ran the popular epitaph. It cannot be disputed that hunting and love-making have always been close friends. Mrs. Markham will have nothing to do with Cytherea. When pressed by the intelligent questions of Richard and George and Mary, she falls back upon the French horn explanation of his death. It is true that Ambroise Paré, Charles' physician, told Brantôme 'qu'il estoit mort par s'être trop fatigué à sonner de la trompe à la chasse du cerf, qui luy avait trop gâté son pauvre corps.' The king's 'trompe,' it appears, was larger than anybody's, and quite an encumbrance to his person; but the note could be distinguished above all the others, and the temptation to rally and direct the hunt, says a contemporary authority, was too great for him to resist.[1]

However, the hunting literature of the day was not confined to serious prose. The Pleiad deigned to shine upon the chace; its poets illuminated its triumphs, hazards, and delights. Baïf extols the feat of his royal patron, who brought a stag to bay with a single hound, 'sans levriers, sans clabots.' Ronsard immortalised the drive and stoutness of a bitch hound called Courte and a dog called Beaumont, and bewails in an elegy Charles IX.'s untimely end. Even the High Almoner, Gaucher, who should have known better and minded other things, spent much of his time, and indirectly, no doubt, much of the king's money, in composing bad verses on the different kinds of hunting.

During his captivity in England, Sir John Chandos made King John of France a present of a brace of greyhounds.[2] There is a curious letter in the British Museum from Louis XIII. to the King of Aragon, thanking him for the gift of a white falcon. 'Il m'a plut,' he writes, 'tant par la beauté et l'estrangeté qu'aussi il vient de vous.' Royal personages have always been great hands at this admirable sort of intercourse. They have always been willing to receive such presents from their subjects—sometimes they have

[1] I remember hearing Mr. Browning say, in conversation with Mr. Gladstone upon the particular point whether or not many great men had been great chess-players, that Charles XII. of Sweden was a great chess-player, but spoiled his game by insisting on always making use of his king, and refusing to recognise the limits of his possibilities; and I dare say Charles IX. often played the mischief with what might otherwise have been a good day's sport.

[2] Notes et Documents relatifs à Jean, Roi de France, et sa captivité en Angleterre, par S.A.R. le Duc d'Aumale. *Philobib. Soc.*

given in return. Thus George III. recognised Arthur Young's services to agriculture by the gift of a Spanish merino ram.

Indeed, assuming a happy selection of examples, an interesting chapter might be written on the antiquity and modernness of this kind of present. From Solomon's Temple to the stud farm at Sandringham, gifts of this kind and exchanges of blood may easily be traced back authentically to the very earliest times, and can be brought as easily up to date. It is a note of the inclinations and pursuits of a large section of human beings in all times. Like playing the trumpet, the habit has neither gained nor lost by the progress of civilisation and the frequent reconstruction of human ideas and societies.

The French hound of high degree to this day claims descent from the gift of a subject to his sovereign. I am not sure of the date, but in the latter half of the fifteenth century a poor country gentleman of Poitou gave a hound called 'Souillard' to Louis XI. There was nothing remarkable in the colour. The white St. Huberts were already an ascertained breed, and although the Duke of Burgundy of Quentin Durward's time hunted the 'Rouge Sanglier' with the mastiff-like hounds I alluded to in the last chapter, his successor in 1608 kept a strong pack of twenty to twenty-five couple of notable staghounds. 'Chiens merlants issus de la variété blanche des chiens de St. Hubert.'[1] But this particular hound came to Plessis les Tours with the reputation of being something quite out of the common. As Louis XI. liked greyhounds better than line hunters, very little further notice was taken of Souillard. However, he

[1] A royal pack of this strain was held in great esteem in Louis XIV.'s time. Unlike most French hounds, they went a great pace, and were said to bay their stag in twenty minutes. In 1709 orders were given by the king to M. de la Rochefoucauld, the Grand Veneur, to slow down the 'grands chiens blancs,' as they went too fast for him as he got older. (Baron Dunoyer de Noirmont, *Hist. de la Chasse en France.*)

had been noticed and appreciated ; so one day the Seneschal de Gaston asked the king to let him have the dog. The king, who was not a cheerful giver, asked why and for whom he wanted him. The seneschal replied that it was for 'la plus sage dame' in the kingdom. Louis, who had a poor opinion of women, was curious to know who the lady might be. On hearing that it was his own daughter, Anne of Bourbon, he only said, 'Dites moins folle que les autres, car de sage femme il n'y en a point au monde,' and, recompensed by the epigram, made no further objection to Souillard being drafted to her kennel.

Anne of Bourbon knew what she was about, and a bitch called Baudé was mated with Souillard. Baudé's litter by Souillard vindicated her selection. In France a good tufter to this day is always supposed to go back to Souillard. He is Corbet's Trojan and the Beaufort Justice rolled into one. Souillard should always be pointedly referred to somehow at the meet, or, better still, at the brisée, by the intelligent sporting tourist.

In the footnote I have given, with the late Duc d'Aumale's permission, a list of French books on Vénerie, which his Royal Highness very kindly sent me, in his own handwriting, from Chantilly in December 1895.[1] The

---

[1] Le plus ancien des traités de vénerie est celui de Gaston-Phébus, comte de Foix, mort en 1390, mon ancêtre et celui de tous les veneurs. L'édition imprimée par Vérard à la fin du xve siècle n'en donne qu'une faible idée. Il faut se reporter aux manuscrits et surtout aux enluminures qui les décorent. J'en ai un fort beau. Il y en a plusieurs à la Bibliothèque Nationale.—Intéressant.

Presque contemporain, mais moins important, le 'Livre du Roy Nodus et de la Reyne Racio,' imprimé à Chambéry en 1486, avec de curieux bois, et plusieurs fois réimprimé depuis. J'en ai un joli manuscrit et la très rare première édition.—Plus curieux qu'instructif.

Signalons encore le 'Livre des Déduitz,' par Gace de la Buigne, écrit en Angleterre pendant la captivité du roi Jean pour enseigner la vénerie et la fauconnerie au jeune duc de Bourgogne. J'en ai un manuscrit original et j'en ai parlé dans un 'Essai' inséré au tome II des 'Philobiblon Society's Miscellanies,' tiré à part sous le titre ' Notes et Documents relatifs au Roi Jean,' etc.

comments are valuable, backed by his eminent authority not only as a man of letters, but as a judge of hunting. But a book which interested me very much is not on this list— namely, 'Meuttes et Vénerie' of M. Jean de Ligniville, which was published in 1635, although I do not think the book enjoys the authority of Du Fouilloux or D'Yanville works.

M. de Ligniville was born in 1580, and became Grand Veneur to the Duke of Burgundy. Lorraine was in those days a jealously preserved hunting country. Only the reigning house, the great nobles, and the chief priests hunted and sported. The clergy, as we understand the term, never hunted in France. Arthur Young contrasts them favourably with our parsons in this respect. 'Such advertisements,' he writes, speaking of the pre-Revolution clergy, 'were never seen in France as I have heard of in England—"Wanted, a living in a good sporting county where the duty is light and the neighbourhood convivial."' The great ecclesiastics, however, hunted on a very large scale. 'I am told, Monseigneur,' said Louis XV. to the Abbé Dillon, Archbishop of Narbonne, 'that you hunt. Is it not a bad example for your clergy?' He replied: 'Sire, for them it would be undoubtedly a grave fault to go hunting; for me it is only a taste I have inherited from my ancestors.'[1] The law was express, and recited its prohibitions with a clearness unknown to modern parliamentary draftsmen. 'Sauf aux prélats et aux gentilshommes défense de fréquenter aux arquebuses et rouet

La 'Vénerie de Jacques du Fouilloux, dédiée au roy Charles IX.' Poitiers, 1560. Avec de très belles figures. Beaucoup plus rapproché de nos procédés que la date ne le ferait croire. Nous sommes ici dans le vif et presque dans l'actualité.

Robert de Salnove: 'La Vénerie Royale,' 1665.—Classique, mais a vieilli.
Le Verrier de la Conterie: 'Vénerie Normande,' 1778.—Très complet.
Le comte Desgraviers: 'Essai de Vénerie,' 1804.—Bon résumé : très pratique. Instruction pour chasser à Ermenonville et à Chantilly, pp. 310 à 327.

D'Yanville, premier veneur: 'Traité de Vénerie,' Paris, 1788, in 4°. Le livre classique par excellence.

[1] *Jerningham Letters.*

par les bois, forests, tailles et garennes, plaines et campagnes.' As far back as 1605 a work had been published at Spires in which the question was discussed, 'Quod sit venatio et quotuplex; utrum venatio liceat clericis'; the conclusion being that, though fishing was allowable, hunting was too expensive and venison too heating a diet for holy men.

When Ligniville was about eighteen he was sent with letters of introduction to great people by his relative and patron, the Comte de Vaudemont, to the court of Henry IV., to finish his polite, that is, his hunting, education. He had special instructions to try to learn something of the woodcraft of M. le Comte de Vitry, who hunted the king's hounds after the roe-deer in the forest of Fontainebleau ; the roe-deer being then, as now, in France esteemed by the great Nimrods to be the most guileful of all the beasts of chase. His good looks, his gentle birth—for he came from the most ancient and exclusive chivalry of Lorraine—

> Chastelet et Lenoircourt,
> Ligniville et Haraucourt,
> Grands chevals et chevalliers
> De Noblesse sans esgalle,

his fondness for hunting, and a superlative tufter got him on. He enjoyed himself thoroughly, and writes home to his people, 'Tantost je vas à la court, un limier à la main, une autre fois habillé en veneur, et selon les occurrences vestu en courtisan préparé à aller au bal : le lendemain disposé à monter à cheval,' &c. This was all very nice, and M. de Ligniville made such good use of his advantages and ' occurrences,' that on the retirement of François de Beaufort from the post of hereditary Grand Veneur, he was appointed by Charles III. of Burgundy to the vacant office.

And now for his book. The first thing that made me like it is that he goes out of his way to tell us that a favourite hound of his, called Mouille, came ' de la contrée de York.'

Mouille was so fond of him that she would leave the most ravishing line if she heard his voice; an amiable peculiarity which he admits does more credit to her heart than her perseverance, and which would have profited her nothing with the late Mr. G. Lane-Fox at Bramham. But I like the book for its rather particular and unusual style and flavour. It is too long; most books on sporting subjects, and especially mine, are. Very often we lose sight of the forest for the trees. It is too allusive, thanks to a mixed cargo of classics, ethics, scripture, and philosophy, which the author carries and unloads at every port, but only to take in fresh stores. Saints and sages and public characters of all sorts and sizes are squeezed into his service and into all sorts of ineligible places. But what gives the book the particular and unusual quality I have just referred to, is his treatment of the subject throughout in the spirit—if I may say so without irreverence—of the hundred and fourth Psalm.

When Mr. Jorrocks got lost and benighted on the moor on the Pinch-me-near forest day, the spectacle of nature caused him a homesick alarm. He could only think of Betsy and the Torbay soles he had ordered for dinner. But in similar circumstances M. de Ligniville would have looked at things very differently.

Nature to him is the splendid nature of Addison's hymn. I do not say that at times the sylvan piety is not a little overdone. Every incident of a day's hunting is not susceptible of being read into a sublime and everlasting context. A luxury of horror at Nature's frown, an overdone thanksgiving for her smile, easily become mannerisms, and M. de Ligniville is not frugal enough of realising his feelings in type. But, on the whole, the fault is on the right side. Possibly, the manufacture into words of thoughts about Nature and her divine message is too sustained. But it is

the drift which the benefits of Nature should give to the
thoughts of people who hunt and stalk, and shoot and fish.
I only hope he was not a humbug.

M. de Ligniville is quite as fond of hunting as Captain
Doleful declared himself to be when he took his gods to witness
that it was the only thing worth living for. Not to hunt is to
be a miserable fellow, and he is always demolishing the objections of an hypothetical fainéant who is shirking the rigours
of the game. He is much afraid lest the rising generation
whom he admonishes in every page may be led away by
these specious home-loving gentlemen, and he equips his
disciples with suitable retorts for times of temptation. Tell
the fainéants straight out, he cries, that hunting is the way
to heaven, and stopping at home to somewhere else. Hunt
six days a week if you can ; blow the expense and the waste
of tissue. Remember that Xenophon (a prime favourite
and authority with M. de Ligniville) lived till he was ninety,
and that you will have plenty of leisure to rest yourselves at
the proper appointed time, where beyond these voices there
is peace.[1]

M. de Ligniville's appreciation of English hounds,
English hunting, and English ways have been cited in a
preceding chapter. He visited England. He tells us how
he went there to some extent entangled in preconceptions
and prejudices about English hunting, hounds, and hunters.
He returned to France in quite a different frame of mind.

'Cross the Channel,' he says to his chosen audience, the
youth of his nation, 'you smart young gentlemen who think
you know so much about hunting. If you can manage it,
stay in England for a full hunting season. I cannot find
you in wits as well as in counsel ; some people, of course, can

---

[1] 'Respondez hardiment aux fainéants que pendant la vie vous avez con-
tentement en vostre travail et qu'après la mort vous reposerez et dormirez du
sommeil de l'aix avec Dieu.'

neither learn nor forget, but such of you as can do both or even either will benefit much by following my advice.'

Many things have changed and happened in France since Louis XVI. entered ' rien ' in his hunting diary on the day the Bastille was taken. The charming old names like the Cabinet de Monseigneur, the Route du Vert Galant, the Bouquet du Roi are only names and memories. Hunting is, alas! no longer the occupation of kings or the pastime of a Court. But a Bourbon prince still hunts the stag at Chantilly according to the ideas of the sixteenth century. Gaston-Phébus, his distinguished ancestor, is still the suzerain of vénerie. In this country, less than one hundred years has revolutionised—speaking broadly—our horses, our hounds, our methods, and our hunting fashions—least of all, perhaps, strange to say, our hunting dress. But in France, to have recourse to a metaphor, the valse seems never to have ousted the minuet and the pavane.

CHAPTER XV

THE EMPIRE AND THE REPUBLIC

Remembrance wakes with all her busy train

IN the following pages I only propose to make good some bird-of-passage impressions of a few days' hunting in the neighbourhood of Paris. They were most enjoyable days, and I cannot speak too gratefully of the kindness and courtesy shown me everywhere and by everybody. I shall not attempt to establish comparisons between French and English stag-hunting. They are things to be avoided by the writer, as, provided he can describe what he has seen, they may safely be left to the reader. Besides, where outdoor amusements and many other things are concerned, people should rest satisfied with contrasts. The comparative method often plays the deuce with one. You can, for instance, get a great deal of fun out of the Calpe hounds at Gibraltar, or, as I am told, out of punt fishing in the Thames. But both must be accepted as things by themselves. It will not do to be always comparing the Queen of Spain's chair to the Burton Flats, or a baited swim to the Thurso or the Awe. Instinctively, I suppose, a process of comparison is always going on. You cannot at will make your mind as blank and virgin as a sensitive plate. What you may have seen and done is always thrusting its more or less apt impertinences into what you may be seeing and doing; but, like Colonel Thornton of

Thornville Royal in Yorkshire in similar circumstances, I set out for Calais with the open mind of 'a citizen of the world,' with nothing English about me except my accent.

The shortness of my stay and the comfort and ease of modern travelling did not involve the preparations which Colonel Thornton saw fit to carry into execution in 1801. The Colonel, it may be remembered by those who have read of his exploits and appreciations, took a travelling carriage, six or eight couple of hounds, two valets, a gamekeeper and a huntsman, a terrier and a pointer, Mrs. T.,[1] as he persists in calling her, her trunks, and her maid, and he was much incensed with his coach-builder at having to leave behind a boat and a boat-carriage, owing to these carefully designed necessaries not being finished. All this was in my case meagrely represented by a pair of my own stirrup irons and long leathers; but I inspected my hunting wardrobe with very particular care, inspired my valet with a due sense of the issues at stake, and, of course, had my hair cut by a special artist.

French stag-hunting was not new to me; in a sense I was about to renew an early and affectionate friendship. My riding and hunting education began in France. When I was about eight years old we went to live at Fontainebleau, and we lived there a great deal till the war of 1870 drove us away in a hurry. We only just got through Paris. The gates were closed a very few days later, and cattle were being driven into the fortified *enceinte* and were grazing in the ditches and on the slope of the *glacis* when we passed

---

[1] There were several quasi-Mrs. Ts, but I fancy this one was the lady who in 1806 rode a four-mile match on one of the Colonel's horses against a gentleman whose name I have forgotten on York racecourse. An immense concourse assembled, and great admiration was expressed at Mrs. Thornton's riding and the chasteness of her bloomer costume. She made too much play however with her horse and was easily beaten. Poor Mr. —— , who probably could not help himself, was censured by public opinion for his lack of chivalry.

through; people used to drive out to see them. Our house in the Rue Royale was actually tenanted by Prussian officers, who behaved very well and made a sensible use of everything and of the servants. Fortunately my father prudently buried a recent consignment of claret in the garden before he left.

My first pony was black—a mare called Mignonne. She was bought at Chéris. I don't know how she was bred, but her shoulders were good enough to permit of her kicking high. Our groom—who used also to *cirer* the parquet floors—was an ex-dragoon, an Alsatian. If the day was cold, clear, and sunny, he always warned me that Mignonne might be *gaie*. He was often right about this, and I was often kicked off. My father did not care much about the hunting. 'One fool follows another,' he used to say, and he seldom came out, or if he did went home early, so my education in *vénerie* was left to Isidore, who prided himself upon a complete knowledge of its martial observances and excellent mysteries. We had great fun together, and we were great friends.

Isidore was not an over-confident rider, but in his shiny peaked cap, alpaca coat, white duck trousers and straps, which was his costume on sunny spring days, he circumvented an academy canter down an alley as well as his neighbours. When I first went to school in 1864 Mignonne was sold. However, I always got out hunting when I came home for the holidays. I was soon promoted to independence and an animal called 'Enguerrand,' just out of training, and after Enguerrand to a three-year-old called 'Flambeau,' and sometimes I was allowed to hire. Flambeau had a chequered career. He could 'run a bit' —an expensive accomplishment—and once managed to win a match either at Chantilly or Longchamps. Then he used to go stag and boar hunting, which he liked better

than the last two or three furlongs. When we all had to
flit, bag and baggage, before the Prussian advance, my father
did not go with us, but rode a clean-bred and most fractious
chestnut mare named Catalina to the coast from Fontainebleau. I think it was to Dieppe. Isidore accompanied him
on Flambeau. It was lovely weather, and both horses had
good legs and feet, so they enjoyed it. Once they were all
but shot at as spies by a zealous *franc-tireur* from behind a
tree, but explanations were quickly forthcoming from the
startled Isidore. Flambeau was soon after raffled for an
unflattering amount at a bazaar in aid of an organ fund
in Yorkshire. By that time he made a cheerful noise
himself.

The Fontainebleau hirelings were very moderate animals
and suffered from chronic sore backs, but I remember one, a
reputed 'Irlandais,' which was held in high esteem and
request; and another of the now scarce colour known as
porcelaine—a creamy white with black spots and flecks and
a very pink nose. He was a well-shaped, self-advertising animal, and made a great show and commotion. Louis XIV.,
who liked pied chargers, would have looked capital on
him, and Loutherbourg or Vander Meulen would have
been pleased with their model. There was plenty of hunting; M. M. Aguado hustled the boar about; the Imperial
Vénerie hunted the stag. The late Baron Lambert, as
Lieutenant de la Vénerie, was for all practical purposes
Master. He was very kind to me, and I looked up to him
as one upon the pinnacle of human greatness. He invited
me once or twice to the Vénerie, took me out for a ride on a
Vénerie horse, and gave me a Swaine and Adeney cutting
whip. Speaking from memory, I think he bought nice
horses with plenty of quality for the men, and he always
rode lean-necked, clean-headed, conspicuously coloured
horses himself. I remember in particular a charming white

Le Rendezvous

PIQUEUR DE LA VÉNERIE IMPÉRIALE
AFTER A. DE DREUX

mare. I would not swear to it, but I think she was called Regina. The first Latin declension was in great request for the names of mares in the hunt stables; the Roman Empire and the Punic wars being placed under heavy contributions in the kennels.

Baron Lambert was quite a character and a wit. Lord Byron never would speak French because he declined to speak it like a German waiter; but the Baron had no such fastidiousness about his English. He spoke it as freely and graphically as any Mr. Tiptop in Melton, and could slur the *h* in horse and hundred, and shunt the *g* in hunting with the refined subtlety of a Lord Scamperdale.

He rode about 12 st., à l'Anglaise, in an English pain-flap saddle, double bridle, and hunting spurs. In those days these were all looked upon with only half-approval, for *haute école* riding made her concessions slowly. But Baron Lambert's English ways were never overdone, and he quite suited the frame of his circumstances. His legs were perhaps a trifle short for elegance, but he sat well on his horse, and well-blacked jack-boots —which looked like having been made somewhere near the Marble Arch—did wonders for him. White hair, a clean-shaven actor's face, but as fresh and ruddy as Simon Lee's or Michael Hardy's, the becoming *vénerie* dress, and everything put on and worn and held right. There you have his portrait. He carried an English horn, but I have no recollection of his using it much; and he knew how to catch hold of a horse and balance him on a long rein as we do here, and as even in these days few know how to do there. I saw no one like him, when I was over the other day, tried by the conventions of English hunting riding form.

Napoleon III. liked the thing to go. His hunting notions and sympathies were English. So long as hounds ran on he winked at their having changed their deer, and paid very little attention to the moralities and the purists. He would often gallop like steam for a few minutes along the alleys as they came in his way—the tuneful operations of the chase being a matter of no importance—and then, relinquishing all interest in the proceedings, relapse into conversation with somebody he liked talking to. Sometimes, however, he would electrify M. de la Rue, who held a Woods and Forests appointment under the Second Empire, and has chronicled its *chasses*, by asking him where on earth the hunt had got to. On such occasions M. de la Rue used to lead the way to the Etang de Sainte-Perrine, a favourite soil, and hope for the best. On one occasion he was much annoyed with things having gone wrong, and sent for Baron Lambert, and found great fault with his arrangements. If it should happen again, he told him in my father's hearing, 'Je raye la Vénerie d'un trait de plume.' I never saw him out hunting, and he very seldom hunted at Fontainebleau, but I remember his seat on horseback perfectly. He sat right down and into his horse, and looked exceedingly well on horseback. He was probably not as good a school rider as the Prince Imperial, but I liked his seat and style better. Of course, as everybody knows, he rode exceedingly well to hounds over here, and on moderate horses. On one occasion he showed the whole Queen's field the way, including, I believe, Charles Davis, for the first two or three miles from Pole Hill in the Harrow country.

The old school were scandalised by the full-steam-ahead ways which, under the Second Empire, jostled the stately and classical proceedings of the Valois and the Bourbons. Grave fault was found in the loss of music and the decay of sylvan arts and sciences. England was held to blame. Fifty or sixty couple of hounds had been got together in a 'sic volo sic jubeo' sort of way by Comte Edgar Ney, the Grand Veneur. A few couple of entered hounds came from M. de l'Aigle's pack, but most of them were draft hounds got together in a hurry from England; and entered draft hounds which go to France are sometimes not good enough to earn their keep in their own country.

As far as I remember, I think the hounds were wanting in music, but the men did their best to make up for the deficiency. There was one particular *piqueur* whom Isidore held in high esteem, and who was much admired for the stirring way in which he could wind his horn at full gallop. On such occasions, M. Eugène, as Isidore and I always called him (of course we never dared speak to him), would come through the horsemen and carriages in a crowded carrefour standing up in his stirrups, and leaning over to the off side until the bell of his horn was on the level of his right stirrup. I think M. Eugène seldom knew where he was going, but we all used to gallop after him. '*Rendez la main, Monsieur Thomas; voilà M. Eugène qui sonne*,' Isidore used to say, getting his own horse well on the bit nd giving him the full benefit of a muscular calf.

However, I must now relate my more recent experiences, and say something about the hounds, the horses, and the men I hunted with last November, and the country they hunt.

The Channel was kind, and after travelling all night I arrived at Laversine, a delightful destination, in comfortable time to devote proper and particular attention to the ceremonies of boots and breeches. Now for what I saw and noticed and did.

As compared with those of most travellers and sportsmen my adventures were insignificant. But I was lucky. In these large forests it is not often that a stag will face the open, but the day I hunted at Halatte and the day I hunted at Fontainebleau we got out. This is, of course, a matter of general congratulation, and everybody sits down to ride with refreshed determination and proper regard for cultivation and the damage fund. This is the worst of it. The *plaine* or open is not good going; it is very deep, with that protesting deepness of spade cultivation. I do not know how the land is held, whether in small or large holdings. Of course it is the sort of thing I ought to have asked and did not ask; but the *plaine* shows the honourable symptoms of small ownership. Riding over it gave me the same feeling of doing unkind damage to poor people's pains as riding over allotments or cottage gardens would give me. It has neither the look nor feel of a hunting country. Of course I am only speaking of what I saw, as I fancy in some parts of France, notably the Landes and La Sologne, there is plenty of rough country, although not so wild as in the beginning of this century, when land was sold *au son de la voix* and the stretch of ground reached by a man's voice sold for a few francs.

1 only had four days' hunting. Two in the forest of Chantilly with the Duc de Chartres and the Prince de Joinville; one in the forest of Halatte with the Halatte hounds, kept by M. le Marquis de Valon; and one at Fontainebleau with M. M. Lebaudy.

On the Halatte day we had an excellent hunt. It was a very wet day, but only began to rain about 8 o'clock A.M., after several sunny days with white frosts at night. There was a capital scent, and I was very pleased with the hounds —the way they were hunted, or rather not hunted, and their style and character. I was very unlucky in not seeing M. de Valon hunt his hounds; he had broken two ribs just before I arrived. We ran through some beechwoods something like the birdless grove at Goodwood, and, just as I have noticed in the Goodwood and the Buckinghamshire beechwoods of the Queen's country, the hounds ran a great pace over the thick carpet of wet beech leaves. I do not know what sort of point the deer made, but it seemed to me a long zigzag.

Our stag was harboured in some young oakwood with thick undergrowth, and at first had several other deer with him—I mean he was joined by these, or pushed them up, after the pack was laid on. The *compagnie* went ringing and lurching about together in a thinned *enceinte* with very strong undercover. I rode with the huntsman through the stuff on a nice active horse which a kind friend at Laversine, M. Lambert, had mounted me on, and which would have found his way through Oustwick Whin or Ranksborough; and although, owing to the stubborn undercover, you could not have 'sheeted' them, their cry was beautiful, and each hound hunted the line as if everything depended on his individual performance. We were often within a few yards of the deer, who kept turning as short and stupid as rabbits in the corner of a warren; and the hounds must have constantly seen them, but they showed none of the demoralisation of view. Taking nothing for granted, they stuck to the line religiously, almost fanatically; I do not think you could have lifted them if you had tried. At last they got the stag—an eight-pointer—away with one nobber, who soon got dropped, and stuck to him like wax till they forced him over three or four marshy fields into the Oise and drowned him. I think we were running about two and a half hours.

M. de Valon never touches hounds; that is, they get no assistance of any kind. They have crosses of English blood; and, like M. de Chezelles, he is especially fond of the Duke of Beaufort's blood. But they are essentially French hounds, and personally I liked them much better in their work, their appearance, and their style, than any other pack I hunted with. They are on the long side and a little slab-sided, but of charming quality and no lumber. Over here we should not like the colour. There is a great deal of black and hardly any tan. But this marks and preserves the French foundations of the pack. I saw no regular Badminton badger pie, but several hounds were of a dark mousey colour, which they call *souriot*. This means plenty of Badminton blood, and M. de Valon especially esteems the *souriots*. The Halatte kennel is the only one I saw, as I went to pay the master a visit, and to tell him how much I had enjoyed my day. I went down to look at the young entry—*les chiens M.*—as in many French packs the names of the young entry of each year all begin with some particular letter of the alphabet. As purists the French would be more particular than the fox-hunting English Baronet, who, wishing to name three own brothers in the usual way, called them Govial, Gowler, and Galloper, but they stick to this so religiously that some of the names of a large entry do not strike upon the ear agreeably. It is, however, eminently practical, and better perhaps than some of our names, which are quite senseless. I am reminded of a story of a gentleman who heard his huntsman cheering a hound by the name of 'Lyman.' 'What,' he asked, 'does Lyman mean?' 'Lord, sir,' said the huntsman, 'what does anything mean?'

It was a very wet afternoon, but the establishment struck me as being purpose-like and practical. They do not enter their young hounds until February, as they usually come in from the walks in poor condition. I noticed two things particularly about the Halatte hounds—their ability to gallop fast with their noses down, and their whip sterns. As to the latter, I said to myself, here at last are the whip sterns which were Charles Davis's secret, and which gave the Queen's hounds their particular distinction in the days of the giants. I was much disappointed when I found that their racy appearance was the result of scissors and a fortnightly trimming. As to the other point, I instanced it to a hunting gentleman with whom I travelled up from Chantilly two or three days later, and he said he had observed the very contrary, and that, thanks to scent lying on the bushes more comfortably than on the ground, their tendency was to look for it breast high. I do not know how this may be ; and I dare say he is right and I am wrong. My preference is to let things strike me through the eye, and to be satisfied with what I see if the sight is pleasant. Anyhow, I will not be robbed by my reason-giving travelling companion of the picture left upon my memory of the whip-sterned *souriots* and magpies with their noses to the ground, racing under the high beeches.

At Chantilly we had a good hunting run of about three hours, and killed. It was a very bright sunny day, and the scent was moderate. There was a long check at ' la table du roi,' which carriages, conversation, and luncheon baskets made very tolerable for many of us. Our hunted stag had contrived to associate several other deer with his difficulties, and the horns blew the *accompagné* from every point of the compass. However, tactics and venery prevailed. They managed to cut him out again, and hunted him cheerfully at a steady pace until he stood to bay. The scent, I thought, improved in the afternoon, and I hazarded this rather conventional observation to the head *piqueur*. He said '*Au contraire*,' and gave reasons which he politely explained, but which I imperfectly grasped. They certainly ran with more cry and confidence, but I dare say they were closer at him. Fortunately there is no inevitable agreement about scent, people, novels, and sermons.[1]

Perhaps it may be well to say a word or two here upon

---

[1] H.R.H. the Duc de Chartres most kindly sent me the foot of this good stag beautifully mounted, with a plate bearing the particulars of the day, as follows :

' Rendezvous à la baraque Nibert ; attaqué au trou des Braconniers ; pris au poteau St. Léonard après 4 h. de chasse ; laisser courre par Chéri.
27 Nov. 1895.
Les honneurs du pied à Lord Ribblesdale.'

the qualities and defects of French hounds, and the qualities and defects of English hounds according to French ideas.

French tradition clings to line hunting, drawing and perseverance. It has little patience with the arrogance and fling of a foxhound. M. de Chezelles, a high authority, thinks that a good modern *bâtard*, which is to all intents the French hound, hunts more *gaiement* than an English hound. He is busier: throws his tongue incessantly, and wishes everybody to share in his opinions, perplexities, and triumphs ; and there can be little doubt that a good *bâtard* is probably a better hound for forest hunting than a draft hound from the Holdernesse or the Tedworth. I have already referred to my predecessor, Colonel Thornton. The Colonel, although he tells us that his hounds always outpaced the French hounds—in spite of their rather confined quarters in the travelling carriage with Mrs. T.'s trunks and bonnet boxes—and that he himself performed feats, and exhibited a fertility of resource which made his hosts stare, acknowledges very handsomely that the French surpass us in science. Without pausing to inquire whether or not hunting is a science, be it in France or anywhere else, I am quite willing to agree with the Colonel that now as then the French know a great deal about woodland hunting and woodland hounds. The same candour, however, compels me to say that they have some strange prepossessions about English hunting, English hounds, and English requirements.

As Lord Byron said of the Venetian ladies, the French, as regards their hounds, have ' awful notions of constancy.' A hound must stick to a hunted deer like a limpet. They think that in England a change on to a fresh fox is not only connived at, but encouraged, and English blood is always looked upon with suspicion as willing to cheerfully compound such felonies. Some of the characteristics of English hounds, as noted by writers of authority on sporting subjects in France, are novel and astonishing. According to one authority we care little for music, or for the way a hound draws, or for his staunchness on a scent. The foxhound is represented as a sort of sylvan hedonist. His morals are indifferent, and his character selfish. Tested by French standards of hound probity, it appears that he detests thick cover, and under such circumstances merely follows the ridings, and cuts in with the other hounds or with the deer when they leave it. If the deer stays in cover, he often abandons the pursuit altogether. Bested by slower but more virtuous hounds which have the knack of straining through the wealth of bramble and blackthorn and *ajoncs* which distinguish a French forest, he makes the most of a *débucher*, goes straight up to the front, stays there, and spanks along at such a pace that he makes the industrious *bâtards*, faint but pursuing, bleed from the nose. He only likes a plain-sailing hunt, hates a twisting deer and a stale scent ; one boar is quite as good as another—although it is admitted that his courage makes him a good boar-hound—and he is useless for roe-deer hunting. Here is another bit of news about necks and shoulders : the experience of an expert. It appears that the English insist upon a hound with a long neck, so that he can stoop to a scent ; this is a proof, according to the oracle, that most of our foxhounds have not very good noses. The Saintonge hound—an ancient and eminent French breed— hunted with his head up (*le nez au vent*), without deigning to stoop. This is still a characteristic of a well-bred hound— both in pointers and hounds—but M. de Chabot goes on to say that he has often remarked slow-looking hounds keep right up at the lead, and throw their tongues admirably owing to the way they carried their heads and the way their heads were put on. In our love of drive and pace the French think we have sacrificed nose ; and nose has for centuries been the *bon sang ne peut mentir* test in France.

LE RELAIS VOLANT

Thus M. de Ligniville tells us how a neighbour of his in Lorraine had a *mâtin*—which I take to be a half-mastiff, half-hound or pointer animal—which was a capital tufter; but he goes on to say that he never saw a tufter speak to a line at three o'clock on a hot afternoon which was not 'a highly and a nobly' bred one. The French judges do not like our catlike feet—a Saintonge hound has a hare's foot—and the lameness which besets English hounds after four or five seasons' work in France is attributed to the shape of our foxhounds' feet. After all, if they get four or five seasons out of a hound, he owes very little at the price Wilton sold him ' to go abroad.'

M. de Couteulx is a great believer in the assured future of the French hound. In his *Manuel de Vénerie* he says : 'Nous commençons à ne plus être tributaires de l'Angleterre, et je vois avant peu le moment où celle-ci pourra bien nous prendre plus de chiens que nous ne lui en prendrons.' This is a comfortable and patriotic conjecture, but still in the region of prophecy.

At Chantilly they still hunt with relays. This leads to hounds getting scattered, *semés* as they say, over a wide area. Like Virgil's seamen, *apparent rari*, all over the place and quite unexpectedly, many of them taking but a partial interest in the chase.

In this country we had given up relays as far back as the seventeenth century. M. de Ligniville cites this with approval as a point of acute difference between English and French hunting principles of his day. At Chantilly they are rather a pale survival of more splendid Bourbon days, when relays of hounds with their gaily dressed *valets*, led horses with their attendants, gamekeepers and foresters, all contributed pomp and circumstance, purple and gold to the scenic display. Under the Empire they were still popular stage properties. *Valets de chiens*, in their grey-blue worsted stockings and buckle shoes ; extra horses, in check cotton quarter-sheets, for the swells and the hunt-servants, military-looking greenclad *gardes*, lent colour and animation and importance to the alleys and *carrefours* of Fontainebleau or Compiègne. I remember well the *relais volant*—it sounds like an inn sign or the title of a ghost story—that is, the mounted yeoman pricker, with five or six couple of hounds, theoretically straining on plaited hair rope but really much embarrassed by his horse's heels. But the *relais volant* was always an exciting apparition, as he hastened hither and thither on the spur in response to some distant challenge from his compeers of the horn. To judge by the appearance of the little band, it was hot work for all parties.

Now that hounds are bred and entered to hunt together, it is hardly possible to defend the relay system, and its vogue is very limited. The objections are numerous and obvious. It is difficult enough under any circumstances to keep fifteen or eighteen couple of hounds together in varied and extensive woodlands, even when they are laid on all at one time. It must be nearly impossible to keep twenty-five or thirty couple together laid on at different times, and laid on in a way which must be offensive and disappointing to high-mettled, painstaking hounds; for a relay is always laid on, if possible, with the leading hound as he crosses an alley, and a clever *valet de chiens* is the man who can get all his relay off and on the line at the very head of the hunting pack.

Relays, apart from pageantry, may have had their uses in old days, before constant crosses of English blood bred the fast *bâtard* of to-day. The old French hounds hunted all the better for being in great numbers. They were always uttering speech and certifying knowledge to one another; the chain of communication could hardly be too long. In voice and gesture there was little to choose between the leading and the tail hounds, and a deer was probably seldom at the pains of exerting himself. They killed him very possibly as often, or oftener, than the faster packs of the present day, but they killed him by the same means as the tortoise defeated the hare. His self-confidence led him to take liberties with their perseverance.

The French are an exact people. You should, I am told, read high mathematics in French, rather than in English or in German, because the French language and the French *ingenium* guarantee a correct nicety of expression. They are, as we know, in arts and crafts, sticklers for form and precision. Hunting procedure is no exception. It has a formidable grammar and a prosody. Even to freeing the horn from the results of your efforts, there is an ascertained right and wrong way of doing everything. The late Vicomte H. de Chezelles, a most competent authority, devotes some pages of his interesting book to what he calls the *grandes façons* handed down in certain families of professional huntsmen from generation to generation. M. de Chezelles instances the Namurs, Obrys, Duvals, under the Monarchy, La Trace and La Feuille of the Imperial Vénerie, as all having the grand style, but La Trace is his Charles Davis. When Napoleon III. reconstituted the Vénerie, La Trace was growing vegetables, and marrying people who wished to marry, as the mayor of his native town, Dangu. His country and his Emperor's need called him, like another Cincinnatus, to higher things. The manner in which he made his report to the Grand Veneur, the noble simplicity of his approach, the poise of his whip, the elegant gesture of his saluting hat, the bow with which he decorated the instructions he might receive or inspire, were things, M. de Chezelles tells us, once seen never to be forgotten.

Now, I dare say I may have missed the subtleties of doffing the *lampion*, or of the deployment of the whip-lash. They would appear to be things only to be spiritually perceived. But there is a certain kind of form which is quite independent of dress regulations and the classical unities. You will encounter and recognise what I mean in a stage-coachman, or a shikari in the Himalayas ; in a cricketer or a waiter ; in a gondolier or in a jockey—something which distinguishes the individual from his fellowcraftsmen, which jumps to your eyes and your brain and makes you say, ' This is the real thing.' I admit it may be an external, that often, like many ideals, things are not what they seem. The apparent Crichton breaks down in practice; the bright particular star gives no better light than the meaner people of the skies. But I am only laying stress on externals, and, tried by that test, I saw no La Trace during my stay in France. The eternal principles of French *vénerie* —once the pack has settled to a deer—seem to offer but few opportunities of emerging from a mere character part ; and the professional huntsmen I saw made none for themselves. At his best the huntsman appeared to be a mounted and picturesque master of the ceremonies, the Lord High Chamberlain of the Forest ; at his worst he is a peasant or a stableman dressed up in an *opéra-comique* attire.

Although Arthur Young was given a white pony and a pointer and a gun when he was quite a little boy, and enjoyed the usual outdoor opportunities of English country life, I do not think he ever quite liked hunting. Possibly he could not have loved farming so well had he done so.

When he went to France he was shocked at ' the mischievous animation of a vast hunt ' which the great properties exhibited, at the sovereignty of the game, and the privileges of the *capitaineries*. ' The crop of this country,' he said of the district round Senlis and Chantilly, ' is princes of the blood—that is to say, hares, pheasants, deer, and boars.' He is always noting and regretting the absence of farm buildings and farming energies. At the expense of his political economy, a cowhouse at Chanteloup gives him more satisfaction than Condé's hunting stables at Chantilly with their

240 English horses, and the trade they meant to the English breeder. He calls the cowhouse 'noble,' and he means what he says; but all the beauties of Versailles and St. Germains make no amends for royal and noble indifference to the complete system of turnip cultivation which he held so near his heart. But the most utilitarian side of Mr. Morley's 'wise and honest traveller' would have been gratified by the forests of to-day. Thrift and forestry have tamed Chantilly and Halatte, but especially Chantilly, until it is difficult to trace a vestige of what we understand over here by natural woodland. Even the Scotch firs are shaven to the geometrical alignment of the alleys and to the perspective of a point of sight. I could not help feeling that the deer were a sort of well-to-do colonists living under an ordered dispensation and ascertained conditions. Fontainebleau is different: in spite of economics there are desolations of sand deserts and heather, confusions of grey rock, splashes of lonely water, which belong of right to the tall deer, and which still set at nought the estimates and votes on account of a department.

I have said little or nothing in this chapter about horses and riders, and I have confined myself to observations upon the hounds. In France the hound is the Paramount. In the next chapters I will try to contrast French and English ideas of horses and riding, suggested by my own personal experiences.

CHAPTER XVI

FRENCH HORSEMANSHIP

Jamais bon veneur ne fut mauvais capitaine

HAVING nothing else to ride, I determined to renew my youth by riding a hireling at Fontainebleau, and I carried this sentimental resolution into effect through the telephone of the Hôtel Continental. It is not a modern improvement I understand, but, after the interchange of many 'Holàs,' 'qui est-ce?' 'est-ce vous?' the evening before, I had at last been brought into relations with the local Percival, and expounded my wants, my inches, and my weight; a reassuring 'Comptez sur moi' concluding the transaction.

The next morning broke like a hunting day. Tender grey clouds brooded low over the Tuileries gardens, and moved slowly across a spacious rain-washed sky. The Gare de Lyon was not as animated as Paddington or Euston on a hunting morning. Well-cleaned—even badly-cleaned—boots and breeches are an immediate introduction to the platform of a London terminus and most provincial stations. They secure at once the particular attention of the guard, the smartest services of the porters, and a meed of goodwill and interest all round. But the general public in France have no part or lot in hunting. It has never been popular in the Latin sense of the word. The chasse à courre is a vestige of privilege which has outstayed the ancient régime. Over here the public hunts by right. Over there the individual hunts by invitation.

In this country the varied vicissitudes of the hunting-field are the playground of anecdote and imagination. Even if we have not ourselves owned him—and at times most of us have done so—we are all familiar with the exploits of the old horse. He has invariably only given his owner one fall; even that, poor old chap! was not his fault. Or worse still —for in her case the tender grace of a day that is dead encourages more elaborate sentiment—the old mare; she has never turned her head or missed her turn. Indeed, she often insists upon anticipating it in conversation.

Mr. Disraeli's fine observation told him that something to do with riding across country and falling on your head must come into any true picture of English society in the most national and unrestricted sense of the word society. What can be better than the steeplechase in ' Coningsby,' the after-dinner discussion over its impromptu conditions, and the emergencies of the water-jump ? I do not know whether people read Mr. Disraeli's novels now. They should. But, in this particular book, nine Englishmen out of ten will admit Mr. Guy Flouncey to be a more lifelike figure than Sidonia, merely because his horse lay across his diaphragm in the brook. Although upon one occasion he settled the field on his Arabian—a mare, of course—I cannot suppose that Mr. Disraeli had any personal experience of steeplechase riding ; yet his artistic sense enables him, as it were, to ride a capital race home, and indeed gets him over some little solecisms, such as the yeoman's white mare making the running at a severe pace, lying at the time third or fourth—which would have been fatal to a less gifted writer. All this sort of thing, which makes the characters breathe, and which oxygenises the atmosphere in a story of English life, can contribute nothing to a French novel. So far from that, I even remember M. Octave Feuillet playing the deuce with the disturbing conception he had given me of one of his most charming heroines, by taking her out riding. After hearing that she ' bondissait légèrement sur sa selle,' I confess I took less interest in her perplexed future.

There is no room either for horses in the French novel heroes, excepting perhaps for the brougham horse who devours the paved street on his way to an assignation. Provincial celebrities like the stout yeoman's white mare in ' Coningsby' ; character parts like Mr. Sponge's Multum in Parvo or like Marathon in ' Market Harborough,' can never hope to emerge into real life from the horse community as they do here. The French have never had—it is equivalent to saying that they have never wanted—a Whyte Melville or a Surtees. There is never any story in modern French books about hunting. They discourse of its etiquette and technicalities. To warrant his writing at all, a French writer on sport must write as a scientist, and evolve a textbook. Nor is this to be wondered at. Kate Coventry, Lord Scamperdale, the Hon. Crasher, would be unintelligible marionettes in a French novel. Mr. Sponge would never have set out upon his tour, Mr. Jorrocks never have left Great Coram Street. Hunting and all that has to do with it is popular in England, in the sense of its being in the bone and sinew of the people at large. In France it is the exclusive amusement of a small class and in no sense national. Mme. Bovary and M. de Camors, Sappho and Bel Ami did not hunt. Their tastes and talents lay in other directions.

However, I must remember I have a train to catch. Three or four gentlemen in moderate boots and velvet caps were unostentatiously keeping their toes warm on the platform. On the other hand, the observed of all observers, two sportsmen with high-hammered pin-fire guns en bandoulière, and a pigeon-toed liver-and-white pointer called Byron, had gathered around them a knot of well-wishers. Byron meanwhile assiduously quartered the platform in fine style, in spite of being repeatedly called to heel. I overheard snatches of an evidently exciting conversation. Notes of an excellent breeding season were being freely exchanged. 'Chez nous,' said one, 'ce qu'il y a d'extraordinaire c'est le faisan'; in our part of the world said some one else, 'le lièvre est en masse.' It is true that the arrival of my linen apron created some little interest in favour of horse and hound, but although it was quite courteous, I cannot flatter myself that it was altogether respectful. Even in England, outside a twenty-mile radius of Melton, the compulsions of leathers in this matter of aprons are but imperfectly understood.

I arrived at the Hôtel de France in ample time for a capital breakfast. Here things looked more like business, and the waiter recommended me a Graves which he assured me was much esteemed by the gentlemen of the hunt. The meet was at the Belle Croix, within half an hour's ride of Fontainebleau, and at the telephone-appointed hour I was informed that my horse was at the door. I have never yet got over the pleasurable feeling caused by this familiar announcement—I hope I never shall—so I rushed out full of curiosity. 'Le cheval de Monsieur' proved to be a fine bay Prussian. A brand-new bridle with many buckles caparisoned his lusty neck; a glossy ultramarine frontlet adorned a pensive brow; a burly saddle surmounted his thick withers. The manager of the livery stable had courteously ridden round in order to show me the way, and we looked him over together before mounting. I remarked with deprecation upon his very German appearance, at the same time paying a flattering tribute to the nice horses bred in France. 'Now this horse,' I said, 'was never bred in the Nivernais'—this happened to be the only district which occurred to me at the moment; 'a heavy horse like this can only be a Prussian.' I saw at once that I had made a point. 'Ça se voit que Monsieur est connoisseur. Dame, c'est un cheval qui vient d'un peu partout.' From that moment the manager and I understood each other, and we set off together, excellent friends. The manager himself, who sat as he should, was riding a gay little brown horse with a cock-tail, all quality, and quite a stag-hunter. As I watched his gay movement and the vein tracery starting into relief on his clean neck, I made up my mind to swop horses, and so to be quit of the cosmopolitan. After some more slighting remarks upon the Prussian, I explained within the limits of my French that he was riding my sort of horse, and that he ought to have sent him for me instead of the Teuton. 'But,' objected my companion, 'you said you weighed over one hundred kilos.' This was the telephone guess at my weight made by my representative at the Continental. 'That is so,' I admitted, 'but blood and action carry weight. Can you expect either from "un cheval qui vient d'un peu partout "? ' He knew quite as well as I did that it was not to be done. And after loyally citing the merits of my mount as a ' cheval de retraite,' an equine type that needed explanation, but which turned out to be a good hack home, he agreed to change horses at the Belle Croix after he had shown the brown horse to a client. The client was not out, so we changed at once. I had a charming ride, which, as he assured me the brown horse was ' parfait pour les dames,' was not to be wondered at.

The Belle Croix stands high and deserves its name, but I will not depict the landscape. 'D——n description ; it is always disgusting '—I am sure my readers will agree with Lord Byron.

After the ceremonies of introduction and compliment, Monsieur Lebaudy invited me to go with him to see the stag unharboured. As I was anxious to see his huntsman Hurvari at work, I very willingly did so. Hurvari, who was for many years the Duc d'Aumale's huntsman at

Chantilly, has the reputation of being a sort of residuary legatee of the 'grandes façons' to which I alluded in the last chapter. I can offer no opinion on his woodcraft. As I have already said, the strict 'laissez-faire' principles of French hunting and the colourless conditions of riding[1] to hounds in these large forests give little opportunity to the huntsman of singling himself out, and a stranger is hardly competent to appreciate the niceties of scientific venery. Even on an average day, every huntsman in this country has at least one or two chances of signalising himself by some cast of daring talent, luck, or folly, or by the successful liberties which he takes with a clever horse and forbidding obstacles. Indeed, to professional or amateur alike, the conditions of an English country make a day's hunting a 'carrière ouverte aux talents.' Thus Snob's plucky horsemanship and the little bay cocktail get him asked to dinner by the Melton swells with whom he tries conclusions in the famous pages of the 'Quarterly.' In the alleys and carrefours of a French forest he could not have hoped to enjoy so pleasant a recognition of his performances.

Hurvari wears, I believe, with perfect professional propriety, long and flowing whiskers of the old Piccadilly weeper sort. His style was decorous to the point of frigidity. He belongs, I should imagine, to the older school, which looks upon the horse as a mere means of getting about. Hurvari was riding the only really well-bred hunt horse I saw; but the animal seemed very stale, and they never abandoned a trot. His mind seemed singularly unclouded by enthusiasm. To make up for this, M. Lebaudy and one of the piqueux never stopped galloping from point to point, crossing and recrossing each other incessantly, M. Lebaudy addressing abrupt inter-

[1] I remember reading in a hunting classic of a French huntsman who told an English visitor, when they arrived together at a bank and ditch, that it was no part of his bond to jump. Mr. Beckford—for I think it is in his book—is highly indignant about it; but after all we all shrink from the unfamiliar.

pellations and questions to anybody he happened to encounter. It is true he never waited for an answer, but this always looks business-like, and I dare say he lost nothing.

There were very few people out, but within an hour or so we were joined by a contingent of officers in smart undress uniform, riding flippant horses in plain saddles and bridles. Several ladies graced the scene, and I was pleased to recognise a well-preserved specimen of the 'Princesse' habit of my youth, thought by some to be extinct.

Fontainebleau is a large garrison and school of military instruction. A great deal has been done in late years to encourage unprofessional riding in the French army. 'Le dresseur le plus sage instruit en amusant,' and the French authorities are of that opinion. Our late Military Attaché in Paris, General the Hon. R. Talbot, who now commands the Cavalry Brigade at Aldershot, writes to me in this connection : 'The old haute école seat, as practised in France, has given way to a hunting seat modelled upon the English style of riding in the hunting-field. The man sits back on his horse, rides with a shorter stirrup, and with a bent instead of a straight leg. Instead of riding upon the bit with a tight curb, men are instructed to use both bit and snaffle, the former being less severe, with a comparatively loose curb. The man who made a revolution in French riding was General L'Hotte, who introduced the hunting seat and made jumping and riding across country take the place of the manège and haute école style of riding. He was backed up by General de Gallifet and all the best cavalry officers in France. He altered the whole system of instruction at the Cavalry School of Saumur, which is now as good a military school of riding as can be imagined. There are about four to five hundred thoroughbred horses kept specially for teaching young officers to ride. Every cavalry officer has to spend twelve months at Saumur after being a year with his regiment.

During this twelve months' course he has to ride four or five different horses every day. One horse is a trained charger of his own; a second is a young thoroughbred horse which he has to handle from the first, and break and make into a charger; the other two or three horses are varied every day, and chosen by the instructors. Great attention is given to jumping and out-of-door training. On all the roads round Saumur there are jumps along the sidings. Steeplechases

M. DUTECH CLEARING THE GATE AT A LEVEL CROSSING UPON PAPILLON
From ' Le Sport Universel Illustré,' December 1, 1896.

are constantly run, prizes given by the Government, and the officers are allowed to ride Government horses. I consider that the present generation of cavalry officers below the rank of colonel ride remarkably well, with graceful easy seats and light hands as a rule. I do not think that there are nearly so many really fine riders as in the English cavalry, but there is more uniformity. Young fellows who are clumsily built and unlikely to make cavalry soldiers are not allowed to enter the cavalry, instead of, as with us, being eliminated subsequently, often after many years' service.'

In the English army it is always taken for granted that the major will know how to ride. Thus some of the mounted officers of an Infantry Brigade at Aldershot, or rather the vagaries of their seats and of their chargers, are often exceedingly diverting. I remember occasions when they have made quite tolerable the interminable pauses and contradictions of a review in the Long Valley or a field-day on the Fox Hills. We were often grateful to these eccentric horsemen. Nothing is taken for granted about riding, or indeed about anything else in France. A mounted officer must know how to ride his horse. The French cut of booted over-all rather smothers a plain saddle, and their short-waisted many-buttoned tunic seems to cock a man too much up on his horse. Indeed, with the exception of the long undress frock-coat and close over-all of our own hussars, no uniform looks really well with civilian saddlery. But I have no hesitation in saying that the forty or fifty officers I saw out with Monsieur Lebaudy's hounds rode quite as well as, *mutatis mutandis*, the corresponding contingent from Aldershot do with Mr. Garth or the Queen's.

But to return to my captains and colonels and subalterns and the glades of Fontainebleau. Uniform out hunting was not unfamiliar to me. In the old days 'mon capitaine' or 'mon colonel' occasionally came out hunting, but his punctilio was tremendous. I am not at all sure he did not always wear his sword. At all events he maintained throughout a strictly barrack-square demeanour, or at the best seemed to be bent on a reconnaissance. When we encountered this image of war, at a carrefour, 'le brave Isidore,' as he was honourably dubbed at 'Le Cheval Noir' and other houses of call, used instinctively to pull himself together, straighten his leg, drop his heel and right arm, and coerce into an extra curve his left wrist. All this is changed. I feel certain that had it been our lot to be translated into a gallop over the Berkshire banks, the military would have given an excellent account of themselves. One young officer in particular, on a sticky, inquisitive, clean-bred chestnut horse, rode the actual line of hounds all day, and squeezed him in and out of the man-traps of the rock-strewn Vallée de la Sole in a way which looked like getting the very last stride out of a Lanercost at the judge's box.

Now, a word or two on what I will call secularised French riding. As far back as 1878, M. Le Jeune, in a pleasant article in 'Lippincott,' devoted some attention to establishing the existence of a bruising school of French horsemanship, and he records almost controversially, in support of his proposition, several moving incidents by flood and field. Such, for instance, as a M. de Pully pounding two Lincolnshire fox-hunters in Le Berri by swimming the Creuse on a cold November day, and of the same gentleman —who appears to have been quite a customer—being all but drowned in a mill-race. And here it may be observed that the French are almost over-conscious of the fact that a well-rided forest involves a lack of suitable risk and adventure. It was evidently supposed that every Englishman is thirsting for a five-barred gate or some equally congenial obstacle. Most courteous apologies were frequently made to me for the absence of these luxuries, and as nothing I could say to the contrary seemed to dispel this flattering hypothesis of my habits, I at last threw myself into the spirit of the thing, acquiesced in all sorts of foolhardy desires, and rode over some enormous places in the course of much conversation. Indeed, when at last we got out into the open I was quite relieved at seeing there was nothing to jump.

But to go back to M. Le Jeune's contention. Without in any way generalising from the signal exploits of individuals, I feel there can be little doubt that the old school of

horsemanship, whether military or civilian, has been gradually
superseded. Early in the sixties hunting dress began to
change, and new dress regulations found their way into the
hunting text-books. Many of the gentlemen who hunted
with the Imperial pack and M. Aguado's boarhounds had at
this time taken to scarlet coats, blue bird's-eye neckcloths,
cords of a horrid ochre hue, and top-boots. Neither they
nor their valets managed very well at that time, and the
result was neither one thing nor the other. They would
not have looked right at Kirby Gate, and somehow they
looked wrong at La Croix du Grand Veneur. Style and
saddlery followed suit—the whip was carried differently, no
longer up like a drawn sword, or poised to a discreet parallel
with your horse's crest and pointing to a future between
his ears. By 1870 the rigour of the game had relaxed.
Haute école may still have reigned, but it no longer
governed. Personally I am rather sorry that its glory should
have departed. France used to be its Shiloh. Henri III.,
one of the few Valois who did not hunt, when he heard that
the Duke of Burgundy had accused him of living like a
monk, rode a school horse over a high leaping-bar in the
presence of a gentleman of Burgundy, and bade him go back
and tell his master what he had seen the monk do. The
Duke of Newcastle in his book on manège-riding instances five
French gentlemen 'as the best of his acquaintance and in the
world.' The Connétable Montmorency, he tells us, invented
a bit and spurs which were unrivalled. A school horse commanded a higher price in France than anywhere else. The
Duc de Guise bid the Duke, then plain Mr. Cavendish, six
hundred pistoles for a grey leaping horse 'who could cut
surpassing caprioles, take the highest and justest leaps without assistance,' and throw himself 'terrâ a terrâ' an incredible number of metres in the riding-school. The main objection Addison's Tory foxhunter urges against France is
the loss of a man's hunting seat. The whole vocabulary of

the manège is French. As I watched the young officers cramming their horses along in a way which argued complete independence of the riding-school and the classics, I wondered what M. Triboulet, a well remembered figure of my boyhood, would have said of it all. M. Triboulet was the respected riding- and fencing-master of the town. He was also versed in the theory of gymnastics and a shrewd exponent of the arcana of dumb-bells. These were his gods, and he had grown old and grey and poor in their service. I am afraid he never had many pupils. To make up for this he exacted from himself all the disciplines he would have imposed upon others, and luckily a clever wife and the popularity of a little café facing the barrack gates helped out the arts and sciences. The 'Spectator' would have proposed him for his club, Daudet in his more clement mood would have introduced him to us, Stevenson must have included him in his 'Memories and Portraits.' Perhaps, though, Sir Walter Scott would have understood him best of all, and done justice to his faithfulness over a few things. Winter and summer his costume never varied. A black velvet postillion cap with a very high crown, a short black justaucorps, tight pepper-and-salt over-alls, square-toed boots, formidable swan-necked spurs, a long rapier-like cutting whip, grey beaver gloves, a high 1830 black stock admirably tied—for, like Beau Brummell, he never had a failure—lent suitable dignity to the inflexible features of an ideal martinet. He lived and thought in cautions, words of command, and well-imagined affairs of honour. They were the chosen companions of his leisure. Triboulet disapproved of hunting, and looked upon the gay company who swept through the alleys as so many lords and ladies of misrule; but he spent much of his time on horseback, and he never spared himself, or the old milk-white flowing-tailed Arab, or the streets or the landscape any one of the due observances of the riding-school.

CHAPTER XVII

FRENCH HORSES

Quant a moi, je suis bien assceuré, qu'il n'y a rien d'universel dans la cavalerie, ni aucume autre chose que je schache . . . Mes vœux seront pour les noble cavallerizzes, à ce qu'ils puissent garder cette profession honorable exempte de tâches et blémissures, afin de s'attirer l'estime des plus grands Roys et Princes.—Methode et invention nouvelle de Dresser les Chevaux, par le Prince Guillaume, Marquis et Comte de Newcastle, &c. (Anvers, 1658.)

M. LE JEUNE laments, in the article I have already referred to, the absence of any hunters of French stock with the fashionable packs round Paris. Everything, he says—this was in 1878—is English. To some extent this is true now. Just as American ladies must buy their clothes in Paris—it is an obligation to be applauded by every man of taste who has not to pay their bills—the cream of Chantilly and Compiègne like to have their horses from England. A Frenchman quite enjoys telling you that the horse he is riding distinguished himself at the Dublin Show, or that he was bred in 'le Yorkshire.' It is a not unpleasing fact, too, that in a show class of harness or half-bred riding horses, the odds are still in favour of the pick of the basket being an English horse. Yet at the same time the average 60*l*. or 70*l*. English horse, which is sold in Paris at 120*l*. or 140*l*., is not a better animal, tested by English standards of quality and action, than the home-bred horse which can be bought for very much less money in France.

But what does M. Le Jeune mean by French stock?

When was there such a thing as a distinct French riding horse? How far must we go back to find the famous breeds of Auvergne and the Limousin, of Navarre and Périgord, in their integrity and vigour?

These are questions which were scrupulously investigated by a strong Commission[1] which went into the whole question of horse-breeding and remounts in 1873. The able and attractive report drawn up by M. Edouard Bocher, who at that time represented Calvados in the Sénat, a great horse-breeding district, is capital reading. The general conclusion arrived at is summed up in one sentence of that Report: 'Elles [the famous French strains] n'ont jamais été que l'objet de souvenirs et de regrets.' Even in Louis XIII.'s reign a M. de Charnizay, in his 'Pratique du cavalier,' anticipates M. Le Jeune and many subsequent writers of authority, and bewails the absence of French-bred riding horses. 'Our own best strains,' says M. de Charnizay, 'are by this time either " abâtardies " or lost.'[2]

If M. Le Jeune is thinking of a Limousin or a Navarrois when he sighs the lack of native-born horses, he will find himself, historically speaking, in the excellent company of Louis XIV. The Preamble of the 'Arrêt du Conseil' of 1665,

---

[1] Commission chargée d'examiner la proposition de loi de M. Delacour sur les Haras et les Remontes, Assemblée Nationale, année 1873. The Loi Organique des Haras, 1874, is based upon the Report of this Commission.

[2] For what a Yorkshire show catalogue would style 'Road or Field,' we were at this time little or no better off in England. Racing appears to have flourished. The satirical writings of Bishop Hall give evidence of a turf sufficiently scientific to ruin a promising nobleman like the Earl of Cumberland. But there are constant anxieties about the scarcity of what we now call —the phrase rather suggests a treatise on Political Economy—'general utility' horses. Coaches were introduced in Elizabeth's reign, and occasioned a sudden demand for horses. The House of Lords rushed to the rescue, and suitably debated whether it would be best to bring up the supply of horses to the new coaches, or to bring down the coaches to the horses. Sir E. Harwood, an authority in Charles I.'s time, laments the increasing scarcity of 'able' horses, and deprecates the growing popularity of racing, and the consequent breeding of horses for speed and not burthen.

which provided for the establishment of Haras throughout the kingdom, sets forth the urgency of the horse-breeding question, and the steadfast determination of the king to come to the rescue of a perishing industry by a large measure of State aid, ' de telle sorte,' says this 'Arrêt,' ' que les sujets de sa majesté ne soient pas obligés de porter leurs deniers dans les pays étrangers pour achats de chevaux.'

Both Louis XIV. and Louis XV. got their horses from England. Their hackneys came chiefly out of Suffolk, and their hunters from Yorkshire—the latter were called ' Courtaults ' from having their ears cropped, and were docked very short. Eight hundred francs was an average price given for hunt horses, and if Oudry's pictures are to be trusted, the royal stud got good value for its money.

The Duke of Newcastle's beautiful book, of which the still more beautiful MS. is now at Welbeck, was published in 1667. It is significant that in his vivid descriptions, or rather narratives, of the various breeds of riding horses, their qualities and their points, he makes no mention of a distinct French breed, whilst he devotes a separate chapter apiece to the ways and uses of the Polander, the Swede, and the Frisian. This is the more significant in view of the ascendency of French horsemanship at the time. As we have already seen, the Duke of Newcastle makes most special mention of individual French horsemen and of French riding generally, but says not a word about French horses. ' Barbs,' he told Don John of Austria with happy courtesy, when he was presented to him at Amsterdam, ' are the gentlemen of horse kind, and Spaniards the Princes.' The Duke also held the Naples courser in honourable esteem, but for his own riding he preferred Barbs, Spaniards, and, it sounds strangely in our ears, Dutch-bred horses.

M. François de Guise, Grand Veneur to François II. and Charles IX., agreed with the Duke of Newcastle in liking

Spanish horses best, and they were popular in England. Don Diego Salgado speaks of them, in a book dedicated to our Charles II., as 'incomparably nimble and pretty.' The Spaniard, till, say, 1650 or so, was probably the best animal to go hunting on. But there are now, and were then, Spaniards and Spaniards. In spite of the sprightly ballotade he is throwing, I never quite liked the shoulders of the animal the magnificent Olivarez is riding so bravely in the great Velasquez at Madrid; but Olivarez evidently rode a great weight, and so had to ride the wrong class of Spaniard. We may feel certain that Rosinante had plenty of quality, for Don Quixote tells Sancho that you can always recognise a gentleman by the smoothness of his seat. This rather formidable and arbitrary formula depends at least as much on the breeding of the horse as on the gentility of the man. It is a Quixotic and therefore attractive way of saying that well-bred people insisted on well-bred horses. They always should. Cumberland remarks that there seems a pleonasm in the manes and tails of Velasquez' horses. There is certainly a want of shoulders; but Sir W. Stirling Maxwell points out that Velasquez was an Andalusian who painted according to the ideas of Andalusia, not of Newmarket; and, speaking of the equestrian portraits of Philip IV. and Olivarez, he goes on to say that they enable us to judge accurately of the Spanish horse of the seventeenth century.

> The bounding steeds they pompously bestride,
> Share with their lords the pleasure and the pride.
>
> (*Anec.* vol. ii. p. 15.)

Odd colours were at this time in great favour: and the old strain of piebalds and skewbalds still flourishes in Holland. Utrecht Fair, held on Easter Monday, is the great market for them, and a great many come over here. They have many merits, and make capital coach-horses. 'Soupe de lait,' a sort of cream colour, 'Tigré' (fleabitten) and 'porcelaine' were colours in great request. Louis XIV. himself always rode a pied horse on parade or at state ceremonies, and would give a high price for a really conspicuous charger.

M. Bocher speaks of the system of Haras instituted by Colbert being maintained with a high hand ('puissamment') for over a century. Louis XIV. certainly liked having things his own way. Yet the measures taken do not appear to have effected the objects in view. They failed most conspicuously in making France independent of the foreign supply. In 1717 a State paper,[1] after a sonorous prelude to the effect that a supply of horses sufficient for all its wants is the chief wealth and honour of a well-governed State, gives practical reasons for further subsidies to the State Haras. The public service, runs the text, is still far from being self-supporting; 'l'on s'est vu réduit à traiter l'argent à la main avec des marchands Juifs pour tous les besoins de la cavalerie, des dragons, de l'artillerie et même de la maison du roi.'

If the Jews acted as middlemen, I dare say the needs of the public service were much better supplied in this way than by the mismanaged Haras, although the objection taken to the ready-money element by the M. de Calonne type of Finance Minister is easily understood. But 'Juifs' here may only mean exorbitant. Fond as they are of horses and of riding, I do not think the Jews of Europe have ever seriously turned their gifted attention to horse-dealing. At the same time, it was a Jew who sold Ivanhoe the black horse he did so well with at Ashby-de-la-Zouch. Sir Walter Scott would never have got the horse into Isaac of York's hands unless he had some historical authority.

In 1790, State-aided horse-breeding as organised by Sully and Colbert was done away with. It was swept away in the catastrophe of institutions, and I imagine it had altogether failed to justify its existence. Besides, to be powerless for

[1] 'Mémoire du Conseil en dedans du Royaume.'

good at that time in France often meant the same as being powerful for mischief, and the Haras system was rife with abuses. The Haras du Roi, which were in theory, at all events, the equivalent of the present well-managed stallion depôts, should have done well enough. Perhaps they even tried to do well: at all events, Arthur Young,[1] who visited Pompadour, makes no direct charge against them. So might the Haras maintained by great noblemen, like the Haras de Chambord and of Rocroy, which professed to be as advantageously at the service of the public as the State establishments. Their regulations and conditions of service seem reasonable and well considered. But the 'approuvé' stallion played the deuce with everything—that is, the stallion owned by a private gentleman and subsidised by the State on prescribed conditions of standard and service had become an intolerable burden and abuse. The conditions were only nominal—a mere question of filling in forms and affixing a signature. The advantages to the stallion owner, on the other hand, were distinctly real. The owner of an 'approuvé' or, as he was styled, a 'garde-étalon,' became at once entitled to considerable remissions of direct and indirect taxation, and to complete exemption from local rates. It will be admitted, particularly in these days of agricultural depression, that these were temptations not likely to be easily resisted.

All the collaterals of the nobles, as well as the nobles

[1] Speaking of the Pompadour Haras, A. Young says: 'There are all kinds of horses, but chiefly Arabian, Turkish, and English. Three years ago four Arabians were imported which had been procured at the expense of 72,000 louis [£3,149]. The price of serving a mare is only three louis to the groom. The owners are permitted to sell their colts as they please, but if these come up to the standard height, the King's officers have the preference, provided they give the price offered by others.' He goes on to say that all the horses had to be taken up at night on account of wolves, which were so common about Pompadour as to be a plague to everybody. On the other hand, he had a very poor opinion of the Chambord Haras—he speaks of it as an extravagant and wretched concern, with 'not a tendency but to mischief.'

themselves, owned stallions, and thereby shifted their rates and taxes in a seemly way to other people's shoulders. The effect of the operation is put by M. De la Font Pouloti in a way which most ratepayers will appreciate, without much knowledge of French or of the incidence of taxation. 'Les privilèges et exemptions des Garde-Étalons sont très onéreux aux communautés, parce qu'étant presque toujours des grands propriétaires, le rejet de leurs impositions sur les autres contribuables cause une augmentation considérable en retombant sur le peuple.'

This was in 1789. No fewer than 3,300 stallions were registered, yet horse-breeding for many years prior to that date had been in a languishing condition. The whole system was a whited sepulchre. Production annually decreased, yet the 'approuvés' and 'garde-étalons' annually multiplied. Every day, too, some fresh and vexatious restriction upon private enterprise came to the further assistance of the 'garde-étalon.' Cunningly drawn regulations, police supervision, pains and penalties denied to private enterprise the bare necessities of life. It is neither to be wondered at nor regretted that this 'ensemble de privilèges et de rigueurs,' again to quote M. Bocher's eloquent Report, received short shrift at the hands of the statesmen and economists of the Revolution.

However, the horse-supply question soon thrust itself again upon the attention of statesmen. The Haras and the gardé-etalons had been got rid of, but the practical difficulty of working up a supply of useful horses to an increasing demand still remained. In the year X. of the Republic, Huzard, in a minute printed and circulated by order of the Minister of the Interior, again calls attention to the decadence of the ancient French breeds. Maledon, in 1803,[1] holds much the same language, but decorates it with poignant

[1] *Réflexions sur la Réorganisation des Haras*, par M. de Maledon, Paris, 1803.

sentiment. He laments the Limousin in quite a brokenhearted strain. 'Le cœur saigne quand on pense qu'elle n'existe plus que dans quelques rejetons çà et là,' and, with a burst of patriotism which is worthy of M. Le Jeune, he goes on to declare that no country in the world can lay claim to a breed equal to the Limousin, or worthy to be compared to it for quality, stamina and good looks.

Something had to be done, and in 1806 there was a man at the head of affairs quite able to do it. That year Napoleon insisted upon the importation of a large number of Mecklenburg, Hessian, and Baden horses. This recollection was the only thing, indeed, which reconciled me for the moment to the Prussian I had to mount in front of the Cour des Adieux, and in view of the long windows of the room in which he signed his abdication a very few years later. The direct and personal interest which the Emperor (who knew little about horses, and was a bad rider) took in the horse question was from the military, or, rather, the national point of view. National, that is, in the best sense. His despatches abound in special instructions to his cavalry generals to make the most of their horses; to Murat especially, who had Rupert-like conceptions of possibilities and functions of cavalry, and the waste of horseflesh in his campaigns was enormous. But the industrial requirements of the country were evidently also present to him when, in 1806, he appointed and drew the instructions of a Commission to investigate and report upon the alleged scarcity of serviceable horses, the extinction of the ancient strains, and the best means of reconstructing a State system of horse-breeding.

It is not my intention to pursue the more modern history of State-aided horse-breeding any further. Suffice it to say that the recommendations of the Report of 1806 were given effect to, that they were amplified in 1815, and again in 1820. Between the year 1830 and the year 1863, when the

Haras system was demolished almost as ruthlessly as in 1790, horse-breeding had a good deal to put up with. According to the Bocher Report, it suffered many things from incessant changes of Government, from the freaks of departmental administration, and from the absence of any continuity of policy. At one time its affairs were committed to the Beaux-Arts, at another to the Minister of 'Marine.'

In 1874 there was another reconstruction based upon the Report of the Bocher Commission; and the troop-horse at Châlons or Saumur to-day is the best test which can be applied to the soundness of the conclusions then affirmed, and given effect to by the 'Loi des Haras' of 1874. He stands it well. It might not do to ask what he now costs or has cost the country to bring to good effect since Louis XIII. instituted a State Haras. But there he is, 'Per varios casus et tot certamina rerum,' a very different animal to the 'Cheval Normand' of Lord Malmesbury's good story.[1] At the same time, I should not say that any of the cavalry horses I saw out hunting were quite up to the best mark of picked troop-horses from the ranks of a crack light cavalry regiment. The conditions of modern warfare have taught

---

[1] 'In 1829, he [Louis Napoleon] used to have several old officers of his uncle, the emperor, about him—men who seemed to me to be ready for anything. I recollect one, an old cavalry officer, who had seen the whole Peninsular war, relating the following anecdote. One day he was reconnoitring with three or four troopers when they came suddenly upon a young English officer, mounted on a superb thoroughbred horse and similarly occupied. Summoned by the colonel to surrender he quietly cantered away, laughing in the Frenchman's face. The dragoon pursued at full gallop of his heavy steed, and when the Englishman had allowed him to get quite close he kissed his hand, and leaving him behind, shouted, pointing to his horse, "Cheval Normand, monsieur." Again the Frenchman pursued, threatening to shoot his enemy if he did not surrender, and pointed his pistol at him, but the weapon missed fire. With a roar of laughter, the young officer shouted again, "Fabrique de Versailles, monsieur," and giving the thoroughbred his head, was seen no more. It was most amusing to hear the old colonel tell this story and describe his rage, adding, however, that he had always felt glad that he had not shot "ce brave farceur."'

us that a cavalry horse can hardly be too good an animal.
It is true that he has not to jump fences, but he has to carry
a weight which from a hunting point of view would be
restrictive; and he must possess all the qualities of a fourteen-
stone grass-country hunter, blood, bone, stoutness, action,
and no lumber. To manage his job at all he must be able,
as dealers say, 'to move himself.' Breechloaders have done
away with the shock action of cavalry and the corresponding
advantages of heavy impetus. Job's war-horse, his neck
clothed with thunder, is as much a thing of the past as
the shouting captains he either carried or unhorsed. Lord
Cardigan led the Light Brigade up the Valley of Death on a
chestnut horse which had often cut out the work amongst
the strongly-fenced enclosures of Northamptonshire, and a
hunting man could pick a stud of horses out of, say, any two
squadrons of any Dragoon or Hussar regiment now stationed
at Aldershot, which he might take down to Tarporley or
Market Harborough without any hesitation as regards looks,
quality, or action. I am not sure that he could quite do this
from the troop stables at Châlons, but I should consider the
horses I saw quite up to the average animal. With one or
two favourable exceptions, like the shifty, long-tailed chestnut I mentioned before, they were all of the same type and
class, and there appears to be a reliable supply of well-bred,
native-born horses, with plenty of scope and quality, good
legs and feet, and particularly good backs and middle pieces.
Shoulders throughout perhaps left a little to be desired.
They often do. Indeed, they were so much of one model
that Géricault and Rosa Bonheur, Fromentin and Meissonier
might perhaps complain of individual character being too
much merged in a general type: but I imagine the French
cavalry horse is a better animal now than he has ever been,
and that he would go faster, carry more weight, and stand
the strain of a campaign very much better than the under-

sized Arabs so much esteemed before the war of 1870, or the plain-headed trooper M. Detaille draws so admirably.

I really think the nicest horse I saw in France—not excepting the one I rode at Chantilly, which had won in a strong four-year-old class at Dublin—was a French-bred horse. He was the property of a M. Kulb, with whom I rode home three or four miles after my day with the Halatte hounds to a village called Fleuriner, where a most excellent refection was laid out for ' messieurs et mesdames les chasseurs,' hot spiced claret and noble baked apples being novel and attractive features of our entertainment. This was a bright chestnut horse, a little on the leggy side, perhaps, but aristocratic and mettled enough for the Quorn Hunt stables under their present sumptuous régime, or to head the Royal Procession at Ascot races. M. Kulb told me that ' fond ' was the prime essential of a French hunter. I do not suppose this can be translated by what we mean by staying power—that can only be tested by having to go fast—but rather by cheerful resistance to long dragging days on springless sand, which must often be very dull for the horses. You do not have to go fast with French woodland packs. Most of the hunt horses I saw must have been as slow as tops. Hurvari, as I have said, trotted about to his hounds. Unless you happen to make a mistake or get into the open, a slow canter with the eye cast well forward, to see if the deer crosses, keeps you comfortably abreast of the leading hounds. And I was hunting with the fast packs. The hounds of the Saintonge, or the Vendéan, or the Bleu Gascon breed walk their deer to death. M. de Carayon Lacour's beautiful pack, which I should much like to have seen, take five or six hours to bay their stag. A good walker, says M. Le Jeune, can keep up with them.

In France the field do not, in our sense, compete. The huntsman or the master sets the pace, usually at a Rotten Row canter, and the field in Indian file or here and there in sociable couples follow suit. The only time I saw a hunt-servant really gallop he did so very much in spite of himself. I suppose the man had got thrown out, and was rejoining us from the rear. The procession was at the time ambling along a narrowish alley, conforming to the painstaking operations of Hannibal and Nicanor on our right flank, when the chestnut horse he was riding took matters into his hands and came through us like a shot out of a bow. Fortunately we were warned of his irresistible approach by the lusty shouts of the rider. We found him at the next carrefour, mopping the honest sweat from his brow, and well satisfied with his adventure.

An open galloping country makes a fast horse, and a fast horse makes a fast hound. We have only to look at Stubbs's and Wootton's and Seymour's pictures [1] to see that our fast half-bred horse had at least a century's start of the same animal in France. The fox-hunting gentry, like the Osbaldistones in 'Rob Roy,' rode galloping horses long before this class of animal was realised in France, which is only quite lately. But the French—witness the cavalry horses I have just been speaking about, and M. Kulb's conspicuous chestnut—are quickly making up for lost time.

[1] I have two or three pictures at Gisburne of members of my family on horseback, coursing and hunting, painted about 1720 or so. The horses are exceedingly well bred and full of character, but narrowish and not up to more than twelve stone. They *all* show much more Eastern blood in their heads—the bump on the forehead, the full eye, which we only find here and there in an individual now. They were, of course, much nearer the blends of Arab and Arabian blood to which we are indebted for everything we prize most in horseflesh. J. Ward's best horses are quite a different stamp. By that time we had somehow or other got more substance and size into our breed.

BUT I must get back to England and to Berkshire from my agreeable wanderings across the Channel, and so, as far as these pages are concerned, I will take my leave of the Queen's Hounds, and of Her Majesty's lieges who ride to them. I feel certain that fine runs, a hard-going tireless pack, and—best of all—the old names year after year in the deer-paddock, will continue to do credit to the keenness and experience of the Queen's Huntsman and to the smartness and competence of the whole staff. Nor can I pass by this opportunity of especially thanking the landowners and tenant-farmers of Berkshire and Buckinghamshire, for their unvarying generosity and goodwill. I bade them all good-bye with sorrow in the summer of 1895. Now that I have finished this book, in the same month of June, 1897, and within a week of the same day, I wish them all prosperity, not only on my own behalf, but for the sake of my companions, who, in an unbroken succession, have held the office of Master of the Buckhounds from the reign of Edward III. until this great and acceptable year of grace, and thankfulness, and Jubilee.

APPENDIX

LIST OF MEETING PLACES OF ROYAL HUNT
(See Map)

Berks

1. Maidenhead Thicket.
2. Brick Bridge.
3. Twyford Station (G.W.R.)
4. White Waltham.
5. Shottesbrook Farm and Park.
6. Hawthorn Hill.
7. New Lodge.
8. Warren House.
9. Dinfield.
10. Warfield.
11. White Hart, Winkfield.
12. Ascot Heath.
13. Bracknell.
14. Wokingham.
15. Swinley.
16. King's Beech.
17. South Hill Gate.
18. Cricketers Inn (Bagshot).

Bucks

19. High Wycombe.
20. Holtspur Heath.
21. Beaconsfield.
22. Gerrard's Cross.
23. Red Hill.
24. Denham.
25. Chalfont St. Peter's.
26. Great Marlow.
27. Wooburn Green.
28. Farnham Common.
29. Farnham Royal.
30. Stoke Common.
31. Iver Heath.
32. Two-Mile Brook.
33. Salt Hill.
34. Slough Station (G.W.R.)
35. Langley Broom.
36. Horton Manor House.
37. Richings Park.

Middlesex

38. Uxbridge.
39. Harefield.

Surrey

40. Sunningdale Station (L. & S.-W.R.)
41. Broomhill Hut.
42. Chobham.
43. Woking Station (L. & S.-W.R.)

Hampshire

44. Yateley Green.

INDEX

Adair, Mr., 27
Addison, 11
Adolphus, Prince, 41
Agundo, M. M., 261, 288
Aldershot Common, 65
Alfonso XI. of Castile, 7, 8
Althorp, Lord, 36
Amboise conspiracy, 246, 247
Ambroise Paré, 249
Anderson, horse-dealer, 67 n, 79, 242
Anet, Diane de Poitiers' estate, 244
Anne, Princess, 234
Anne, Queen, 33, 200
Arabian horses imported into France, 295
Aragon, King of, 250
Army riding in England and France, 284-286, 289
Arnold ('Budge'), 144; his death, 145 n
Arscott of Tedcott, his famous foxhunt, 120 n
Ascot Heath and Course, 39, 70, 78, 108, 156, 158; the position of its stands, 213-218; names of stands, 214; and races, 216; soil and turf, 218; the responsibilities of the M.B.H. at, 219, 220; a curious incident there, 221, 222
Ascot Kennel, 48, 49, 118, 123, 139, 140; established by Queen Anne, 201; kennel lameness at, 201, 202; its cure, 202; description and plans of the establishment, 202, 203; the Queen's visit to, 203
Ashburton, Lord, 97

Baden horse in France, 297
Badminton, 32

Bagot, Colonel Josceline, 232
Baillie, Billie, 147
'Baily's Magazine,' 60 n, 71, 77, 238
Bapst, M., 227
Barbs, 292
Barraud, 70, 71
Barry, Mr., 121 n
Barrymore, Lord ('Hellgate'), 49
Bartlett, George, 56, 60
Bartlett, Robert, 97, 132
Bartlett, William, 172, 198, 201, 202
Batchelor, valet to George IV., 51
Bateman, Lord, Master of the Buckhounds, 237
Beaconsfield, Lord. See Disraeli, Mr.
Béarn, Vicomtes de, 5
Beaufort, Duke of, 70, 98 n, 207
Beaufort, François de, 254
Beaurepaire, 3, 10, 18, 21
Beers, Frank, 76
Belle Croix, 282
Bellingham, Mr., 233
Belvoir, 32
Bentinck, Lord George, 224 n
Bentinck, Lord Henry, 140
Beresford, Lord Bill, 151
Berkeley, Lord, 32, 154 n, 230
Berkshire, as a hunting country, 175, 183, 209, 302
Bessborough, Lord, Master of the Buckhounds, 143, 223 n, 240
Billesden Coplow run, 180
Billingbear, meet at, 41
Blessington, Lady, 226
Bleu Gascon hounds, 300
Blunt, Miss Martha, 42
Bocase stone and tree, 14

x

Bocher, M. Edouard, 291, 294, 296, 298
Boleyn, Anne, 222, 227, 229
Boleyn, George. *See* Rochford, Lord
Boleyn, Mary, 227
Boleyn, Sir Thomas, 227
Bonheur, Rosa, 299
Borhunte, Sir John de. 10, 11
Borhunte, Mary de. *See* Roches, Mary
Borhunte, Thomas de, 11, 15
Bourbon, Anne of, 252
Bracknell country, 64, 65
Bramshill hounds, 225
Brantôme, 249
Bretigny, Peace of, 7
Brighton, George IV. and, 200, 201
Broad Moor, 65
Brocas family and the hereditary mastership, 1
Brocas, Comte de, 4 n
Brocas, Ann, 12
Brocas, Anne, 18
Brocas, Bernard, 18
Brocas, Sir Bernard, 1, 3, 4, 8, 9, 13, 20, 23, 222, 229
Brocas, Sir Bernard, (II.) 9, 12, 17
Brocas, Edith, 12, 18
Brocas, John, 12
Brocas, John (II.) 12
Brocas, Sir John de, 3, 6, 7
Brocas, Sir Oliver, 7
Brocas, Sir Peter Arnald de, 5
Brocas, Sir Pexall, 12, 19, 20
Brocas, Thomas, 12, 21
Brocas, William (I.) 12, 16
Brocas, William (II.) 12
Brocas, William (III.) 12
Brocas Chantry, 1, 10
Brocas College, 19
'Brocas March,' the, 4
Brocklesby, 32
Bromley Davenport, Mr., 175
Brown (of the Old Berkshire), 199
Browning, Mr., 250 n
Brummell, Beau, 224 n
Brunswick, Duke of, 59 n
Bryant, Charles, 211, 212
Buckhounds, Royal; hereditary masters: the Brocas family, 1-21; Mr. Hore's history of, 3; list of the hereditary masters, 11, 12; during the Georgian period, 22-57; lemon-pye v. tan, 56, 57; Davis's, management of, 59-81; the question of their retention, 82-91; masters of, 222-243
Buckinghamshire, hunting in, 172-175, 183, 208, 209, 302

Budé, his treatise on Vénerie, 245
Burghersh, Sir Bartholomew, 8
Burgundy, Duke of, 251, 253, 288
Burke, his letters, 36
Burrows, Mr. Edward, his story of the hereditary masters, 1-21, 23
Burrows, Captain Montagu, his 'Brocas Family,' 1 n, 222
Buscott Reservoir, 198
Butler, Rev. William, and George IV., 52
Butt-Miller, Mr., 131
Byron, Lord, 226, 263

CANNING, LORD, 69
Canterbury, Archbishop of (Dr. Temple), 88, 210
Canterbury, Archbishop of (Matthew Parker), and Lord Leicester, 230, 231
Cardigan, Lord, 69
Carlyle, Mr., as a horseman, 227
Caroline, Queen, 27, 38, 39
Carrington, Lord, 127
Carter, George, 137
Castelnau, his letter to Henry III., 229
Cato, the Prince of Wales's black boy, 49
Cattistock country, 182
Cavalle, on the hunting expenses of François I., 246
Chabot, M. de, 271
Chalon, picture by, 121
Châlons troop stables, 298, 299
Chambord, Haras at, 295, 295 n
Chandos, the Duke of, 155
Chandos, Sir John, 250
Chantilly, 30, 266, 269, 273, 276, 277
Chantonnay, 246, 247
Chapman, Mr., 170, 171
Charles I., 27
Charles II., hunting reminiscences of, 20, 206, 232, 233
Charles III. of Burgundy, 254
Charles IX. of France, 248-250, 292
Charles X. of France, 225
Charles XII. of Sweden, 250 n
Charles the Bold, 247
Charlotte, Queen, 46
Charlton run, 48, 121, 121 n
Charnizay, M. de, 291
Chartres, Duc de (Philippe Égalité), 54, 149, 266, 269
Chéruel, quoted, 230

Chesterfield, Lord, the celebrated, 34, 35, 49
Chesterfield, Lord, Master of the Buckhounds, 238, 239
Chezelles, M., 270
Chiflinch, James H.'s letter to, 233
Chillingham deer, 107
Christian, Dick, 18, 169, 182, 239
Christinu, H.R.H. Prince, 216
Chute, Mr., his hounds, 225, 226
Clanricarde, Lord, 240
Clark, Rev. C. (' the Gentleman in Black '), 71
Clement, Major, 218, 219
Clergyman, hunting, 173, 174
Clergymen, hunting in France, 253, 254
Clermont, Lady, 54 n
Cleveland, Duke of, 174
Clewer-Brocas, 1
Clisson, Oliver de, 8
Coaches, the introduction of, 291 n
Cobden, Mr., tailor to George IV., 55 n, 56 n
Colbert, institutes the system of horse-breeding in France, 294
Collyns, Dr., 115, 120
Colson, Walter, 153
Colville, Lord, 147-149, 207
Comins, the Queen's Huntsman, 140 n, 167
Common hunt, the, 29, 30
Compton, Mr., 69
Connaught, Duke of, 96, 156
Conyngham, Lady, 52
Conyngham, Lord Albert, 50
Cook, Captain, 164
Cope, Sir John, 65, 162, 223
Cordery, Mr., 63, 63 n, 65, 163
Cork, Lord, Master of the Buckhounds, 112, 134, 143, 145, 147, 149, 151, 185, 199, 202, 238
Cornwallis, Lord, Master of the Buckhounds, 237
Cosmo I. de Medicis, Grand Duke, 245, 246
Costumes, hunting, 156, 157, 288
Courtaults, 292
Couteulx, M. de, 273
Coventry, Lord, Master of the Buckhounds, 32 n, 83, 156, 243
Coverley, Sir Roger de, 11
Cox, Mr. F., 151
Crane, Will, 121 n
Crecy, 3, 7, 8
Crichel, George IV. at, 52
Croft, Dr., his hunting reminiscences, 59, 63, 72, 79, 101, 171, 239, 240, 243

Cumberland, Duke of (Ernest), 53, 51
Cumberland, Duke of, 237
Cumberland, on Velasquez' pictures, 293
Cumberland Lodge, stabling and stud-grooms at, 202, 204-207, 209-212
Cuttenden, Mr., 30

D'ALBRET, 5
Daniel, his ' Rural Sports,' 118
Danvers, William, 11
Darby, Mr., 122 n
d'Argenson, Marquis, 54
d'Aumale, Duc, 139, 252, 282
Davis, Charles, and the new school of stag-hunting, 48, 50, 55-58; description of, 59; adopts hunting as a profession, 60; letter to Sir John Halkett, 62, 63; Dr. Croft on, 63; Mr. Cordery on, 65; some of his experiences as a Queen's Huntsman, 66 n, 67; Mr. Bowen May and, 67; Colonel Thomson and, 68; 'Æsop's' anecdote concerning, 70; pictures and engravings of, 70, 71; memoir of, in ' Baily's Magazine,' 71, 72; personal appearance and dress, 72; his abstemiousness, 73; disapproval of ladies in the hunting-field, 73; as a disciplinarian, 73, 74; his racing tastes, 74; as a huntsman and horseman, 75-80; private character, 80, 81; other hunting reminiscences of, 92, 100, 101, 121, 131, 132, 147, 148, 150, 160, 168, 171, 200 n, 201, 202, 238, 239, 264, 268
Deer, things necessary for a successful run, 92; scent and country, 92; methods of noted deer, 92-98, 101, 102, 108, 109; the 'run' the true sport, 98, 99; not to be hunted like a fox, 99; management of deer, 101; tricky deer and how to manage them, 101-104; when hounds fail to realise deer, 103, 104; wet ditches and water-meadows spoil sport, 105; young deer, 105, 106; the Swinley herd, 106; breed, situation, and other influences on deer, 107, 108; lying out and its effects, 109; some master deer and their exploits, 109, 110; liking for society, 110, 111; luxurious life at Swinley; the paddock staff, 111-113; exercise, 113

Deer, noted:
  Bartlett, 93-96, 107 n, 110, 112, 188
  Blackback, 96-98, 110, 194, 198, 199
  Bramshill, 173
  Compton, 39, 45
  Guy Fawkes, 102, 110, 186, 188
  Harkaway, 112
  Hawthorn, 108
  Hide and Seek, 162
  Highflyer, 45
  Highlander, 134
  Lord Clanwilliam, 100, 108-110
  Miss Headington, 154
  Moonshine, 45, 46
  Princess, 98 n
  Richmond Trump, 67, 68
  Runaway, 110
  Sepoy, 93
  Starlight, 45
  Sulky, 102
  The Miller, 100
  Winchelsea, 103
De la Font Pouloti, M., 296
De la Rue, M., 264
Deloraine, Lady, 27
Derby, Lord, 63
Dessy, the trainer, 77
Detaille, M., 300
Devon and Somerset (Old) Staghounds, 116, 122, 123
d'Humières, M., 247
Dillon, Abbé, on hunting, 253
Disraeli, Mr, 36, 227, 242, 279, 280
Dixon, Mr. Hepworth, 228
Dom Miguel, 224 n
Don John of Austria, 292
Donovan, Mr. T., 108
D'Orsay, Count, 226, 238, 239
Drake, Rev. Mr., 173, 174
'Druid,' the, 44, 48, 77, 79, 93, 107, 183
Dufferin, Lord, 60 n
Du Fouilloux, 111 n, 249, 253
Duhallow hunt, 243
D'Urfey, 29
D'Yauville's works on Vénerie, 253

EDWARD II. and the Brocas family, 2, 4 n, 5
Edward III., 2-8, 23, 302
Edward the Black Prince, 8, 9, 10
Edwards, the trainer and jockey, 74
Egham Heath, meet at, 73
Egremont, Lord, 60
Eleanor of Guienne, 4

Elizabeth, Queen, hunting reminiscences of, 18, 19, 21, 29, 229-232, 248, 291 n
Emerson, Mr., 72
Enclosures Acts, their effects on stag-hunting, 23
English horse in France, 295 n
English hounds, 270, 271
Enguerrand, 260
Epping Forest Hounds, 48, 122 n, 130
Eton College, 3
Evelyn, 232
Exmoor deer, 111

FERNELEY, his pictures, 32
Featherstonhaugh, Sir H., 77 n
Feuillet, M. Octave, 279
'Field,' the, 156
'Finsch, Ned,' 24
Firr, 150
Fitt, Mr., his 'Covert-side Sketches,' 116, 121
Fitzhardinge, Lord, 30
Fitzherbert, Mrs., 52
Flambeau, 260, 261
Fontainebleau, 30, 265, 266, 284, 286
Forest, the, and forest hunting, preliminaries of a day's hunting, 158; characteristics of, 158-160; Charles Kingsley and, 160-165; 'Nimrod' on Sir John Cope's country, 162; difficulties of riding forest run, 165-167; hounds and horses in the forest, 167-171
Fowle, Rev. Mr., George III. and, 173
Fox, Charles James, 52
Fox-hounds and fox-hunting, 32, 92, 93, 99, 101, 119, 121, 131, 132, 137, 155, 163, 164, 167, 188
France, England's relations with, in 1734, 38; hunting costume of the Second Empire, 44; the English hound in, 117, 130; the Duke of Wellington hunting in, 225; stag-hunting in, in the sixteenth century, 244; during François I.'s reign, 244-246; in the time of François II., 246-249; and Charles IX., 248-250; hound-breeding in France, 251, 252; French books on Vénerie, 252 n, 253 n; M. de Ligniville, 253-257; changes since the taking of the Bastille, 257; a few days' hunting around Paris, 258-277; horseman-

ship in France, 278-289; and horses, 290-301; modern hunting in, 300, 301
François I., his Court. 241-246
François II. and the Guises. 246, 248, 292
Freeman, Professor. 88
Freeman, J., whip to Queen's hounds, 102, 200 n. 240
Freeman, Luke, 60
French horsemanship. 278; the French novel on, 279. 280; Hurvari at work, 281-284; military schools of instruction in riding, 284-287; secularised French riding, 287-289
French horses, M. le Jeune and M. Ed. Bocher on, 290-292, 296; English hackney and hunting horses used by Louis XIV. and XV., 292; State-aided horse-breeding in France, 292-298; the modern cavalry horse, 299; M. Kulb on French hunters, 300
French hounds, 251, 267, 268, 270
Froissart, quoted, 5
Fromentin, 299
Froude, Rev. John, 123

GAINSBOROUGH, painter, 28
Gallifet, General de, 284
Garth, Mr., 163, 165, 223
Garton, Thomas de, 7
Gaston, the Seneschal de, 252
Gates, Mr., 77
Gaucher, High Almoner, 250
George I., characteristics and reminiscences of, 23-25, 33
George II., reminiscences of, 25-27, 31, 33, 38, 39, 53, 121
George III., reminiscences of, 23, 35, 39, 43-45, 48-50, 60, 63, 116, 117, 123, 130, 251
George IV., reminiscences of, 42, 48-52, 200, 224 n
Georgian stag-hunting. See Stag-hunting
Géricault, 299
Gilbert, Miss, 73
Gilbey, Sir Walter, 49 n
Gladstone, Mr., 82, 102 n, 227, 250 n
Göhrde, his picture, 24
Goldsmith, Mr., of Kemble, 195
Goodall, Frank, 57, 72, 149, 150, 151, 153, 154, 202, 203.
Goodall, Stephen, 51 n
Goodall, William, 135
Goodrich, Sir Harry, 122

Goodwood, 32
Goodwood hounds. 48, 49
Gordon Boys' Home, 160
Gosden (yeoman pricker), 40
Gould, Mr. Baring, 120 n
Grafton, Duke of, 26, 32, 44, 54, 180
Graham, Sir Bellingham, 171, 178
Graham, Miss Catherine, 235
Graham, Colonel James, Master of Charles II.'s Buckhounds, 232-235
Granby, Marquis of, 95
Grant, Sir F., 78, 156, 158
Grantham, Lord, 38
Granvelle, Cardinal de, Chantonnay's letter to, 247
Granville, Lord, reminiscences of, 68 n. 69, 71, 83 n, 222, 223 n, 240-243
Great Western Railway Company, 190
Green, Mr. J. R., on George I., 25
Grenville, Lord, 44
Greville, Mr. Charles, 51, 54, 237
Gronow, Baron, 51
Guest, Mr. Merthyr, 128
Guildford stud, 6
Guilford, Lord, 182
Guise, Ducs de, 246, 288, 292
Gwyn, Colonel, 45

HALATTE, hunting at, 265, 266, 268, 277, 300
Halkett, Sir Arthur, 63 n, 74
Halkett, Sir John, 60, 74, 201
Hall, Bishop, 291 n
Hamilton, Duke of, 234
Hampshire Hunt, the, 52
Hampton Court stud, 24 n, 25 n, 58
Haras system in France, 294-298
Hardwicke, Lord, Master of the Buckhounds, 151 n, 154, 243
Hare-hunting in the Georgian times, 32
Hargreaves, Mr. John, 165 n
Harriers, Royal, 59
Harrow country, its departed glories, 142; reasons for its decline discussed, 143; jumping parties from Harrow School, 144, 145; hunting during Lord Cork's mastership, 145, 147, 149, 151-153; Mr. Higgins's account of a run in the forties, 146, 147; Lord Colville overcomes difficulties, 147, 148; his experiences in 1867 and 1868, 149, 150; Frank Goodall's testimony, 149, 153-155; effect of railways on hunting, 155, 156; the

question of costume, 156, 157; a
  foggy day in, 189-193
Harry's Wood, 13
Harvey, Queen's huntsman, 89, 138,
  139, 166, 173, 195, 197, 203
Harwood, Sir E., 291 n
Hayman's Lodge, 205
Hemans, Mrs., 111
Henri II. of France, 247, 248
Henri III. of France, 229, 288
Henri IV. of France, 249, 254
Henry I., 29
Henry II., 12
Henry IV., 17, 229
Henry VI., 18
Henry VIII., 18, 20, 227-229
Hervey, Lord, 26, 31, 37-39, 53
Hessian horse in France, 297
Heysham, Mr. F. ('Æsop'), 52 n, 57,
  70
Higgins, Mr., 146
Hoare, Charles, 179
Holland, Robert, 8
Hollande, Comtesse de, 9 n
Holroyd, Miss Maria, cited, 36
Holtspur Heath, 209
Holyrood Day, 41
Hompesch, Baron de, Master of
  William III.'s Buckhounds, 234
Hoppner, his pictures, 53
Horace, 192
Hore, Mr. J. P., his history of the
  Royal Buckhounds, 3, 22, 23, 26,
  27, 30, 49 n, 235 n
Horse, the cream, 24, 25
Horse-breeding, State-aided in France,
  294-298
Horses and forest-hunting, 169-171;
  thoroughbreds as hunters, 183, 184,
Horses, noted hunting and other:—
  Agitator, 169, 192, 193
  Bayard, 7
  Black Bess, 182
  Cardinal, 150, 151 n, 154
  Catalina, 261
  Chance, 203, 208
  Charlie, 207
  Clipper, 67
  Columbine, 70, 75
  Countess, 154
  Crusader, 150, 151 n
  Curricle, 51
  Dartmoor, 124
  Dunce, 154
  Firefly, 207
  Hermit, 70, 75-79
  Hobby, 43
  Lanercost, 102

Horses—cont.
  Lebryt, 7
  Lockington, 207
  Lottery, 80
  Mignonne, 260
  Milkmaid, 173
  Norman, 151 n
  Paddy, 207, 208
  Perfection, 43
  Pomers, 7
  Q. C., 207
  Radical, 181, 182
  Rib, 121 n
  Romeo, 195
  Rosslyn, 154, 203
  Rural Dean, 207
  Stag, 128
  Thornton, 207
  Tiger, 53
  Tobacco Stopper, 53
  White Boy, 154
  William, 94, 140, 169, 196, 198, 199
Houdemarre, Baron, 105
Hounds, French and English, 267,
  268, 270, 271, 273, 274
Hounds, noted, and other dogs:—
  Baudé, 252
  Byron, 280
  Cardigan, 137
  Charlie, 113
  Cheerful, 103, 104
  Dash, 122
  Falkland, 105, 139
  Ganymede, 201
  Garland, 134
  Glory, 134
  Grellier, 122
  Hercules, 164
  Hotspur, 166
  Luxury, 118, 118 n
  Merkin, 118, 121, 122
  Minos, 56
  Mouille, 254, 255
  Nellie, 139
  Nemesis, 140
  Norman, 151 n
  Notion, 104, 198
  Needful, 94
  Remus, 137
  Rhapsody, 133
  Rhetoric, 118, 119, 133
  Shot, 122
  Souillard, 251, 252
  Splendour, 172
  Wellington, 94
  Windsor, 116, 121
  Woodman, 139
Howard, Miss Dorothy, 232

Huish, cited, 55
Hunter's Coppice, 13
Hunter's Manor, 10-13, 15
Hurvari, Duc d'Aumale's huntsman, 282, 283, 300
Huzard on horse-breeding in France, 296

ISLE OF WIGHT, 139
Islington fields, hunting in, 29

'JACOB OMNIUM,' 30
James I., 19, 21
James II., 200, 232-234
Jenison, Mr. Ralph, Master of the Buckhounds, 27, 44, 121, 237
Jerningham, Lady, cited, 53
Jersey, Lady, 52
Jersey, Lord, Master of the Buckhounds, 74, 237
Jews as horse-dealers, 294
Jockey Club and the Hampton Court stud, 58; and the stands at Ascot, 214-216
John, King of France, 8, 250
Johns, Rev. C. A., 160, 161
Johnson, Dr., on Sir Joshua Reynolds, 28 n; 37, 56 n
Johnson (the King's huntsman), 39, 40
Joinville, Prince de, 266
Jowett, Dr., 22

KEMPSHOT, George IV. at, 51, 52, 57
Kendal, Duchess of, 24
Kennel lameness, 200
Kennels, at Ascot, 200-203
King, Harry, first whip, 77, 78, 81, 148, 149, 202, 207, 240
King, Mr. and Mrs. James, 66 n
King-King, Captain, 63 n
King's Beech, 75
Kingscote, Mr. Henry, 179
Kingscote, Colonel Sir Nigel, 207
Kingsley, Charles, his love of hunting, 160, 161, 163; expressed in poetry and prose, 163, 164
Kinnaird, Lord, his Mastership, 107, 239
Kintore, Lord, 99, 100
Kulb, M., 300, 301

LACOUR, M. de Carayon, his hounds, 300
Lade, Lady, 12, 42 n, 56 n
Lade, Sir John, 56, 56 n

La Feuille, French huntsman, 275
Lambert, Baron, 261, 263, 264, 267
Lansdowne, Lord, 83
La Trace, French huntsman, 275
Leatherhead, stag-hunt at, 44
Lebaudy, M. M., 266, 282, 283
Lecky, Mr., 23
Leicester, Lord, Master of the Buckhounds, 222, 229-232
Leicestershire horses, 182
Le Jeune, M., on horsemanship and horses, 287, 290, 297, 300
Lely, Sir Peter, his picture of Col. Graham, 234, 235
Les Ormes Kennels, 54
Levens, Westmoreland, 232
Lévriers, of Queen Elizabeth's time, 230
L'Hotte, General, 284
Lichfield, Lord, Master of the Buckhounds, 238
Lieven, Madame de, 242
Ligniville, M. Jean de, 120, 132, 253-257, 272, 273
Limousin, 291, 297
Little Weldon, 12-16, 19-21
Loddon Bridge meets, 209
London, Lord Mayor of, 29
Lonsdale, Lord, 77, 131, 167
Lord's Walk, 13
Lorraine as a hunting country, 253
Louis XI., 247, 251
Louis XIII., 250, 291, 298
Louis XIV., 251 n, 261, 291, 292, 294
Louis XV., 30, 44, 49, 51, 54, 252, 292
Louis XVI., 257
Lovel, John, 11, 12, 14, 15
Lovel, Margaret, 11, 15
Lovel, Osborne, 11, 12
Lovel, William, 11
Lucas, Mr., 122
Luttrell, 234

MACHELL, Captain, 217, 218
Makepeace, 147
Maledon on horse-breeding in France, 296
Malmesbury, Lord, 69, 298
Mandeville, J., 200 n
Mar, Lady, 42
Markham, Gervase, 120
Marlborough, Sarah, Duchess of, 206
Martin, Sir Theodore, on Lord Granville, 243
Mary, Queen, 18, 21, 231
Mary Queen of Scots, 248
Maryborough, Lord. *See* Mornington

Mason, Jem, 80, 81, 147, 150, 152, 176
Massy Buckhounds, 116, 120
Master of the Buckhounds, the office of, considered, 82-92; his stand at Ascot, 214; character of the office, 222; distinguished men as riders, 223-227; particulars concerning past masters, 227-243
Matthews, Reuben, 211, 212
Matthews, Mr. Thomas, 194 n
Maxwell, Sir W. Stirling, 293
May, Mr. Bowen, 60 n, 63 n, 67, 92, 157, 190
Mecklenburg horse in France, 297
Medicis, Catherine de, 248
Meissonier, 299
Mellish, Mr., 48, 122
Melvill, Sir James, 231
Meynell, Mr., the 'Hunting Jupiter,' 54, 77 n, 121 n, 180
Miles, Josiah, stud groom at Cumberland Lodge, 210, 211, 212
Milton, horse-dealer, 53
Montagu, Lady Mary Wortley, 42
Montague, Mr., 82
Montfort, Earl Simon de, 5
Montmorency, Connétable de, 247, 288
Moore, Joseph, 194, 194 n, 195, 199
Morbeque, Sir Denis de, 8
Mornington, Lord, Master of Buckhounds, 50, 66 n, 167, 237
Morrell, Mr., 164
Mount Charles, Lord, 50
Murat, Prince, 139
Musters, Mr. Chaworth, 80
Mytton, Jack, 177, 178

Najara, 3, 8
Napoleon I., his horsemanship, 223; and the importation of horses into France, 296
Napoleon III., his hunting morals, 263-265; reconstitutes the Vénerie, 275
National drag-hunt, proposed, 88
Naunton, Sir Robert, 231 n
Neeld, Elliot, 144
Negus, Colonel Francis, Master of the Buckhounds, 26
Nevill, Mr. Benjamin, 124
Nevill, Mr. T., 98 n, 115, 124-127, 130
Newcastle, Duke of, 206, 288, 292, 293
New Forest, stag-hunting in the, 68, 69
Ney, Comte Edgar, 264
Nicholls, Colonel, 131
'Nimrod,' 32, 99, 100 n, 122, 123, 130, 162, 174, 178, 224 n

Norden, his *Survey of Windsor Forest*, 205, 235 n
Norfolk, Duke of, 229
Nottage (yeoman pricker), 40

Odiham stud, 6
Old Berkshire country, a day's staghunting in, 194-199
Olivarez, equestrian portrait of, 293
Oliver, Tom, 80, 81
Orr-Ewing, Master of the Old Berkshire, 194, 199
Orthez, 5
Osbaldistone breed of pointer, 122
Osbaldistones, the, in 'Rob Roy,' 32
Oudry's pictures, 292

Paris, hunting in the neighbourhood of, 225, 258
Parsons, Alderman Humphrey, 30
Peacocke, Captain, 139
Pecche, John, 4 n, 10
Pedro the Cruel, 8
Peel, Sir Robert, as a horseman, 227
Pembroke, Lord, 44, 225 n
Penton, Captain, 173
Pepys, 200
Pexall, Lady, 12
Pexall, Ralph, 12, 18
Pexall, Sir Richard, 12, 18, 19, 20, 21
Philip IV., equestrian portrait of, 293
Philippe Égalité. *See* Chartres, Duc de, 54
Plantagenet, Lady Joan, 9
Plato on hunting, 90
Pliny on deer, 111 n
Poitiers, battle of, 3, 7, 8
Poitiers, Diane de, 244
Poland, state of, in 1734, 38
Pompadour, the Haras of, 295, 295 n
Ponsonby, Fred, 240
Pope, 34, 37, 42; his 'Essay on Fals Taste,' 155
Porter, Mr., 77 n
Portsmouth, Earl of, 98 n
Poyntz, Mr., 53
Prince Consort, 243
Prince Imperial, 154, 264
Pytchley, 14

Quantock Hill deer, 111
Queensberry, Duke of ('Old Q'), 37, 54
Queen's hounds, the, 131-141
Quorn Hunt stable, 300

RADCLIFFE, Mr. Delmé, 155
Railways, their effect on horses and hunting, 155, 156
Ratford, stud-groom to George IV., 54
Reade, Mr. George, 194 n
Reynolds, Sir Joshua, his pictures, 27, 28, 37, 42 n, 44, 54 n
Rich, Charles and James, 196, 197, 199
Richard II., 2, 11
Richmond, Duke of, 48, 51 n, 67, 118 n, 121
Rivers, Lord, 69
Robinson, Mrs. ('Perdita'), 53
Roche Court, Manor of, 10
Rochefoucauld, M. de la, 251 n
Roches, Mary, 10, 11, 12
Roches, Sir John de, 10, 11
Rochford, Lord, Master of Henry VIII.'s Buckhounds, 20, 222, 227–229
Rockingham, Lord, Master of the Buckhounds, 12, 20, 21
Rockingham Castle and Forest, 13, 14
Rocroy Haras, 295
Roden, Mr. John, 129, 130
Roe-deer hunting, 139; in France, 254
Rogers, Samuel, 85
Romans, hunting among the: their wanton slaughter of animals, 115 n
Ros, Thomas de, 8
Rose, Edmund, 7
Rosey Brook, 194, 195, 199
Rossendale Harriers, 139
Rosslyn, Lord, Master of Buckhounds, 68 n, 72, 146, 239
Rothschild, Baron Ferdinand de, 155
Russell, Lord John, 36, 242
Russell, Rev. Mr., 123, 124
Rutland, Duke of, 118 n

ST. EDMUND'S CHAPEL, 4, 11
St. Giles' fields, hunting in, 29
St. Hubert staghounds, 124, 125, 126, 128, 130, 136, 251
Saintonge hound, 271, 273, 300
Salgado, Don Diego, 293
Salisbury, Lady, 43
Salisbury, Marquis of, 88, 154
Salt Hill, the meet at, and objections to it, 175
Samways, Charles, 191, 192, 199
Sanders, Mr., 153
Sandhurst College, 160
Sandpit gate, royal menagerie at, 55
Sandwich, Lord, Master of the Buckhounds, 39, 237

Sangrado's treatment of deer, 123
Sartorius, his pictures, 120
Sault, 2, 5
Saumur, cavalry school at, 284, 298
Savage, Sir Richard, 12
Saxty, Mr., 240
Schaumberg-Lippe, Prince, 25 n
Scott, Sir Walter, 247
Scrope and Grosvenor Roll, 8
Selwyn, George, 29, 34, 37
Seymour's pictures, 301
Shackle, Mr., 175
Shard, Mr., 122, 123, 237
Sharpe, George, huntsman, 48, 52, 57, 117, 121, 200–202
Sheffield, Lord, 36
Shelley, Sir Thomas, 17
Sheward, Mr., 153
Shirley (senior), 152, 153
Shirley (junior), 238
Shuldham, Lady, 42
Simmonds, Mr. F., 106 n
Simpson, Sir Henry, 209, 210
Sixteen-String Jack, 42 n
Slough country unsuitable for hunting, 175
Smith, Mr. Assheton, 69, 70, 133, 140, 141, 180–182
Smith, Mr. Noble, 190
Smith, Tom, 73
Smith, Mr. Thomas, 99, 136, 137
Smyth, Sir R., 37
Snyder's pictures, 230
Somerville, poet, 163; and Master of Hounds, 30, 32 n
South, Mr. Nim, 223, 224
Sowter, Mr., 207
Spanish horses, 292, 293
'Spectator,' 159
Spencer, Lady Charles, 28
'Sporting Gazette,' 129
'Sporting Magazine,' 39, 42, 43, 116, 117, 121, 200, 223
'Sporting Review,' 118 n
Staghound, the, literature of the subject, 114; predecessors of the modern staghound, 115; Lord Wolverton's and Mr. T. Nevill's packs, 115, 124, 127; the old Devon and Somerset staghounds, 116; the hound Windsor, 116; points of a modern hound, 117; Royal hounds taken to France by Colonel Thornton, 117; Merkin, Luxury, Roman, and Rhetoric, 118, 119; the southern and northern types, 119, 120; the Yorkshire breed, a foxhound type,

120; the 'old Goodwood sort,' 121;
Colonel Thornton's hounds, 121:
the pointer strain,122; Mr. Mellish's
lemon-pyes and the Old Devon and
Somerset hounds, 122, 123 ; Lord
Wolverton's, 127-130; the 'pie'
and 'black-and-tan' varieties, 130 ;
the staghound of the present day :
the Queen's, 131-141. *See* also
Hounds, noted
Staghound of Queen Elizabeth's time,
230; the effect of forest-hunting
on, 168
Stag-hunting, Royal, 22 ; under George
I., 23-26, 30; under George II.,
36-39; and George III., 39-50; the
new school, George IV.'s interest
in, 48-57 ; William IV.'s experiences, 57, 58; breaking up of the
Hampton Court stud, 58; Charles
Davis as Huntsman, 59-81; the
ethics of the sport, 82-91 ; things
necessary for success, 92; a run
from Hawthorn Hill to Stanford
Dingley, 93-95; from Aldershot to
Sutton, 95-98; mettle and fettle
a requisite, 98; fox-hunting *v*.
stag-hunting, 99; Davis's method,
100, 101, hunting tricky and sulky
deer, 102-106 ; good deer only
should be hunted, 106, 107 ; a run
from Cobham, 109 ; in the Harrow
country, 142-157 ; in the Forest,
158-171 ; the banks and ditches
of Bucks and Berks, 172-188 ;
masters, 222-243; hunting in
France: vénerie and the Valois,
244-257; under the Empire and the
Republic, 258-277
Staines, stag-hunt in, 41
Stanhope, Lord, 233
Stanhope, Mr., 178
Stanhope, Sir John, 20
Stanley, 'Ben,' the Whig Whip, 223 *n*
Starkie, Colonel Legendre, 122
Stevens, Nancy, 52
Strathavon grouse moor, 122
Strathfieldsaye coverts, 225
Stratton, Rev. Mr., 84, 88-90
Strickland, Charles, 185
Stubbs, his pictures, 42, 70, 120, 122, 301
Sturges, Mr., 196
Suffield, Lord, Master of the Buck-
hounds, 154 *n*, 243
Suffolk, Duchess of, and Queen Eliza-
beth, 231
Suffolk, Lady, 26

Suffolk and Berkshire, Lord, 235
Sully, organiser of State-aided horse
breeding in France, 294
Sutton, Sir Richard, 71
Swift, 200
Swinley, 45, 93, 131, 235-237, 201 ;
paddocks, 106, 106 *n*
Sykes, Sir Tatton, 77
Symons, Sir R., 122

TAILBY, Mr., 149
Talbot, General the Hon. R., 284
Talbot, Mr., 153
Talbots (hounds), 130
Tankerville, Lord and Lady, 27
Tattersall, Mr , on Black Bess, 182
Tattersall, Mr. Edmund, 79
Thackeray, Mr., 46, 55
Thistlethwaite, Dr., 37
Thomson, Colonel Anstruther, 63 *n*, 68, 72, 240
Thornton, Colonel, 30, 117, 121, 130, 258, 259, 270
Thrale, Mr. and Mrs., 56 *n*
Throckmorton, Sir Robert, 68 *n*, 248
Titian, his 'Charles V.,' 70
Tornabuoni on François I., 245, 246
Triboulet, M., 288
Trouttes, Bernard de, 8
Tubb, Mr. John, 126, 127, 157
Turberville on staghounds, 115 *n*
Turkish horse in France, 295 *n*
Tuscany, Grand Duke of, 121 *n*

UTRECHT FAIR, 293
Uxbridge, the water at, 66 *n*

VALON, M. le Marquis de, 266, 267, 268
Vaudemont, Comte de, 254
Vavasour, Agnes, 10
Velasquez, painter, 28, 70, 230, 244, 293
Vendéan hounds, 300
Vénerie and the Valois, 244-257
Venour, Hamon le, 11, 12
Vernon, Dianna, 32
Verulam, Lord, 74
Victoria, Queen, her visit to Ascot
Kennel, 203
Vine hounds, 225
Virginia Water, 40
Vitry, M. le Comte de, 254
Vyner, Mr., 201
Vyse, Captain (Dicky), 147, 240

INDEX

Wales, Prince of (Albert Edward), 119, 156, 207
Wales, Prince of (Frederick), 19, 53
Walpole, Horace, 26, 27, 42, 51 n, 82, 235
Walpole, Sir Robert, 26, 27, 31, 35, 38, 39, 53
Waltham Common, meet at, 43
Waltham stud, 6
Ward, Captain Henry, 127
Ward, Mrs. Humphry, 36
Warham, George, 12
Warner, Dr., 34, 85 n
Waterer, Mr., his 'Nurseries,' 160
Watson, Sir Lewis. See Rocking-ham, Lord
Waveney, Lord, 28
Webb, Byron, 79, 182
Weldon. See Little Weldon
Wellington, Duke of, 5, 50, 55, 223-225
Wellington College, 65
Westminster Abbey, 1, 11
Westminster, Duke of, 208
Wyger, Mr. Van de, 176, 194
White, Captain J., 122
White, Mr. J., 180
Whitfield, Mr. Robert, 194 n
Whyte Melville, Major, 129, 132, 142, 192
William the Conqueror, 3
William of Wykeham, 6, 7
William III, 33, 121 n, 223, 284
William IV., 57, 287

Williamson, Mr., his hunting experiences, 179
Wilson, Mr. Griffin, 41
Wilton, Lord, 224 n
Winchester, Marquis of, 21
Windham, Mr., 56 n
Windsor Castle, 2, 3, 175
Windsor Forest, a Royal hunt in, 10
Windsor Great Park, hunting in, 59 n
Windsor Park, stud in, 6, 7
Woburn deer, 107
Wolverton, Lord, 115, 127, 130
Wolves in France, 295
Woodland Pytchley, 167
Woodstock stud, 6
Wootton, his pictures, 49, 120, 301
Wraxall, his description of George IV., 58
Wyatville, Sir Jeffry, 206
Wycherley, Mr., 31
Wyndham, Sir William, Master of the Buckhounds, 35, 222

Xenophon, 111 n, 161, 256

York, Duke of, 74, 232
Yorkshire breed of hound, 120
Young, Arthur, 54, 251, 258, 276, 295

Zoological (Gardens), 57

www.ingramcontent.com/pod-product-compliance
Lightning Source LLC
Chambersburg PA
CBHW032042220426
43664CB00008B/829